Discover

Malta

Cover: The Azure Window, Gozo, in November — and divers about to take the plunge.

Discover
Malta

Terry Palmer

HERITAGE
HOUSE

DISCOVER MALTA First published March 1987
Second edition, revised and extended, January 1988
Third edition, revised and extended, March 1991
ISBN 1.85212.0211
Typesetting extrapolated in 8.5 on 9.5 Rockwell on
Linotronic 300 by Anglia Photoset, St Botolph Street,
Colchester, from in-house computer setting.
Printed by Colorcraft Ltd, Hong Kong.
Distributed in the UK and major outlets overseas by Roger
Lascelles, 47 York Rd, Brentford, TW8 OQP. Distributed in
Malta by Progress Press Ltd, 341 St Paul St, Valletta.
Published by Heritage House (Publishers) Ltd, King's Road,
Clacton-on-Sea, CO15 1BG

Acknowledgement. The author acknowledges the help of Brian
Crickmay of Worthing, Sussex, formerly of Mellieħa; Isabella Vella, Malta
National Tourist Office, London; Mr and Mrs Carmel Casaletto, Mellieħa;
and Nick Bonello of Dingli. Also, Ernle Bradford's book *The Great Siege,*
Hodder & Stoughton, 1961, and Joseph Micallef's *When Malta Stood
Alone,* published by the author in Malta, 1981.

Titles in the 'Discover' series, in print or in preparation, include:

Discover The Channel Islands	Discover Cyprus & North Cyprus
Discover Czechoslovakia	Discover The Dominican Republic
Discover Florida	Discover The Gambia
Discover Gibraltar	Discover The Grand Canyon State
Discover Iceland & The Faeroes	Discover Malta
Discover Morocco	Discover Sardinia
Discover The Seychelles	Discover South Africa
Discover Tunisia	Discover Turkey

Also by Terry Palmer: *The Ghost At My Shoulder,* (Corgi), *The Ghost
Who Loved Me,* (Heritage House), *The Cairo Alternative,* (Heritage
House).

Exchange rates used throughout this book are £1 = Lm0.60 =
DM2.95.

CONTENTS

Malta: 208-9
        210-1
        212-3
        214-5
        216-7
        218-9
        220-1

200-1

Terry Palmer, his wife Joan, and a knight's suit of armour in the
Verdala Palace.

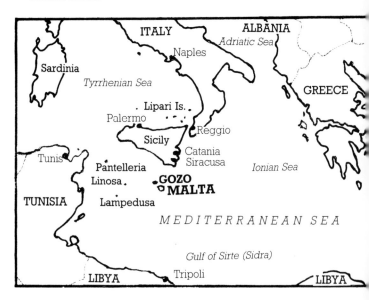

1: WHY MALTA?

The honeyed isles

MALTA IS AN OPEN-AIR MUSEUM to the history of mankind. The Republic of Malta, a cluster of European islands with African overtones, is unique in several ways. It has its own language and alphabet, used nowhere else on earth; it is one of the most densely populated countries on this planet and yet it retains miles of open countryside; it has one of the world's most impressive natural harbours; it had its own civilization while primitive man was still a hunter-gatherer in northern Europe; and it has a history that can be read in hundreds of buildings across the archipelago.

Malta's people have their roots in every Mediterranean country from Spain to Palestine, plus Britain, and they have built in their tiny island home the biggest and most impressive display of parish churches in the world; it's not surprising that among them are the third and fourth largest domes in Europe.

Oversized history. Malta's history is far bigger than the islands themselves, embracing two creeds, two of the greatest sieges in the annals of mankind, two distinctive crosses, and an elected French monarch who turned the tide against the Ottoman Empire, then built a second capital and gave it his own name.

The Maltese islands today offer the north European visitor a happy compromise of Mediterranean sun with almost all the comforts of home. Britons in particular benefit from the colonial legacy as nearly every Maltese can hold a conversation in English, the roads carry a far higher percentage of British-built cars than in Britain itself, and the people drive on the *left* . . . most of the time, but we'll come to that later.

European. Malta is geographically European. During the interglacial periods of prehistory, animals from Europe left their bones in Malta's caves, and today the island sits on the continental shelf that extends south of Sicily, with a deeper channel separating it from north Africa. In 1801, before continental shelves were known, the British Parliament passed an Act 'to regulate the trade and commerce . . . of Malta . . . and to declare the isle of Malta to be part of Europe.'

The Maltese people adamantly consider themselves European; at one time they considered becoming a county of Britain rather than going for independence, but now that they are independent, membership of the European Community is an ambition.

Where? The north coast of Gozo is 50 miles (80km) from Sicily, the south coast of Malta is 198 miles (320km) from Tripoli in Libya, and the western tip of Gozo is 172 miles (275km) from Cap Afrique in Tunisia.

The archipelago lies in the central Mediterranean, its northernmost point being at 36° 6' N, its southernmost at 35° 48'N, its westernmost at 14° 10' E, and its most easterly point at 14° 35' E. The 14th line of eastern longitude runs through Valletta – and through Prague (Czechoslovakia) and Walvis Bay (Namibia) – while the 36th parallel of northern latitude which touches Tarifa in Spain, continental Europe's most southerly point, runs through the South Comino Channel.

But you would be wrong in thinking Malta is therefore Europe's most southerly island, as Crete, which also sits on the continental shelf, is at latitude 35°.

What? The Republic of Malta is a group of three inhabited and several uninhabited islands with a total area of 121.9 sq miles (315.59 sq km). The main island, Malta, covers 94.9 sq miles (245.73 sq km), Gozo is 25.9 sq miles, (67.08 sq km) and tiny Comino sandwiched between them is 1.1 sq mile (2.78 sq km).

The others are Cominotto and its two un-named islets; St Paul's Islands on the north coast of Malta where the apostle is believed to

Villegaignon Street, Mdina, has some of the best statuary in Malta.

have been shipwrecked; the craggy Filfla south-west of Malta, used occasionally for gun practise; Fungus Rock at the west of Gozo, noted for its health-giving green algae; and the insignificant Fessej, Taċ-Ċawl and Ġebel tal-Ħalfa rocks off Gozo's southern shore.

The highest point is a clifftop pinnacle 826ft (251m) above sea-level, south of Dingli.

What to do and see. There are numerous good beaches around the islands, although most of them are small, and there is a wide choice of nightlife in Sliema and St Julian's − or at the other extreme there are quiet villages and rustic peace.

Malta is a good holiday location if your interests include sunbathing and water sports; a busy nightlife with smart restaurants, nightclubs, cabaret, theatre or casino, but it is not in the same league as Torremolinos or Benidorm, nor does it want to be.

Many visitors come to explore the ancient ruins, as Malta is renowned for its Neolithic temples, several of which predate the First Pyramid at Giza. Or you can study medieval and modern history where it happened, notably the Great Siege of 1565, one of the bloodiest battles in history and comparable with that of Gibraltar in 1779-1783 and Leningrad in World War Two; and the Greater Siege of 1940-'42, one of the biggest *Blitzkriegen*, in which the Axis forces dropped 16,000 tons of bombs on the islands, far more than was unleashed in the London and Coventry blitzes and second only to the reprisal attacks on Dresden and the Ruhr. Malta's ordeal during these years earned it the George Cross, still seen in the left canton of its flag.

Or perhaps you're a lover of rural solitude, which should take you to the smaller isles of Gozo and Comino.

First impressions. Assuming you come between May and September your first impression of the landscape will be its predominant yellowness, with summer-dry crops standing in now- arid fields − there is little irrigated land − and even the houses are built of a warm yellow stone. Malta in summer is a mosaic of yellows, taking its cue from the honey-coloured globigerina limestone, a sedimentary rock laid down in seamless beds a hundred or more feet thick and hewn from several large quarries.

This honey-yellow rock is singularly apt, for in ancient times Malta and Gozo were known as the 'honeyed isles' and the name 'Malta' may well have derived from the Greek word μξλι, *meli*, meaning honey.

The Eye of Osiris. Many fishing boats around the coast of Malta have a pair of human eyes carved or painted on the bows; and a single, ever-watchful, never-closing eye can be found in many unexpected places, such as a watchtower in Senglea overlooking Grand Harbour.

This is the Eye of Osiris — or both eyes on the boats, for symmetry — a symbol which is almost as Maltese as the cross of the Knights of St John.

Osiris began his divinity as Busiris, the Egyptian deity who, centuries before Christianity, brought agriculture to the Lower Nile. The agricultural link brought Osiris in contact with Ra, the Sun God, so Osiris gradually became the God of the Moon. He was then seen as one of several children of the union of Earth and Sky, others being Isis and Set.

Ignoring their kinship, Orisis and Isis married, becoming the parents of Horus, the human god with the head of a hawk. But their brother Set, the God of Darkness, slew Osiris, cut his body into 14 pieces and scattered them across Egypt. Isis gathered them and brought Osiris back to life, which led to his being considered the God of Resurrection and Eternal Life, as well as Lord of the Underworld.

With Osiris holding the secret of eternal life, the ancients held him in great esteem, creating images of his all-powerful eye which could foresee dangers in the lives of mortal men.

Modern Maltese fishermen put their faith in the Virgin Mary, but there's no harm in giving old Osiris a small place aboard their boats.

The Eye of Osiris on a watchtower in the Safe Haven Garden Senglea. But are those Osiris's ears as well?

2: BEFORE YOU GO

Paperwork and planning

MALTA IS AN EASY DESTINATION for European visitors: its season is long, its formalities short.

HOLIDAY SEASON

The main holiday season stretches from early May to late September, with peak season being mid-June to early September. The usual factors govern these dates; school holidays and hottest temperatures dictating the peak, and the rainfall, almost totally confined between mid-October and late March, dictating the off-season. The tourist industry on the island, reluctant to see hotel rooms standing empty, is now promoting Malta as a winter resort for golfers and hikers, and is boosting the conference business.

Malta re-entered the holiday market in the mid-1980s after a period in the doldrums caused by an earlier government's flirtation with socialism, but it has rapidly made up for lost business, which means there is great tourist pressure on hotels, airlines, and particularly on hire cars, in July and August: advance booking is essential.

Peak period. If you can avoid this peak period you can risk arriving with nothing booked except your return passage, and you'll be able to shop around for bargains, especially if you're looking for self-catering accommodation. Away from the island's airport at Luqa, you can also negotiate terms for hiring a car — but don't use the argument that the vehicle isn't new: even the internationally-known car rental companies offer vehicles that have lost their showroom smartness.

Discount airfares. Malta is not an easy destination if you're seeking a bucket-shop flight, but discounted fares are occasionally advertised in the quality press. Flight-only aboard tour operators' charter aircraft is available, with notional overnight accommodation included to avoid breaking the law. People seeking just an air passage and whose timetable is flexible, could try the Air Travel Advisory Bureau on ☎071.636.5000, or Trailfinders on ☎071.938.3232.

Package or solo?. If you've never been to Malta, have no contacts there, and are going in peak season, you must reserve your accomodation in advance, either by buying a package or by making your own booking — which this book will help you do.

Some of the tourist hotels are owned by tour operators or deal exclusively with the package holiday business, but there are many which are glad to take bookings from private individuals.

Self-catering. Self-catering accommodation is in two distinct classes: privately-owned apartments or villas sleeping from two to ten guests and found mostly in St Paul's Bay, Buġibba, Sliema, Mellieħa and Gozo; and the company-owned apart-hotel found mostly in St Paul's Bay, Buġibba and Sliema. The package tourist will inevitably go to a company-owned property, while the independent traveller will often find an apartment in a private house.

Budget hotels. There are no budget hotels offering bedrock basic services, such as you find in north Africa and Turkey: Malta is not that kind of country.

Camping and caravanning. Caravanning is out of the question in Malta for both trailer and motorised caravans: the vehicles are not welcomed at the port and there are no sites whatever. Camping is discouraged because of the fire risk, and there are no camping sites either.

Backpackers' dilemma. The absence of basic accommodation and campsites tends to exclude the backpacking traveller, the person who favours sleeping on the beaches, and by extension the hitch-hiker. These people support the adage that to journey is better than to arrive, but Malta is definitely a destination in its own right, not a stopping-point en route to somewhere else.

There are hostels at Marsaxlokk, Floriana, Paceville, Buġibba and Rabat; details are in chapter 7.

TOURIST OFFICES

The Maltese National Tourist Office has bureaux in:

Austria (also covering Hungary): B.T.R. GmbH, Hilton Center, Top 1730-Am Stadtpark, A-1030, Wien, ☎222.7134051.

Belgium: Aviasales, International Rogier Centre, 3me étage, Boîte postale 33, B-1210, Bruxelles, ☎2.182286.

Germany (also covering Switzerland): Fremdenverkehrsampt Malta, D-6000, Schillerstr 30-40, Frankfurt am Main 1, ☎069.285890.

Irish Republic: Sean Carberry Associates, 2 Ely Pl, Dublin 2, ☎611044.

Netherlands: Nationaal Verkeersbureau Malta, Geelvinck Gebouw, 4te étage, Singel 540, 1017 AZ Amsterdam, ☎20.207223.

Sweden (for Scandinavia): BNL Information AB, St Michaels Grand 1, S-62157 Visby, Sweden, ☎0498.71100.

United Kingdom: Malta National Tourist Office, Mappin House, Suite 300, 4 Winsley St, London W1N 7AR, ☎071.323.0506.

United States: Permanent Mission of Malta to the United Nations, 249

St Paul's Parish Church in the centre of Rabat. The door on the right leads to St Paul's Catacombs.

East 35th St, New York, NY 10016, ☎(212).725.2345~9.

Tourist offices in Malta. The head office is at: M.N.T.O, 280 Republic St, Valletta, ☎224444. Branch offices are at: Luqa Airport (☎239915); City Gate, Valletta, (☎237747); Balluta, St Julian's, (☎342671−2); Bisazza St, Sliema, (☎313409); Mġarr Harbour, Gozo, (☎553343); and Victoria, Gozo, (☎556454).

PASSPORTS and VISAS

Citizens of most British Commonwealth countries, all EEC countries, plus Scandinavia, Iceland, Bulgaria, Hungary, Yugoslavia, Switzerland and the USA, the north African states, Japan and a few others, can enter Malta for up to three months without a visa; Britons can also travel on a one-year visitor's passport.

Visas. Visitors travelling on other passports, including Israeli and South African ones, need a visa, available either from a Maltese consulate or from the Commissioner of Police, Floriana (or fax 247777), giving your full passport details, duration and purpose of visit, and proof of funds and onward or return ticket.

HEALTH REQUIREMENTS

Injections. There is no need for injections against yellow fever, typhoid, polio or cholera, or any other disease, and Malta is well clear of the malaria belt. As Malta is not in the EEC the E 111 'health passport' does not apply, but British and certain other nationals staying for up to a month can receive free medical and hospital attention at the **Government Hospital, St Luke's, Gwardamanġa** (☎241251), or at Victoria on Gozo. **Private hospitals** include St Catherine of Siena at Attard and the Irish nuns' Blue Sisters Hospital in Sliema.

EMBASSIES and CONSULATES

These embassies, consulates and high commissions in Malta should be able to provide a certain amount of help for their nationals in distress:

Australia: Ta'Xbiex Tce, Ta'Xbiex, ☎338201.

Germany: Il-Pjazzetta Building, Entrance B, 1st Floor, Tower Rd, Sliema, ☎336531.

United Kingdom: 7, St Anne St, Floriana, ☎233134.

United States: Development House, St Anne St, Floriana, ☎243653.

Diplomatic and consular representatives for Belgium, Canada, Cyprus, Denmark, Hungary, Netherlands, New Zealand, Norway and Switzerland, are at the appropriate embassies or high commissions in Rome.

TOUR OPERATORS

Malta is a popular destination for package tourists. This list of tour operators is compiled from several sources but cannot guarantee to list every one.

The Selmun Palace in Northern Malta has been extended to become a fashionable hotel. And the views are splendid.

British: Airsavers, Birmingham; Airtours, Rossendale; Aquasun Holidays, London; Belle Air Holidays, London; Bonaventure Holidays, London; Burstin Travel, Southend; Cadogan Travel, Southampton; Chevron Air Holidays, Windsor; Cosmos Air, Stockport; Falcon Leisure, London; Global Air, Bromley; Gozo Holidays, Chipperfield; Harlequin Holidays, Sheffield; H.F. Holidays, London; Horizon Holidays, Birmingham; In Style Holidays, Exeter; Intasun Holidays, Bromley; Inter Church Travel, Folkstone; Lancaster Holidays, Bromley; Malta Movement Holidays, London; Malta Plus Holidays, London; Malta Sun Holidays, London; Martini Holidays, Wembley; Medallion Holidays, London; Melita Holidays, Kingston on Thames; Meon Villas, Petersfield; Multitours, London; Owners Abroad, Ilford; Page & May, Leicester; Pan World Holidays, London; Portland Holidays, London; Prestige Holidays, Ringwood; Purevalue Travel, Newcastle upon Tyne; Quest Travel, Brighton; Raymond Cook Holidays, Bedford; Redwing Holidays, Crawley; Saga Holidays, Folkestone; Select Holidays, Hertford; Seasport Holidays, London; Serena Maltavillas, London; Skytours, London; Sol Holidays, Bromley; Solo's Holidays, London; Speedwing, London; Sunseeker Travel, Huddersfield; Sunset Holidays, Manchester; Sunspot Tours, London; Thomson Holidays, London; Tinos Travel, Bolton; Tjaereborg, London; Transair, Birmingham; Vella Holidays, Newcastle upon Tyne; Waymark Holidays, London.

Danish: Dansk Folke Ferie, Kobnhavn; Globetrotter Tour, Kobnhavn.

Dutch: Allair Internationaal, Maastricht; Amiticia, Zwijndrecht; Bex Reizen, Alphen aan de Rijn; Concord Reizen, Baarn; EPC Reizen, Huizen; Educational Holidays, Den Haag; Future Line Travel, Amsterdam; Holland International, Rijswijk; Hotelplan, Rijswijk; Island Travel, Nieuwkoop; Jet Travel, Rotterdam; M 2000, Veenendaal; Mille Idée Vacances, Utrecht; NBBS, Leiden; Neckermann Reizen, Diemen; Nouvelles Frontières, Amsterdam; Pluto International, Amsterdam; Sinbad Tours, Eindhoven; Sonar Reizen, Utrecht; Sportreizen Service Oudenbosch; Stijcting 55+ Reizen, Baarn; Sunglobe, Monnickendam; Talma Tours, Sneek; Top Travel, Bergen op Zoom; Travel Connections, Maastricht; Travel Service, Oudenbosch; Travel Time, Voorburg; Unitravel, Leiden; WC Speciale Reizen, Rosmalen.

Finnish: Matkapiste Oy, Helsingfors.

German: Air Konti Flugreisen, München; Airtours, Frankfurt-a-M; Akademische Studienreisen, Heidelberg; ATS Reisen, Saarbrücken; BAG, Köln; Bontours, Köln; Conti Reisen, Köln; Elizabeth Ellul, Messel; Euro Sprachreisen, Aschaffenburg; Fee Sprachreisen, Stuttgart; Feria, München; Fischer Reisen, Hamburg; Frosch Touristik, München; Germania Reisen, Berlin; Hetzel, Stuttgart; ISI, Bad Neuenahr; Ikarus Reisen, Berlin; Intercontact, Remagen; Jahn Reisen,

München; Jet Reisen, Frankfurt-a-M; Jet und Bett, Düsseldorf; Kreutzer Touristik, München; LAL, München; Meiers Weltreisen, Düsseldorf; Nur Touristik, Frankfurt-a-M; RFG Reisen, Dortmund; Ruth Rick Reisedienst, Aachen; S R Sport und Reisen, Koblenz; Studiosus, München; THR Touristik, Düsseldorf; Transair Flugreisen, Düsseldorf; Tjaereborg, Mönchen Gladbach; Teddys Reisen, Stuttgart; Dr. Tigges Fahrten, Hannover; Unger Flug Reisen, Berlin; Wolters Reisen, Bremen.

Irish: Abbey Travel, Dublin; Global–Intasun, Dublin.

Norwegian: Globetrotter Tour, Oslo; Prisma Tours, Oslo; Gullivers Rieser, Drammen.

Swedish: Atlas Resor, Stokholm; Globetrotter Tour, Stokholm; Sun & Snow, Malmo; Kulturresor, Malmo; Resekonsulterna, Goteborg; Europabuss, Malmo.

Swiss: Airtour Suisse, Bern; Baumeler, Luzern; Beach Travel, Basel; Cosmopolitan Reisen, Zürich; Decco Tours, Genève; Delphi Reisen, Zürich; Dr. Steinfels Sprachreisen, Zürich; Esco Reisen, Basel; Geriberz Reisen, Wettingen; Helvetic Tours, Zürich; Holiday Maker Reisen, Zürich; Holiday Maker Voyages, Genève; Hotelplan, Zürich; Imholz Reisen, Zürich; Interstudy, Basel; Irene Tourism, Zürich; Isi Sprachreisen, Zürich; Jelmoli Reisen, Zürich; Jet Tours Suisse, Genève; Jugi Tours, Bern; Kuoni, Zürich; Nouvelles Frontières, Genève; Popularis Tours, Bern; Reisebüro Kundig, Zürich; RHZ Reisen, Zürich; Rolf Meier Reisen, Neuhausen; SSR Reisen, Zürich; Sundoor Travel, Kirchberg.

United States: Archaeological Tours, New York; Cavalcade Tours, Seccaucus, NJ; Jetaway WorldVacations, Rockville, MD; Perillo Tours, Woodcliff Lakes, NJ; Pleasure Break, Des Plaines, IL; Ribair Holidays, Rutherford, NJ; Saga, Boston, MA; African Explorers, Parlin, NJ.

MONEY MATTERS

British cheques. Taking money to Malta is ridiculously easy. Traveller's cheques in your native currency are welcome in all banks, most hotels and car rental companies, and the larger shops; Eurocheques are equally acceptable. Britons can draw cash on Barclays Bank cheques with a Barclaycard as guarantee; cheques on many other major European banks can be cashed with the Eurocard as guarantee, to a limit of Lm70 per cheque. Keep your receipt as you may need it for reconverting spare liri.

Plastic money. A credit card is perhaps the most convenient way of drawing funds, with both the Bank of Valletta and the Mid-Med Bank taking the major international cards: Access, Visa, MasterCard and American Express. With all but Amex, amounts more than Lm35 have to be referred to head office for clearance, usually a matter of minutes.

Comino is off the beaten track, so where better to build this isolation hospital?

Banks. Two banks share the money market in Malta: the Mid-Med Bank with 46 branches and the Bank of Valletta with 44. Most branches have simple road maps of the islands available free to tourists, but the Mid-Med's map also has a good street plan of Valletta. The Lombard is a merchant bank not involved with small-time currency exchange.

Banking hours. Banking hours are moderately complex. Both banking companies are open *only in the morning,* but special **foreign exchange bureaux** in selected branches also open during the afternoon; the Mid-Med has 11, the Valletta 15.

In broad terms, the **summer** business hours, from 15 June to 30 September, are 0800-1200 Mon-Fri, 0800-1130 Sat, but the Bank of Valletta has variations in Dingli and Senglea. In **winter,** from 1 October to 14 June, the banks open and close half an hour later — 0830-1230 Mon-Fri, 0830-1200 Sat.

Foreign exchange bureaux. Foreign exchange offices usually open in **summer** afternoons from 1600-1900, Mon-Fri, but there are several variations. **Winter** afternoons are 1500-1800 Mon-Fri, but several don't open at all.

Always open. Both banks operate exchange bureaux at Luqa

Airport, and both are open around the clock all the year.

Lira or pound? The island currency is the Maltese lira, indicated by Lm, fixed at parity to the pound sterling on independence as was the Cyprus pound; now they are among the few currencies in the world worth more than the pound sterling.

The lira is divided into 100 cents with each cent divided into 10 mils. Inflation has almost finished the mil, but you can still find many cash registers in Malta that work to three places of decimals. While the official name for the currency is the *lira*, plural *liri*, many Maltese still think of it,and call it, the pound.

Notes and coin. The Lm1 note was phased out in the 1980s, replaced by the Lm2 note which joined the Lm5, Lm10 and the new Lm20. Coins have the value of Lm1, 50c, 25c, 10c, 5c, 2c and 1c — and you might occasionally see the 5, 3 or 2 mil coins.

The lira is the only legal currency on the islands, but no Maltese will turn down the offer of cash in any other negotiable form, be it sterling, dollars or Deutschemarks: the banks show exchange rates in many currencies, including the *ecu*, the European Community unit, and many Maltese have foreign currency accounts.

If you're dealing in anything but Lm, note the offered exchange rate at the outset; large shops usually have it posted in the window.

COST OF LIVING

The former Labour government had a strict price-control policy, with a list of the maximum permitted retail prices for basic foodstuffs

The Maltese lira has proved resistant to inflation.

18

published in the press. The Nationalist government, believing in a free economy, has let prices find their own level. This is an idea of the cost of living:

Nescafé classic coffee, 200gm 79c, **£1.32** DM3.90
Typhoo tea bags, 160 . . . . Lm1.63, **£2.70** DM10.65
Homepride cook-in-sauce, 385gm 39c, **65p** DM1.90
Heinz soups, 425gm 30c, **50p** DM1.48
HP sauce, 255gm 42c, **70p** DM2.06
corn-oil margarine, 400gm 41c, **69p** DM2.03
Flora margarine, 500gm 59c, **98p** DM2.90
Danish Brie cheese, 125gm 58c **96p** DM2.83
local honey, 185gm 36c, **60p** DM1.77
ice cream (large wafer) 25c, **41p** DM1.20
Snickers or Mars bar 25c, **41p** DM1.20
cigarettes, international brands, pkt 20 . . . .
                                        35c−43c, **58p−71p** DM1.70−2.09
Martell cognac, 75cl Lm5.25, **£8.75** DM16.95
Gordon's gin, litre Lm6.80, **£11.33** DM33.42
Cutty Sark whisky, litre Lm6.40, **£10.65** DM31.40
Smirnoff vodka, litre Lm4.75, **£7.92** DM23.36
Black & White whisky, 75cl Lm5, **£8.33** DM24.55
whisky in airport duty-free shop . . . .
                            Lm3−Lm3.50, £5−£5.83 DM14.75−DM17.20
Bristol Cream sherry, 70cl Lm3.30, **£5.50** DM16.22
★local wine, 75cl . . . . 25c−75c, **42p−£1.22** DM1.23−DM3.68
★local lagers, 50cl 23c, **38p** DM1.12
Perrier water, litre 34c, **57p** DM1.68
pomegranates, kg . . . . 30c−35c, **50p−58p** DM1.47−DM1.71
tomatoes, kg . . . . 25c−35c, **42p−58p** DM1.23−DM1.71
honeydew melons, kg 35c, **58p** DM1.71
bananas, kg 35c, **58p** DM1.71
Women's leather boots, high fashion Lm24.50, **£40.85** DM120.50
Kodak gold film, 36exp Lm1.60, **£2.65** DM7.80
bus fare, Valletta−Siġġiewi 8c, **13p** DM0.38
taxi fare, Luqa−Mellieħa, night Lm8, **£13.30** DM39.25
gallon of 4-star petrol Lm1.20, **£2** DM5.90
Cinema performance, adult 45c, **75p** DM2.20
3-bed, 3rd-floor flat (apartment), Sliema . Lm13,000, **£21,600** DM64,000

Salaries: Police constable, 1st class, per annum . . . .
            Lm2,153−Lm2,576, **£3,588−£4,293** DM10,585−DM12,655
Highest civil service pay scale, ... Lm5,107, **£8,510** DM25,100
Roadsweeper, basic pay . . . . Lm1,810, **£3,016** DM8,900.

★*plus a 5c or 2c refundable deposit on the bottle*

Looking for the Turk? It was once a deadly serious task from these ramparts at Gozo's Citadel.

DRESS

The Maltese are conservative in their dress. Only recently have men appeared on the streets without a shirt, and it's still not accepted behaviour in Valletta and other urban areas. Shorts are popular wear for both sexes — but not when visiting churches or smart restaurants.

Bikinis are fine for the sands or the hotel pool, but are unacceptable anywhere else, although there is a growing movement for women to wear bra and shorts in the resort areas, and they occasionally visit Valletta in a halter top with bare midriff. Women, therefore, do not go topless on any beach.

There is no longer any strict formality for evening dress unless you are attending a really special function; you don't need to dress for dinner at the smartest restaurants or the casino, but don't expect to be admitted wearing jeans and a tee-shirt.

Many Maltese men wear woollen pullovers even in high summer, and the older women in the countryside always appear overdressed for the climate, with a few widows still clinging to the Mediterranean tradition of wearing black for the remainder of their days.

DISABLED &

Numerous wheelchair travellers holiday in Malta and while there is little outward show of catering for them there are few hazards.

The visitor in a wheelchair can, of course, travel as a passenger in a rented car, go on the ferries to Gozo even without a car, visit some of the beaches and all the ancient monuments except Ghar Dalam and the Hypogeum; pass through Luqa Airport both ways and use its toilet but not its restaurant; and visit all the towns and villages with the possible exception of Valletta city centre, Mdina, and the Gozo Citadel. Bus travel is totally impossible and so is a visit to Comino.

The disabled symbol used in the following pages indicates places which the wheelchair-bound tourist can visit easily with the help of a mobile companion; the symbol is also used to indicate hotels which publicise their ability to cater for disabled guests.

WHERE TO GO

Bustling. The greatest concentration of tourist hotels in Malta is in the Sliema and Paceville area, which is where you will also find the most restaurants, the casino, much of the night life, and the terminals for cruises around the harbour and to the islands; Sliema is also a good shopping centre. It's worth remembering that nowhere in the Maltese islands will you find the pace of life, for the Maltese or for the visitor, approaching the razzmatazz of Spain's Torremolinos or Benidorm, and the further you travel from Sliema the slower that pace becomes.

Quieter. For a slightly quieter time, choose Buġibba or its twin, Qawra.

Quiet, with beach. If you're looking for a quiet resort with a decent beach your choice is from Mellieħa, Birżebbuġa, Marsaxlokk, Marsascala or St Paul's Bay.

Beach above all else. You want a fine sandy beach with good watersports, but aren't worried about the absence of shops? Try Golden Bay on the west coast, or Għadira on Mellieħa Bay, from where Mellieħa village is half a mile, mostly uphill.

Self-catering. There are 380 privately-owned self-catering apartments in the St Paul's Bay to Qawra area, 220 in Sliema — Paceville, 120 in Mellieħa, 80 on Gozo and 150 elsewhere. You'll need to make your own arrangements to rent one of these, but the advantage is you'll meet the Maltese in their own homes.

Company-owned self-catering accommodation in apart-hotels or hotel apartments specialises in package tourists. There are 320 in the St Paul's Bay to Qawra area, 240 in Sliema — Paceville, and 120 elsewhere.

Relaxation. The relaxing holiday can be summed up in the one word Gozo. The unspoiled island is much quieter and has the feel of being a Peter Pan living permanently 50 years in the past, without being backward. It has several good but small beaches, and you'll probably have to make your own entertainment.

Ultimate escapist. A stay on Comino is the closest you can come to the ultimate in get-away-from-it-all breaks, but there is some commercialisation: the Comino Hotel has a pool, there is a small holiday village in the next bay, and the Blue Lagoon draws cruisers from Sliema each afternoon.

History. If you plan to soak up Malta's history, try for Rabat, Victoria on Gozo, or Floriana which is on the doorstep to Valletta and Grand Harbour.

WHEN TO GO

The islands are a year-round holiday destination, but catering for differing tastes between summer and winter. As the summer is hot — see chapter 3 for a weather chart — there is little incentive for using much energy and from noon until mid afternoon most people look for the shade. This is the best season for sunworshippers and swimmers, although temperatures allow swimming much of the year.

Malta is promoting itself as a winter resort for sportspeople, notably golfers and hikers, and for conference organisers.

WHAT TO TAKE

For summer visitors, rain will be a rarity and the temperature can easily top 95°F (35°C) with very low humidity, so light cotton clothing is the order of the day. But see the paragraph about *dress,* above. Winter brings the wind and rain — do you remember the meeting that Reagan and Gorbachev had in a stormy Marsaxlokk Bay? — but without the penetrating chill of northerly climes, and there's never any frost or snow. A good raincoat and some woollen garments are all that's needed.

Biting insects after dark can be a problem for sensitive skins, and the sun-worshipper should have a good barrier cream, but these preparations are readily available in Malta.

All types of film are on sale throughout the tourist areas.

CONFERENCES

Malta has entered the conference market in a big way, beginning with the conversion of the Hospital of the Order of St John in Valletta in 1979 into the **Mediterranean Conference Centre.**

The Government has increased hotel standards and introduced the international star rating for conformity, with all the five-star, most of the four-star and a few of the three-star establishments catering for conferences.

Air Malta offers off-airport check-in and upgrades its economy class or club class service for conference delegates, which other airlines serving Luqa Airport are also finding necessary. Around 17 destination-management companies arrange everything else, from airport transfers and press conferences to providing secretaries and luxury coach tours of the islands.

Does it work? Ask such corporations as Birds Eye, Eurocard, Ciba Geigy, Ford Motors and the Kölner Bank.

3: MALTESE FACTFILE

Facts at your Fingertips

AFFILIATIONS

Malta is a member of the United Nations, the Commonwealth, the Council of Europe and the Non-Aligned Movement. It applied on 16 July 1990 to join the EEC but doesn't expect an answer before 1992.

ARMED FORCES

Since independence Malta has been responsible for its own defence, for which purpose the Armed Forces of Malta was created. The force is also prepared to offer immediate help in any national emergency and is organised and trained with this role in mind. AFM has as its main divisions the Second (Support) Regiment and the Task Force. There is no ceremonial role.

BUSINESS HOURS

Banks. See 'Money Matters' in chapter 2.

Post Offices. The General Post Office in the old Auberge d'Italie in Merchants St, Valletta, is open in **winter** 0800-1830 Mon-Sat, and in **summer** (15 June-30 Sep) 0730-1800, Mon-Sat. Sub post offices, in most of the villages, 0730-1900 Mon-Sat all year. They are closed on public holidays.

Telephones. See 'Telephones' further in this chapter.

Shops. Most shops open Mon-Sat 0900-1900, but the siesta can vary from two to four hours; expect some to close at 1200 and all to be shut by 1300, with reopening between 1500 and 1600. A few open at 0800 and a few others stay open until 2000, but only the bakers and the duty pharmacists are open on Sundays or public holidays, all closing at 1200.

Business offices. The core opening time is Mon-Fri 0800-1230, 1430-1800, Sat 0800-1300, with few of them opening in the afternoons in summer – mid June to the end of September.

Government offices. Mon-Fri 0745-1230, 1315-1715, but not opening in the afternoon from mid June to the end of September.

Museums and neolithic temples. Times vary, but usually the hours are Mon-Sat from 0830 to late afternoon in summer, to midday in winter; Sunday hours are usually slightly less.

Petrol stations. Usually 0600-1800 Mon-Sat. Sunday opening stopped with the oil crisis of 1979 when double pay for the attendants proved uneconomic, but when automatic pumps and self-service filling stations are introduced, Sunday opening may return. The rare Sunday-opening filling station charges up to 10c a gallon extra although this is illegal.

CINEMAS

The number of cinemas has slumped in the past few years although television is not a strong rival. The survivors are in Valletta and Sliema, usually screening English-language films and frequently some while after their release in the USA or Britain.

CLIMATE

The climate is typical of the Mediterranean type, with warm wet winters and hot dry summers. The small area of land prevents **temperatures** soaring into triple figures Fahrenheit (more than 38°C) but a persistent wind off the Libyan desert can make the island very hot in high summer. In winter, high humidity is the main characteristic, caused by the hot *sirocco* wind coming from Africa and picking up moisture.

	mean daily range °C	mean daily range °F	sea temp °C	rainfall in mm.	bright sun hrs
January	15−9	60−48	14.5	88	5.3
February	15−9	60−48	14.5	61	6.3
March	16−10	61−50	14.5	44	7.3
April	19−11	67−52	16	27	8.3
May	23−15	74−60	18.5	10	10
June	27−18	83−65	21	3	11.2
July	30−21	86−70	24.5	1	12.1
August	31−22	88−72	25.5	9	11.3
September	28−20	83−79	25	44	8.9
October	24−17	76−63	22	118	7.3
November	20−14	69−58	19.5	75	6.2
December	17−11	63−52	16.5	96	5.2

Rainfall. The average annual rainfall is 22 inches (570mm), about the same as London, but in 1934 there were 32.2in (995mm) and in 1947 just 8.3in (210mm).

ELECTRICITY

Electricity is at 240v AC single-phase everywhere, with British-style fittings: bayonet-fixed bulbs and three-pin power plugs. Continental Europeans and Americans need adapters.

Gozo has power failures of irregular length at random intervals, and the voltage anywhere in the islands is subject to occasional surges, which have been known to destroy television sets. Customers can not sue Enemalta, and the official response is to recommend each installation be fitted with a mini-transformer; before you re-charge your video camera, check that your accommodation is protected against surges.

FESTIVALS

The Maltese love festivals. From May to October every village celebrates the *festa* of its patron saint, the most important event in the year. The parish church is decorated with flowers and its treasures are displayed; outside, the church front and the village streets carry thousands of light bulbs, ribbons and bunting, with the processional route having the biggest and brightest flags and banners.

After a three-day preparation the villagers carry their saint's statue through the streets to the accompaniment of church bells and brass bands, reaching a climax as the saint returns to the church amid a display of fireworks.

National festivals. The main national festa is **Imnarja,** a corruption of the Italian word *luminaria,* 'illumination.' Imnarja, held on 29 June, celebrates the completion of harvesting and features a mass serving of the national dish, stewed rabbit, served with wine as a prelude to an all-night picnic in the grounds of Buskett Gardens. On 30 June the celebrations continue with bare-back horse and donkey races on the road to Rabat, the winners receiving *palji,* embroidered banners, which they usually give to their parish church.

The Valletta **Carnival,** held for 15 years in May to boost tourism, is back in February where it traditionally belongs. It is one of the ancient festivals of Malta, marking the end of the dark days of winter — but they're not very dark in these latitudes — and the beginning of spring. It is now a marvellous excuse for thousands of children, and their parents, to put on fancy dress while exotic carnival floats parade through the streets of Valletta and Floriana.

The **Regatta** on 8 September in Grand Harbour marks the end of the Great Siege of 1565 and the Greater Siege of 1940-'42, both of which ended on this day. The main event is a series of rowing races between the towns around the harbour.

This list contains the most important festivals:

February: Valletta Carnival; St Paul's Shipwreck, Valletta; Jesus of Nazareth, Sliema.

Easter: Good Friday processions at Qormi, Naxxar, Mosta, Siġġiewi, Valletta, and other places. Palm Sunday procession of Our

Lady of Sorrows, Valletta; five weeks later, St Publius festa, Floriana.

May: Our Lady of the Rosary, Marsaxlokk; St Philip, Żebbuġ. Processions on Sunday after Ascension Day at Għar Lapsi, and on Trinity Sunday and Holy Trinity at Marsa; Corpus Christi in most villages.

June: St Joseph the Worker, Birkirkara; Martyrdom of St Paul, Rabat.

July: Visitation of Our Lady, Valletta and Għarb (Gozo); Sacred Heart, Sliema; Our Lady of Mount Carmel, Valletta, Gżira; Mdina; St Joseph, Kalkara, Msida; St George, Victoria; Our Lady of Sorrows, St Paul's Bay; Kingship of Christ, Paola; Santa Venera in Santa Venera.

August: St Joseph, Qala (Gozo); St Peter, Birżebbuġa; St Gajetan, Ħamrun; St Lawrence, Vittoriosa; Our Lady, Star of the Sea, Sliema; Our Lady of Loreto, Għajnsielem (Gozo); Conversion of St Paul, Safi; Assumption celebrated in many villages.

September: Our Lady of Victories on 8th marks the defeat of the Turks in 1565, the end of the German Blitz in 1942, and the Feast of the birth of the Virgin Mary, and is marked in most villages, particularly in Mellieħa where Don García's relief troops landed, and in Senglea. Also Marija Rejina, celebrated in Marsa.

November: St Catherine, Żejtun.

FLAG

Legend claims that Roger the Norman, Count Roger I of Sicily, created the original Maltese flag. When Roger seized the Christian island from its Arab overlords in 1090, he tore off part of his red personal standard and gave it to the Maltese people as their own; they added an equal-sized white section to bring the flag to an acceptable shape.

The motif in the left canton is the George Cross, awarded to the island in 1942 after the Greater Siege; don't confuse it with the Maltese cross which the Order of St John also presented to the island. See the rear cover of this book.

GAS

The 190-gm canisters of butane gas used on camping stoves are not readily available in Malta: there are, of course, no camping sites. The fuel is widely available in quantities ranging from 13kg to 12-ton static tanks for home and industrial use.

Enemalta. Electricity, gas and petrol are all provided by the Enemalta Corporation which has a storage capacity of 100,000 tons of diesel oil, plus other fuels, at Kalafrana on Marsaxlokk Bay. Enemalta generates its electricity with two thermal and two steam-turbo power stations with a total capacity of 175 megawatts; one of the stations distils sea-water as a by-product, giving 4,500,000 gallons of drinking water a day; a fifth station is being built on the Delimara Peninsula. Cables carrying 11kv run under the sea to Comino and Gozo.

GOVERNMENT and CONSTITUTION

Malta achieved independence on 21 September 1964, and became a republic on 13 December 1974, remaining in the Commonwealth. Under former Prime Minister Dominic Mintoff the country adopted a non-aligned policy which was often seen in Britain as courting communism and socialism. Mintoff's successor Mifsud Bonnici reversed the trend and thus brought back the visitors.

The constitution states that the House of Representatives must have an odd number of seats with not less than nine nor more than 13 constituencies, each of which must return not less than five and not more than seven members. This obviously means that Malta has proportional representation, and for the record it uses the single transferable vote. The minimum age for voting is 18 years.

There are five years between elections, the latest being on 9 May 1987 when the Nationalist Party polled 119,721 votes, (50.91%) and won 31 seats; the Malta Labour Party polled 114,937 (48.87%) and won 34 seats. The previously-revised constitution, seeing this type of result as a possibility, had decreed that the number of votes, not of seats, should decide which party governed — so the Nationalists were awarded four extra seats.

Maltese society is so split across this political divide that people

The walls of Mdina deterred Mustapha Pasha during the Great Siege — and that was before they looked this formidable.

often refuse to marry into the opposing camp; not surprisingly, the small parties fare badly — the Malta Democratic Party got 380 votes (0.16%), the Communists 119 votes (0.05%), and independent candidates scored 12 votes (0.01%).

President. The president, currently Dr Vincent Tabone, has executive authority, and the Cabinet consists of the Prime Minister and 12 ministers.

Contacts. The Office of the Prime Minister is in the Auberge de Castille, ☎243026; the Minister of Foreign Affairs is at the Palazzo Parisio, and the Minister for Gozo (a new appointment which is proving popular and successful) is at the Pjazza San Frangisk, Victoria, Gozo.

MAPS

You have a choice of three maps of the Maltese islands. The Clyde Leisure map is at a scale of 1:50,000 (around 1.25in to the mile), for £3.50 in the UK; it lists hotels, restaurants and places of interest, and has street plans of Valletta, Mdina, Rabat, Sliema and Victoria. The Hildebrand map is on the same scale for the same price, and offers a street plan of Valletta; Intermap's publication is at the larger scale of 1:40,000, also for £3.50, and with street plans of Valletta, Mdina, St Paul's Bay, Sliema and Victoria, with separate maps showing bus routes and historical sites. Edward Stanford Ltd of 12–14 Long Acre, London, WC2E 9LP (☎071.836.1321) stocks them all and sells by mail order, with post and packing as extras.

The Directorate of Overseas Surveys in London no longer stocks maps of Malta at 1:25,000 (2.5in = 1 mile), as the latest survey was done by a French company with the results due to be on sale in 1991. The Malta National Tourist Office issues street plans only of Valletta, Buġibba and Sliema, with a simple island map at around half-inch to the mile (1:120,000). The Mid-Med Bank and the Bank of Valletta give customers simple road maps of the islands.

Beware of maps marking a good road from the Roman baths by Għajn Tuffieħa south to the Zammitello Palace: it doesn't exist — a pig farm blocks the route. Beware, also, of maps not marking the St Paul's Bay and the Mellieħa bypasses.

NEWSPAPERS

The Times is Malta's English-language daily newspaper, founded in 1978 from *The Times of Malta* and published from Strickland House, 341 St Paul's St, PO Box 328, Valletta, ☎224032, for 10c. Its policies are strongly independent, and the paper was originally founded by Mabel Strickland, daughter of Lord Strickland, the island's prime minister 1927-'32. Weekly papers in English are *[erratum added by Heritage House, with apologies to Allied Newspapers] cle, The Democrat,* and *The Sunday Times.*

Malti papers are the daily *In-Nazzjon Tagħna* published in Pietà, and *L-Orrizont* from Valletta; there are five Malti weeklies.

Foreign newspapers. Newspapers from continental Europe are on sale on the day of publication or the day after, but American newspapers don't get this far.

POLICE

The *pulisija* is based on the British police force with its officers wearing near-identical uniform. The force is unarmed and performs the same role as its British model: crime detection, law enforcement and traffic duties, plus immigration control, with no political involvement. Its officers are pleasantly unobtrusive, though they can issue on the spot fines for parking and similar minor offences. The police headquarters is in Floriana and there is a police station in almost every village.

POPULATION

The islands had a population of 314,216 in 1967, 340,907 in 1983, and 345,418 at the 1985 census — of those latter, more than 305,000 lived on Malta and only a dozen or so on Comino. Of the total, 98.6% were Maltese nationals.

The 1983 figure gave an average density of 2,833 people per square mile (1,094 per sq km) which is one of the world's highest; for comparison, Belgium has 838p.s.m. (323p.s.km), the United Kingdom (including Scotland and Northern Ireland) has 603p.s.m. (233p.s.km.) and Montana, USA, has 5.5p.s.m. (2p.s.km.). Valletta had 14,040 people in 1983, the small figure dictated by the size of the city.

Paola, Ħamrun and Sliema are crowded, with frequent minor traffic jams although seldom with a major blockage. Despite the population density, nowhere else on the islands gives the impression of having crowds of people, and in the rural areas you can get right away from the human race.

POST OFFICE

Rowland Hill and the old British General Post Office still influence Malta's postal services, and British-style collection boxes dot the islands, but the Mediterranean influence comes through because shops and hotels join the Post Office with the right to sell stamps. The Maltese GPO — even the original name is retained — has its head office in a former *auberge* (hostel) of the Knights of St John, in Merchants St, Valletta.

Letter deliveries are made to private and business addresses, but there is no parcels delivery: the addressee must come and collect.

There are sub post offices in most villages.

PUBLIC HOLIDAYS

January	1: New Year's Day
February	10: St Paul's Shipwreck
March	19: Feast of St Joseph (husband of Virgin Mary)
	31: Freedom Day (Jum il-Ħelsien, National Day)
	Good Friday ✝
May	1: Workers' Day
June	7: Commemoration of this day in 1919
	29: Feast of Sts Peter and Paul
August	15: Feast of the Assumption of Santa Marija
September	8: Feast of our Lady of Victories
	21: Independence Day
December	8: Feast of the Immaculate Conception
	13: Republic Day
	25: Christmas Day.

(✝ Easter Day is the first Sunday after the first full moon after 21st March.)

When a public holiday falls on a weekend there is no compensating day's holiday on the nearest working day, but all employees qualify for a day's paid holiday at their convenience.

St Paul's shipwreck commemorates the presumed date of the event, believed to be on St Paul's Islands; Freedom Day marks the closure of the British military base; and on 7 June 1919 British marines shot four Maltese in food riots.

The only businesses open on public holidays are restaurants, bars, emergency pharmacies, car hire agencies, the Gozo ferry, buses, and

The New Dolmen Hotel in Qawra has an original old dolmen in its grounds.

the exchange bureaux at Luqa Airport.

PUBLIC TOILETS (Restrooms)

Malta has plenty of public lavatories, either labelled in English or in symbols. They are free and adequately clean, but few are adapted for the disabled. In the villages, lavatories are usually near the church.

RADIO and TELEVISION

Malta Broadcasting Authority. The broadcasting authority, which is independent of government control, supervises **Television Malta,** which started transmissions in September 1962. TVM operates one channel, in colour since 1981, starting with a satellite relay of CNN (Cable News Network) from the USA at 0700 then coming back on air around 1625 with its own schedule — some in Malti — until shutdown before midnight. Some of its programmes are bought from the BBC and British independent television. But the Maltese aren't short of television entertainment as they have up to 15 foreign channels available, depending on the weather. Most of these are Italian, where the airwaves have been deregulated; Libyan is occasionally available, with French a rare luxury.

The broadcasting authority is also in charge of **Radio Malta's** National station which broadcasts 18 hours daily on 998 KHz, 310m, medium wave; the Second station offers music on 87.9 KHz, VHF; and the Third station is international. Radio Malta National is also available as Cable Radio Two — there *is* a Cable Radio One — and the Third band puts out weekly programmes to Maltese expatriates in Britain and Germany. There are large Maltese communities in Australia and the United States, but they're too far to reach economically by radio.

Radio Mediterranean broadcasts daily from Malta on 1557 KHz medium, and 6110 KHz short wave, in English, French and Arabic. The station opened in 1978 but failed, and was reopened in 1983. **Voice of the Mediterranean** began in 1988, jointly owned by the Maltese and Libyan governments. Its English-language output is brief, and aimed at intellectuals.

The **BBC World Service** is available from the East Mediterranean Relay station at Zygi, Cyprus, on these frequencies:

	0200	0300	0400	0500	0600	0700	0800	0900	~	1000	1400	1500	1600	1700	1800	1900	2000	2100	2200
25.75 MHz																			
17.64 MHz																			
15.07 MHz																			
12.09 MHz																			
9.41 MHz																			
6.19 MHz																			

RELIGION and CHURCHES

The Maltese people are staunchly Catholic, with 92% of the population members of the church, but there is complete tolerance of other Christian sects and other religions. Religion plays an important part in the life of the average Maltese villager and communities have been known to impoverish themselves in order to build a larger and finer church than the next village has — which is why the islands are blessed with such elegant and enormous buildings.

Protestant Churches. Among the few protestant churches in Malta are the Bible Baptist in the St Andrews Barracks area, ☎410833 any time; St Paul's Pro-Cathedral in Old Theatre St, Valletta, ☎225714; Holy Trinity in Rudolph St, Sliema, ☎330575; and the Church of Scotland, South St, Valletta, which is amalgamated with the Methodist and Free Churches.

For Anglicans, Malta comes in the Diocese of Gibraltar in Europe, with its bishop resident in Britain. For Catholics, the Archbishop of Malta is based in Floriana, with a Bishop of Gozo in Victoria.

SOUVENIRS

You want something typically Maltese for a souvenir? Try an embroidered tablecloth from Lm12, Gozo knitwear up to Lm20, leatherware such as belts, bags and wallets, or glassware and pottery from Ta'Qali.

Maltese churches are in the superlative. Mosta's dome can be seen for miles around.

TELEPHONES

The Telemalta Corporation's offices are: **St Julian's:** St George's Rd, near Styx disco and Palladium night club, open continuously; **Valletta:** St John's Square, Mon-Sat 0800-1830; **Luqa Airport:** daily 0730-1845; **St Paul's Bay:** Main St, daily 0830-2230; **Sliema:** Bisazza St, Mon-Fri 0800-2100, Sat 0800-2000; **Victoria, Gozo:** Republic St, Mon-Sat 0800-1930.

In addition, there are international phones on Gozo at Xlendi, Marsalforn and Mgarr's tourist office, and several shops and post offices in Malta let you make international calls, charging around double the Telemalta rate. Hotels may actually double the rate.

Making a call. The procedure for making an international call is simple: go into a kiosk, dial the number you want, and pay at the desk afterwards.

International codes. The international access code is **00**; after that, dial the code for the country you are calling:

Australia	71	Netherlands	31
Austria	43	New Zealand	74
Canada	1	Norway	56
Czechoslovakia	66	Sweden	46
Denmark	45	Switzerland	41
Germany	49	United Kingdom	44
Hungary	61	United States	1
Ireland	500		

Phone boxes. Phone kiosks in the street are for local calls only, with a major overhaul of the system ending in 1991. Calls were priced at 3c, then rose to 5c: five one-cent coins, changing to one 5c coin. Phone boxes are either the old-style British cast-iron kiosk, a ligher-weight structure, or modern cubicles built of the local limestone. Sadly, they're often out of order.

Telephone number changes. The revision of the system involved changing several thousand numbers. Those which began with **226** are now 236; **227** numbers are 237; **228** are 238; **229** are 239; **470** are 520; **531** are 431; **62** are 24 (except in Rabat where they're 45); **64** are 46 (except in Rabat where they're 45); **67** are 45. In addition, many hundreds of numbers have been changed out of recognition. This book has used the **new numbers** but there may be some old numbers which have slipped in.

Cheap rate. Cheap rate for calls is from 2100 to 0800 nightly, and all day Sunday.

TELEVISION

See 'radio.'

TIME

Malta is on GMT+1 in the winter. The Maltese advance their clocks one hour for summer time (daylight saving time) on the last Sunday in March, making their time GMT+2 until they put the clocks back one hour on the last Sunday in September. Note that the end of summer time in Malta coincides with everywhere else in Europe *except* Britain and Ireland.

TIPPING

You will be expected to tip in restaurants and taxis, where the tip should be no more than 10% of the charge, but if you feel the service didn't warrant a tip don't be afraid to withhold it. Tips are also expected with porters and waiters in hotels where you must use your discretion.

Certain car parks, such as on Sliema's Strand and in Valletta, have attendants; I feel that a short stay on the Strand is worth 10c, but all-day parking by the Lascaris War Rooms in Valletta, with valuables left in your car, is worth at least 50c. A few other places, such as the Verdala Palace, have no entry fee but rely on tips instead; by careful observation I feel 25c to 50c per couple is the going rate.

WATER

Water is difficult to supply on heavily- populated islands with virtually no rainfall for six months of every year and with no permanent stream. There are a few tiny reservoirs near Rabat but most water comes from boreholes, supplemented in summer by desalination, using reverse osmosis.

Until the early 1980s when tourism became important once again, each village was cut off for several hours at a time to conserve supplies. The situation is now greatly improved, but mains pressure is not sufficient to guarantee a permanent supply of water to upper floors or to houses on high ground.

Mains water is now available virtually everywhere, including Comino — you can see the pipe at the island's south landing — but in certain areas, notably in the south of Malta, it may taste slightly brackish and alter the flavour of tea and coffee. It is, however, safe. Many Maltese families buy bottled water, such as Fontana brand from Baħrija north of Naxxar, for their babies.

WEIGHTS and MEASURES

The metric system operates throughout, with milk sold in litres, distances measured in kilometers, and potatoes priced in kilogrammes. But you can buy petrol by the gallon until self-service pumps are in wider use.

The pre-colonial system is almost defunct, but you may read of the *rotolo* of 1lb 14oz (800gm), the *wizna* of 9lb (4kg), the *terz* of 1.½ pints (.33 litre), or the *tomna* of 174sq yds (.11ha).

Clothing sizes. Continental measures apply in Malta.

	SHIRTS					DRESSES				
British	14½	15	15½	16	16½	10	12	14	16	18
Continental	37	38	39	40	41	40	42	44	46	48
N. American	14½	15	15½	16	16½	8	10	12	14	16

	MEN'S SHOES					WOMEN'S SHOES				
British	7	8	9	10	11	3	4	5	6	7
Continental	41½	42½	43½	44½	45½	36	37	38	39	40
N. American	8	9	10	11	12	4½	5½	6½	7½	8½

WILDLIFE

Malta is sadly short of wildlife, due to the lack of summer rainfall, the absence of rugged country remote from human pressures — and also to the Maltese man's love of shooting and trapping birds particularly during the spring and autumn migrations. In the remoter parts of the islands you will see small columns of stone slabs, topped by a larger stone with a nail fixed to its centre. This is where song-birds are tethered so that they may lure in others of their kind, to fall victim to the mist net or the gun. The saddest sight I have seen in the Maltese islands was two rows of wild songbirds kept in tiny cages on a garage wall in Comino; innocent creatures of the air, condemned to life imprisonment for their beauty and their song — or to be eaten.

Go to any isolated clifftop and you will find empty cartridge cases as a silent testimony to the annual slaughter of other birds, purely for the 'sport.'

When I raised the issue with the Ministry of Education and the Interior, a spokesman explained: "Legislation on the matter of bird trapping exists in this country, and reguates both the species of bird that may be trapped, and the type of trap that may be used, besides requiring a police licence for the activity. Enforcement of the law has been strengthened by setting up a section of the police with the express purpose of clamping down on offences of bird shooting and trapping, and results are being obtained.

"In general, the policy is to discourage these activities as far as possible. One cannot move at the pace one would wish because bird-trapping is a custom in these islands dating back to the rule of the Knights and possibly further. Government is doing its best to educate the people, especially in the years of schooling."

In a perfect world, *no* bird should be trapped or shot. But neither should foxes, deer and badger be hunted for sport.

Rabbits. Large mammals have been extinct since shortly after the Ice Age, and the only wild mammal of any size now is the rabbit; wild rabbits are confined to the St Paul's Islands, where they are legally protected, and to Comino, but domesticated rabbits are bred in many smallholdings for their meat.

The winds bring an occasional locust over from Africa, there are no scorpions, and snakes are rare — but I have seen one on Comino which moved with incredible speed. In season, butterflies abound, with some of the swallowtail species quite common.

Your greatest surprise may come on the ferry crossing to Gozo when hundreds of six-inch (15cm) flying fish leap from the water by the ship's bows and fly or glide for fifty feet (15m) before plunging back into the sea, but you could make the crossing a dozen times and not see one.

Fort St Angelo in Birgu was once a 'stone frigate' in the Royal Navy.

4: MALTI

Malta's unique language

MALTI IS AN ARABIC LANGUAGE, spoken by Christians and written in the Latin alphabet, which makes it doubly unique. It's in the Semitic group along with Amharic, the language of Ethiopia, as well as Hebrew, and Arabic itself. The Semitic tongues are claimed to be spoken by descendants of Shem, one of Noah's three sons; the Hamitic languages, descended from Noah's son Ham, include Cushite, spoken in Somalia, and the Berber of north Africa. Malti is confined to the Maltese islands where it is learned in the cradle and is the republic's official language — although most people speak English as well, and a large number have Italian as a third tongue.

The people of Malta were the first in Europe and its offshore islands to accept Christianity, only a short while after it had taken root in Cyprus, the world's first Christian country, and they held on to their religion even after the Arab conquest of 870. But they lost their Latin language.

Arabic was the language of commerce and government, and it endured later conquests probably because no ruling power stayed long enough to implant its own culture. Norman French, Catalan, German, Italian, Turkish, and English, were all heard in Malta; each contributed to the growing vocabulary of Malti but none was dominant enough to break down the strict rules of Semitic grammar.

Modern Malti, which became a written language only at the beginning of this century, still retains that Arabic structure which alters words more by changing their vowels than by adding bits at the beginning and end, as is more common in European languages. German uses the vowel shift, as in *Vater, Väter*, 'father, fathers,' but is notorious for its agglutination, while English has many examples of agglutination such as *fit* giving 'refit, misfit, unfit, fitted, fittingly.'

Thus the Malti word for *a dog*, specifying the animal's sex, is **kelb** which changes for *the dog* to **il-kelb** and for *the bitch* to **il-kelba**. Straightaway you learn that nouns have gender (how fortunate is the English language!) that there is no word for 'a, an' — and that *il* and its variants mean 'the.'

The word for 'the,' *il*, comes in ten other forms. Whenever it stands before a word beginning with *ċ, d, l, n, r, s, t, x, z, ż*, it drops the 'l' in favour of the first letter of the following word, thus *iċ ċimiterju*, 'the cemetery.' These are called 'sun letters,' and it follows that the other consonants, *b, f, ġ, g, għ, h, ħ, j, k, m, p, q, v, w*, are 'moon letters.'

The word for 'one' has gender, as in all European languages except English, and is *wieħed* in its masculine form and *waħda* in the feminine.

Conjugating Malti verbs (going from 'I am' to 'he was' to 'they would be') is highly intricate, which makes learning the language other than at your mother's knee a daunting task. If you want to take it further, try *Teach Yourself Malti* by Joseph Aquilina (EUP 1965), but for casual use here's a basic vocabulary and a rough guide to pronunciation.

A is short, as in *cat*, not *car*; **Ċ** is the 'ch' in *church*; **C** is a borrowed letter and is always hard, as in *cat*, never pronounced 's' as in *city*; **E** is short as in *let*; **Ġ** is soft, as in *giant*, but **G** is hard as in *go*. It's possible to put the two letters together without a vowel between them, making 'Ġgantija,' the name of a Copper Age tomb, which is pronounced 'jig–an–teea'.

H is mute except at the end of a word when it is aspirated, making 'Misrah' sound *mis-rahhh*. **Ħ(ħ)** – note the horizontal stroke – is harsh like the Arabic ح or the 'ch' in the Scottish *loch* or the German *machen*. **I** is short as in *pin*; **J** has the Germanic sound of 'y' as in *Ja!* **M** is spoken normally, but note that initial M followed by a consonant sounds like 'im' as in *imdeena* for Mdina and *imnaydra* for Mnajdra.

GĦ(għ) counts as a single letter and is slotted between N and O in the Malti alphabet. On the island of Malta it has no sound of its own, but acts as a glottal stop, making the Maltese village of 'Għargħur' sound like *:aar:ur*, with a total silence at the start and in the middle of the word. But on Gozo it has a faint rasping sound, making the Gozitan village of Xagħra sound like *sha-hhhra*.

O is straightforward, as in *not*.

Q is another difficult letter and never has a U after it. At the beginning and middle of a word it is a glottal stop, the ع of Arabic, the brief pause marking where a Scot drops the 'tt' from *butter*, or between the words *Herr Ober!* when a German calls the waiter, and often shown by the symbol ¦. At the end of a word, Q is pronounced as 'k,' so in normal English 'to Qala, Luqa and Żurrieq' which would sound 'tookala, lookaran Zurreek,' should sound 'to ¦ala, Loo¦a and Zurriek.'

U tends to be medium-long as the vowel in *put* or southern-England *soot*, not as in *cup*. **X** is as *sh* so that 'Xemxija' is *shem-shi-ya*. **Ż** is soft as in *Zanzibar* while **Z** is hard as in the German *Zimmer* or the 'ts' in *nuts*.

BASIC VOCABULARY

The Maltese appreciate your using a few words of Malti, and it's one way of making friends among a people who are already very friendly.

Please	**jekk jogħġbok**	*ee-eck yawj-bok*
Thank you	**grazzi**	*grats-tsee*
Goodbye	**saħħa**	*sahh-ha*
Today	**illum**	*ill-loom*
Tomorrow	**għada**	*¦aa-da*
Yesterday	**il-bieraħ**	*ill-bee-erahh*
Lunch	**l-ikla ta'nofsinhar**	*lee-kla ta nofs inn-aar*
Dinner	**l-ikla ta'filgħaxija**	*lee-kla ta fil¦a-shee-ya*
Tomato(es)	**tadama, tadam**	*ta-dam-a*
Orange(s)	**larinġa, larinġ**	*la-rinn-ja*
Apple(s)	**tuffieħa, tuffieħ**	*tuff-ee-eha*
Melon(s)	**bettiegħa, bettiegħ**	*bett-ee-eha*
Cheese	**ġobon**	*jaw-bon*
Bread	**ħobż**	*hhops*
Wine	**imbid**	*im-beet*
Water	**ilma**	*il-ma*
Ice	**silġ**	*seelj*
Hotel	**lukanda**	*look-an-da*
Bathroom	**kamra tal-banju**	*kamra tal-ban-yoo*
Bedroom	**kamra tas-sodda**	*kamra tass-sodda*
Shop	**ħanut**	*hhanoot*
Chemist	**spiżżerija**	*spizz-er-eeja*
Bank	**bank**	*bank*
Church	**knisja**	*k-niss-ya*
Beach	**plajja**	*pla-eeya*
Cliff	**irdum**	*ir-doom*
Island	**ġzira**	*j-zeera*
one (masc, fem)	**wieħed, waħda**	*wee-e-hhet, waahh-da*
two	**tnejn**	*t'nayn*
three	**tliata**	*t'lee-etta*
four	**erbgħa**	*errb-¦a*
five	**ħamsa**	*hham-sa*
six	**sitta**	*sitta*
seven	**sebgħa**	*seb-¦a*
eight	**tminja**	*t'min-ya*
nine	**disgħa**	*dis-¦a*
ten	**għaxra**	*¦ash-ra*
eleven	**ħdax**	*hhuh-dash*
twelve	**tnax**	*t'nash*

thirteen	**tlettax**	*t'lit-tash*
fourteen	**erbatax**	*err-bat-ash*
fifteen	**ħmistax**	*hh'mis-tash*
sixteen	**sittax**	*sit-tash*
seventeen	**sbatax**	*sbat-ash*
eighteen	**tmintax**	*t'min-tash*
nineteen	**dsatax**	*tsat-ash*
twenty	**għoxrin**	*ˌawsh-reen*
thirty	**tletin**	*t'let-teen*
forty	**erbgħajn**	*err-baˌeen*
fifty	**ħamsin**	*hham-seen*
sixty	**sittin**	*sit-teen*
seventy	**sebgħajn**	*sebˌa-een*
eighty	**tmenin**	*t'men-een*
ninety	**disgħajn**	*disˌa-een*
(one) hundred	**mija**	*mee-ya*
three hundred	**tlett mija**	*t'let mee-ya*
(one) thousand	**elf**	*elf*
five million	**ħames miljuni**	*hham-ess mil-yoonee*
Left	**xellug**	*shel-loook*
Right	**lemin**	*lem-een*
Near	**viċin**	*vee-cheen*
Far	**bogħod**	*bawˌt*

What is the time, please?	**X'ħin hu jekk jogħġbok?**
It is three o'clock.	**Huma it‑tlieta.**
It is ten to four.	**Huma l-erbgħa neqsin għaxra.**
Where is the bank?	**Fejn hu l-bank?**
Where is the hotel?	**Fejn hi l-lukanda?**
Which way to . . .?	**Minn liema triq ngħaddi għal . . .?**

I am English (*m, f*)	**Jiena Ingliż, Ingliża**
I am Scottish	**Jiena Skoċċi , Skoċċiża**
I am Irish	**Jiena Irlandiż, Irlandiża**
I am American	**Jiena Amerikan, Amerikana**
I am German	**Jiena Germaniż, Germaniża**
I am Dutch	**Jiena Olandiż, Olandiża**
We are on holiday	**Qegħdin vaganza**
What is your name?	**X'ismek?**
My name is . . .	**Jisimni . . .**

5: GOING TO MALTA

Air or sea crossing

THE GREAT MAJORITY OF TOURISTS go to Malta by air. Sea travel is confined to southern Italians taking their cars; to people of any nationality taking up residence ('residence' must be interpreted in its strictest sense; see chap 10) or going for up to three months; backpackers travelling overland and making a brief call at Malta (but Malta is not for the backpacker); and passengers on cruise liners. And, of course, for Maltese drivers exploring Europe. The lack of foreign-registered vehicles on Malta's roads shows that the airlines reign supreme.

BY AIR

Scheduled services. Scheduled services operate between Luqa, Malta's only civil airport (it's pronounced *loo¦ah* and the European cities of Amsterdam, Athens, Belgrade, Berlin, Brussels, Catania, Frankfurt, Geneva, London (Gatwick and Heathrow), Manchester, Moscow, Munich, Paris (Orly and Charles de Gaulle), Rome and Zurich, with feeder links to the remainder of Europe and to North America.

Air Malta, the national carrier, added two Airbus 320s to its fleet in March 1990, with three Boeing 737s for 1993.

Charter services. The majority of package tourists arrive on charter flights, which touch down at Luqa at almost any hour of the day or night, thus many visitors find the airport lights are their first glimpse of the island.

Package tourists are, of course, met at the airport with coaches to transfer to their hotels even at 2am, but the independent traveller on a flight-only ticket must arrange in advance for his hire car to be at the airport, or wait for the working day to begin before he makes a move. The bus service starts around 0530, but taxi drivers are there to meet every arrival; it costs around Lm8 to hire a *cab* to Mellieħa at this hour of the morning, but before you climb aboard make certain the rate won't jump to Lm8 *per person* when you arrive.

LUQA AIRPORT

Luqa was one of three RAF bases built on Malta during the days of empire, and its main runway is now 10,000ft (3,000m) long, dominating the south-centre of the island. Another airfield at Ħal Far has remained as the Maltese military base, while the third aerodrome, at Ta'Qali (*ta'ahly*) has become a craft centre.

Five miles south-west of Valletta, Luqa Airport's terminal was extended and modernised in 1990–'91, giving exclusive parking for 80 coaches outside the main door, separate floors for arrivals and departures on the American system, and a large restaurant and roof garden on the top floor. The roads in the immediate area have also been improved.

Services. The two main **banks** are at the airport, open 24-hours, but you can get cash on your credit card only between 0745-2000 Mon-Sat. The **tourist office** is open round the clock and may be able to help with car hire and hotel bookings even at 1am.

The terminal has toilets (restrooms), including those for ♿ passengers; phones, including an international line (get your coins at a bank); a room for nursing the baby; and one of the world's few duty-free shops for incoming travellers. There's also a duty-free shop for those departing, with both pricing their goods in Lm but accepting any major currency or credit card.

Duty frees. Arriving visitors are allowed to import 200 cigarettes or 250gm of tobacco, a litre each of spirits and wine, perfume worth up to Lm2, and gifts worth up to Lm2.

This Super Constellation serves in-flight meals without ever leaving the ground.

BY SEA

Tirrenia Line. Air Malta's sister company, Sea Malta, operates a container service between Valletta and Felixstowe, but for passenger traffic Catania in Sicily is the main departure point in mainland Europe. Tirrenia Line operates a thrice-weekly service the year round, leaving **Reggio di Calabria** at the toe of Italy at 0830 on Tuesday, Friday and Sunday, calling at Catania (1145-1300) and Syracuse (1515-1630) before docking at Valletta at 2130. The return is on Monday, Wednesday and Saturday leaving Valletta 0845, Syracuse (1400-1530), Catania (1745-1845) and docking in Reggio at 2200. The passenger fare is around £35 one way.

Tirrenia's traffic is handled by Serena Holidays of London ☎071.244.8422.

GNMT. Tirrenia and General National Maritime Transport of Tripoli also operate ferries from **Naples** to Malta with an overnight crossing, and the GNMT then connects with **Libya** which explains how so many Libyans visit Malta. The *why* is another matter: they come for goods not available at home.

Gozo Channel Company. The Gozo Channel Company which, as its name implies, operates the car ferries to Gozo, moved into the foreign market in April 1987 with a summer-only car ferry between **Catania** and Sa Maison, Valletta. Departures are from Valletta at 2330 on Wednesday and Friday, arriving Catania 0800 the next day; Catania departures are at 1500 on Thursday and Saturday, arriving Valletta 2300, same day. Fares start at Lm16 single, with similar prices for cars. The service does not continue to the Italian mainland.

The company's address is Hay Wharf, Sa Maison, Valletta, Malta, ☎243964-5-6; the Italian agent is Signor Luigi Mazzoni, Europa Express SRL, Viale Marco Polo 35B, Rome.

The overland route is undeniably a long haul for north Europeans planning a short stay in Malta, but if you have freight to move it's more convenient and quicker to use the car ferries than to ship the goods on the long sea passage via the Strait of Gibraltar.

Virtu Rapid Ferries. And then came Virtu Rapid Ferries with its high-speed catamaran, operating from 1 April to 15 October from Sa Maison and **Catania,** and on certain days continuing on to **Taormina** (Sicily, Strait of Messina) or to **Pozzallo** (south Sicily). The sailing schedule is complex, with departures every day in high season, sometimes making the round trip twice in a day. One way or day return fares are Lm21, with period return Lm32, making this an ideal day's outing from Valletta. The *Santa Maria* catamaran seats 330 passengers, and at a cruising speed of 47 knots (54mph, 87kph), you are seated: there's no promenading the deck.

The catamaran also sails to Kelibia in Tunisia, not only offering another excursion but also providing an interesting trans-Med link for the backpacking overlander.

Virtu Rapid Ferries is at 3 Princess Elizabeth Tce, Ta'Xbiex, PO Box 285, ☎317088.

Considering the relatively low cost of car hire, driving to Malta is out of the question for normal tourists, but is viable if you're buying property and exporting your car — see chapter 10 — or want to buy some of the classic cars still in daily use in the islands: there are probably more Ford Anglias and Populars, Morris Minors, Triumph Heralds and Austin Sevens in Malta than there are laid up in garages across Britain.

The 'Melitaland' began life in The Netherlands as the 'Dordrecht.'

6: TRAVELLING IN MALTA

Ferries, helicopter, car hire, buses

TRAVEL IN AND BETWEEN THE MALTESE ISLANDS is cheap and convenient. Few places in the world have lower rates for car hire, and the bus fares are among the cheapest in Europe. For a touch of class you can also travel on the flat land around Valletta and along Sliema promenade by *karozzin* (add an 'i' to make the plural), an elegant horse-drawn carriage.

Inter-island ferries give you the option of the short crossing from Ċirkewwa or the long crossing from Valletta, to Mġarr on Gozo; and there's the small passenger-only ferry from Malta and Gozo to tiny Comino. Cruisers ply from Sliema to Comino's Blue Lagoon, or take you around Malta, or Gozo, or both − but these are pleasure trips rather than ferry services, and are priced accordingly. You may also make your own arrangements for a trip around Grand Harbour aboard a *luzzu*, a fishing-boat painted in brilliant colours and carrying the protective eye of Osiris on each bow.

For efficiency, and a touch of adventure, there is also the helicopter link between Luqa Airport and Gozo, which began operations experimentally in the summer of 1990 and went into full service in 1991.

INTER-ISLAND FERRIES

GOZO SHORT CROSSING

The **Gozo Channel Company** operates the car ferry between Ċirkewwa on Malta and Mġarr on Gozo (the names are pronounced *chir-kowa* and *imjar*, and there's another Mġarr on the island of Malta). Departures are year-round unless specified otherwise:

from Ċirkewwa	from Mġarr
0100 (Apr-Oct only)	0030
0300 (Apr-Oct only)	0230
0500 (Apr-Oct only)	0430
0645	0600
0730	0645
0815	0730
0930	0845
1000	0915
1100	1015
1200	1115
1300	1215
1400	1315
1500	1415
1600	1515
1700	1615
1800	1715
1900	1815
1000	1915
2200	2115
2400 (Apr-Oct only)	2315

Fares.

Adult	Lm1.50
Child (3-12 yrs)	Lm0.50
Malta resident	Lm1
Gozo resident	Lm0.30
Car	Lm3.50

GOZO LONG CROSSING.

Valletta-Gozo. The year-round Valletta (Sa Maison) link with Mġarr is now twice a day, leaving Sa Maison at 0930 and 1430, and leaving Mġarr at 0545 and 1200. It's mainly a cargo service but if you can get aboard the fares are the same.

Valletta-Comino-Gozo. The catamaran *Calypso* operates the daily passenger service between Sa Maison and Gozo, with calls at Comino, from mid-June to the end of September on this schedule:

Mġarr	Comino	Marsalforn	Ċirkewwa	Sa Maison	Sliema	Comino
0630	————	————	————	0715	————	————
0815	0830	————	————	————	0915	————
————	————	1000	1015	————	————	————
1300	————	————	————	1400	————	————
1530	————	————	————	————	0615	1645
1700	————	————	1715	————	————	————
————	————	1730	————	————	1830	————

All changes to timetable come into effect on the first Monday of the month. The service operates every day, including bank holidays and festivals, but may be suspended by occasional winter storms.

The Gozo Channel Co's offices are at Hay Wharf, Sa Maison, ☎243964; other contacts are Ċirkewwa ☎471884, Mġarr ☎556114.

The vessels. The Gozo Channel Company operates six vessels, the flagship being the *Ghawdex* – the word is Malti for 'Gozo' – built in Bremen and bought in 1979 as the *Kalle*. It is of 2,310 gross tonnes and is 274ft (83.6m) long. Also bought in 1979, the **Melitaland** was the *Dordrecht* operating in the Netherlands; the vessel was lengthened to its present 231ft (70.4m), giving it a gross tonnage of 1,435. This is an open-sided drive-through ferry, reminiscent of a Mississippi river-boat.

The **Mġarr** came in 1980, changing her name from *Saltholm;* she's a 728-tonner that's 164ft (50m) long. Next was the **Cittadella,** formerly the *Prins Bernhart*, operating in Dutch waters until 1987. She has a displacement of 1,973 tonnes and is 275ft (84m) long, and is a drive-through ship like the *Melitaland.*

The **Xlendi,** formerly the *Royal Sheba*, joined the fleet in 1990 and displaces 1,123 tonnes with a length of 262ft (80m). Finally, the fast catamaran **Calypso,** bought new in 1988, is purely for the tourist market with a stationary displacement of 50 tonnes, a length of 59ft 6in (18.14m), a beam of 19ft (5.9m) and a draft of less than 4ft (1.2m) at speed with her bow cushion in operation.

The company. The Gozo Channel Company, founded in 1979 to replace the previous company operating the ferry, is expanding to meet the growing demand for its services; in 1989 it carried more than 1,700,000 passengers and 324,000 vehicles. As it operates the only year-round link between the islands it offers concessions of up to 70% discount to Gozitan residents as a public service.

Bus connections. Buses on routes 45 and 48 from Valletta run to Ċirkewwa, and those on routes 25 and 26 meet the ferries at Mġarr, Gozo, for the run into Victoria. There are no buses to meet ferries plying through the night.

PASSENGER FERRY TO COMINO.

Visitors' cars are not allowed on Comino, although you may see an assortment of vehicles on the island, including Land Rovers and an occasional bulldozer or a lorry; when the need arises these are shipped in by the Gozo Channel Company to the south landing. The regular passenger-only ferries use the north landing by the Comino Hotel, and the Sliema cruisers moor at a tiny jetty in the Blue Lagoon.

COMINO HOTEL FERRY. The Comino Hotel's ferry service has expanded to become the principal link with the mainland and Gozo. The timber-hulled *Comino* with a capacity of around 40 passengers (although no lifebelts or rafts are visible aboard) was built in Belfast in 1945 and operates the regular schedule; the smaller *Cominotto*, named from the sister island, is the standby vessel, the carrier of stores for the Comino Hotel and other island residents, and is available for special trips.

The Comino Hotel's season is from late March to early November, during which time the ferry is on **summer schedule,** starting from its overnight base on Gozo. These are its **departure** times *to* Comino:

from Malta	from Gozo
0730	0630
0900	0830
1000	(not Wed,Fri)
1200	1100
1515	1430
1715	1615
1900	1800
2230	2145

These are its **departure** times *from* Comino:

to Malta	to Gozo
0645 (via Gozo)	0645
0830 (Wed,Fri)	0800 (not Wed,Fri)
0930	1030
1130	1410
1445	1545
1645	1745
1830	2130
2200	2300

Fares. Adult fares are Lm1 return (either to or from Comino), 50c for a child; a child becomes an adult around 10 years old.

Terminals. The ferry calls at Ċirkewwa on Malta and at Mġarr on Gozo, where the main car ferries dock. Both terminals have public lavatories but as Ċirkewwa has no village nearby it also offers coffee, a restaurant, games room, gift shop and telephone.

Winter schedule. With the Comino Hotel closed, the winter schedule is much restricted. This is what it *may* be in the 1991-'92 season, each time being a **departure** to the next point mentioned, starting at Mġarr, Gozo:

0630 to Comino; 0700 to Malta; 0730 to Comino; 1400 to Gozo; 1430 to Comino; 1450 to Malta; 1545 to Comino; 1645 to Gozo.

ROYAL I. During the summer, a term to be interpreted loosely, the *Royal I* motor launch runs a passenger ferry between Comino and **Ramla Bay.** The skipper has a sign where the main road turns sharp left to Ċirkewwa, pointing right, to Ramla Bay and his ferry. His service is on the hour every hour, subject to passenger load, and his return fare is Lm2, or its equivalent in any other currency.

From this jetty, too, several launches operate for scuba divers in the Gozo Channel. The *Floria* is typical, charging Lm40 for a party, all day, but bookings must be made through a diving club.

CRUISES.

CALLING AT COMINO.

A cruise from Sliema's Strand calling at Comino is essentially a *cruise;* your stay is long enough for you to swim in the Blue Lagoon or stroll to the Comino Hotel but is not long enough to allow you to explore the island in detail and appreciate its solitude.

Captain Morgan: Comino cruise. Captain Morgan's motor cruiser sails from The Strand, Sliema, daily at 1000 and heads directly for Comino, mooring stern-on at the tiny landing in the Blue Lagoon or tying up to a buoy and ferrying passengers ashore in dinghies. Between 1315 and 1400 guests have a cold buffet lunch, followed by 90 minutes to swim or stroll. The little ship sails at 1530, reaching Sliema around 1700. The fare is Lm6.25, including lunch and collection from your hotel or apartment.

OTHER CRUISE ROUTES.

Captain Morgan: Malta circumnavigation. Depart 0915 on a clockwise cruise around Malta, calling at Marsascala and Marsaxlokk bays without mooring; there's a brief stop at the Blue Grotto and a look at Popeye Village before dropping anchor in Comino's Blue Lagoon. The cruiser weighs anchor at eight bells in the afternoon watch (1600) and continues past Mellieħa and St Paul's Islands to reach Sliema at 1730. The fare is Lm7.50, including lunch and collection.

Captain Morgan: Gozo circumnavigation. Departing from Sliema at 1000 on Wednesday (May through Oct), Saturday (June through Oct) and Sunday (July through Sep), the cruiser heads for Aħrax Point and then circumnavigates Gozo clockwise, motoring close to some of the island's splendid cliff scenery, notably the Fessej Rock, the Ta'Ċenċ cliffs, Fungus Rock and the Azure Window, mooring in Comino's Blue Lagoon around 1515 for a 90-minute stay with coffee and cakes. Return to Sliema is scheduled for 1600 and the fare is Lm9.95.

Captain Morgan has three other routes: around Marsamxett and Grand harbours, with daily sailings from Sliema Marina at 1100, 1215, 1315, 1445, 1545 and 1630, for Lm2.50, children younger than ten going free; the Thursday night party leaving Sliema at 1900 and returning at midnight for Lm5.95; and the day or night cruises in a glass-bottomed vessel.

Jylland and Pleasure Cruises. Captain Morgan has wiped out his opposition − not by piracy but by buying them. The Jylland and Pleasure Cruises launches you see at their moorings off Sliema are now incorporated into the Captain Morgan fleet and schedules. Keep a lookout for Jylland's *Almatania,* claimed to be Lord Mountbatten's favourite boat during his stay on Malta in 1940.

Virtu Rapid Ferries. Virtu Rapid, the company which operates the catamaran link with Sicily, circumnavigates the islands on Sun and Mon only (not in winter), leaving Sliema at 0900, calling at Buġibba at 0930 for passengers, then speeding anticlockwise around Gozo and Malta, with a call at the Blue Lagoon, and finishing with a tour of Grand and Marxamsett harbours. The catamaran is the one which cruises at 47 knots to Sicily with up to 330 passengers, so come early for a window seat. Fares are Lm12.50 on Sun, Lm14.50 Mon, and the firm is at 3 Princess Elizabeth Tce, Ta'Xbiex, ☎318854.

THE HELICOPTER LINK

The long-promised helicopter link between Luqa and Gozo began in 1990 with a 13-seat machine which was quickly changed for a 20-seater. Operating in peak season only − July through September − the aircraft follows this daily schedule, *but check for variations* as the service is new:

Flight	depart Luqa	Flight	dep Gozo
H300	0600	H301	0615
H302	0800	H303	0815
H304	1125	H305	1140
H306	1300	H307	1315
H308	1430	H309	1445
H310	1600	H311	1650
H312	1730	H313	1745
H314	1905	H315	1920

All these scheduled flights last for 10 minutes.

Sightseeing. In addition, flight H320 from Luqa at 1015 and H322 from Gozo at 1615 are sightseeing trips taking 30 minutes to make the inter-island journey, with the possibility of asking the pilot to make a special diversion for you alone. You can also charter the machine.

Fares. An open-dated return costs Lm16; a day return is Lm12, one-way is LM8, and a standby one-way is Lm6; children up to 12 travel at half price. The sightseeing fare is Lm15 for adults. The **baggage allowance** is 20kg.

Gozo Heliport. Gozo's heliport is a small patch of tarmac in a field south of the main road linking Victoria and Mġarr, near the Gozo Heritage. Check-in time is 15 minutes, and a taxi service links you with Victoria — or you could walk to the main road and catch a bus.

Contacts. Malta Air Charter, the operator, is available at Gozo heliport on ☎557905, or through the Gozo Channel Co, Sa Maison, on ☎243964, Mġarr ☎ 556114, or through Air Malta reservations, ☎882920-5, or booking offices in Sliema, Valletta and Luqa.

TRAVEL BY LAND

CAR HIRE

The international car hire companies have agencies in Malta. **Avis** is at seven locations but ☎246640 or 225986 (24—hr service) serves them all. **Eurodollar** is on ☎220956 (24-hrs) and **Budget** is on ☎627111 (24-hrs).

You can make your reservation through the company's office in your own country: **Avis,** for example, is in the UK at Hayesgate House, 27 Uxbridge Rd, Hayes, UB4 0JN, ☎081.848.8733; at Mainzer Landstrasse 221, Frankfurt, Germany, ☎069.730081; Neptunus Gebouw, Hagehilweg 7, 1101-CA, Amsterdam ZO, ☎020.564.1641; Biluteleie Postkasse 154, 1312 Slependen, ☎02.847800.

Maltese car hire companies. Malta has more than 100 car rental agencies unconnected with any international chain, most of them being small concerns and some having only one or two cars. To keep this list manageable, the agencies are arranged by area, giving just name, address and phone.

MALTA: Balżan: Emgor Garage, 95 Naxxar Rd, ☎410905; Supermotor Rentals, 64 St Francis St, ☎443129; **Birkirkara:** Ace Car Hire, Windmill St, ☎442795; Jolly Rent-a-Car, Windmill St, ☎499046; **Buġibba:** Agius Car Hire, Pioneer Rd, ☎471603; Alexander's Rent-a-Car, Islet Promenade, ☎471186; Compass Garage, ns in Pioneer Rd, ☎472215; David's Rent-a-Car, Triq Gulju I-Centurjon, ☎475235; Emm Enterprises Ltd, Triq Gulju I-Centurjon, ☎473853; Eurosun Garage, Islet Promenade, ☎472338; Frank's, Islet Promenade, ☎476239; Godwin's Car Hire, St Anthony St, ☎471687; Hideaway, Pioneer Rd, ☎475240; Johncol Rent-a-Car, Triq Il-Ħarifa, ☎474541; Liverpool Car Hire, Upper Conversion St, ☎471668; Victory Car Rentals, Bay Sq, ☎473755; **Burmarrad:** Bluebird Garage, ☎471700; **Fgura:** Marshall's Car Rentals, Triq Il-Liedna, ☎774913; **Gwardamanġa:** Regency Car Hire, Ursuline Sisters St, ☎234532; **Ġzira:** John's Garage, 2, Family Flats, Sliema Rd, ☎334849; Sterling Car Hire Ltd, 100 Manoel St, ☎330925; United Garage, 66 Ġzira Rd, ☎314637; **Ħamrun:** Butterfly Garage, Brighella St, ☎448605; John's Garage, Villambrosa St, ☎238745; Merlin Car Hire Ltd, Mountbatten St, ☎223131; Pat's

Garage, Joseph Abela Scolaro St, ☎239692; Safion Garage, Parish
Priest Mifsud Rd, ☎237400; **Kirkop:** Tony's Garage, Mdina Rd,
☎682183; **Lija:** Percius Car Hire Ltd, Annibale Preca St, ☎442530;
Marsa: Gypsy Garage, 32 Nazzareno St, ☎603500; Paul & Rocco Ltd,
Cross Rd, ☎622267; Unicar Services Ltd, Prince Albert Town,
☎342584; **Marsascala:** BJ Rent-a-Car, Triq Il-Maħsel, ☎816251;
Mellieħa: Al Capone Car Hire, Santa Maria Est, ☎472477; Billy's, Main
St, ☎473308; Drifter Garage, 89 Main St, ☎474022; Fairways Garage,
New Mill St, ☎474570; Henry's Garage Ltd, 10 Mellieħa Sq, ☎474105;
Hirewise, 39 Parish St, ☎473317; JJ Garage, 9 Mellieħa Hts, ☎472048;
Manuel's Garage, 3 Mellieħa Sq, ☎473544; Melita Garage, Saverio
Mifsud St, ☎443698; Mellicħa Garage, 132 Main St, ☎473134; Rainbow
Car Hire, 91 Mellieħa Hts, ☎471184; Roadie's Garage, 78 New Mill St,
☎473321; Xuereb Car Hire, 30 Vista Hts, ☎472638; **Mosta:** CB Rentals
Ltd, 2 College St, ☎445851; Downunder Garage, 6 Alley 2, Bridge St,
☎491057; Nelson's Garage, Rotunda Flat 2, Bridge Junction, ☎497206;
Roma Garage, 6 Main St, ☎410143; **Msida:** Aloysius Garage, Testafer-
rata St, ☎314732; Hiccups Rent-a-Car, Garżin St, ☎340822; JS Garage,
Borġ St, ☎234038; London Services Ltd, Msida Seafront, ☎246640;
Palma Garage, 4 Menoa Sq, ☎335119; Stefan Garage, Box Box Lane,
☎232578; Windsor Car Hire, First St, ☎330046; **Naxxar:** Swift Rent-a-
Car, Triq In-Nissieġ, ☎476816; **Qawra:** Astra Car Hire, Qawra Coast
Rd, ☎475171; London Garage, 17 La Valette Apts, Qawra Pt,
☎472380; **Qormi:** Buvell Rent-a-Car, Triq Il-Ħebbiez, ☎224153; Meli

*Twin cannon guard the main entrance to St John's Co-Cathedral in
Valletta.*

Car Rentals Ltd, Fremond St, ☎487030; Metropolitan Car Hire, Cannon Rd, ☎446532; Virgo Car Rentals, 250 Mdina Rd, ☎491862; **Rabat:** Buskett Forest Garage, ☎454328; Tony Rent-a-Car, Sammut St, Tal-Virtu, ☎682183; **St Andrew's:** Wembley's Car Hire, St Andrew's Rd, ☎335436; Wheeler's Vehicle Rentals Ltd, Triq L-Ibragg, ☎342438; **St Julian's:** Autorentals, St George's Rd, ☎337393; Joe's Garage, Mensija St, ☎314819; La Ronde Garage, Triq Il-Ħawt, Upper Cdns, ☎334079; Pembroke Car Hire, St George's Bay, ☎333641; **St Paul's Bay:** Aquarius Rent-a-Car, 188 St Paul's St, ☎471186; Edlyn's Ltd, Lampuka St, ☎221962; J & S Car Hire, Blacktail St, ☎471841; Night & Day Garage, 19 Toni Bajada St, ☎473459; Peter's Garage, 117 St Paul's St, ☎473474; **San Ġwann:** Alpine Rent-a-Car, Naxxar Rd, ☎337361; A1 Rent-a-Car, Capuchins St, ☎330755; Mr A. Caruana, White Flats, Marsabielle, ☎316861; **Sliema:** Curtis Rent-a-Car, 161 Rudolph St, ☎331614; Driveaway Car Hire, 1 Isourd St, ☎331105; Princess Car Hire, 179 Manwel Dimech St, ☎331368; Qui Si Sana Garage, 50 Qui Si Sana Pl, ☎330995; St Patrick's Rent-a-Car, 28 Windsor Tce, ☎330927; Steve's Garage, Creche St, ☎318712; Stivala Garage, 95 The Strand, ☎318704; U Rent-a-Car, Dolphin Ct, Tigné Seafront, ☎335689; Mr J. Żammit, 48a Tower Rd, ☎338905; **Tarxien,** Reno's Rent-a-Car, Żejtun Rd, ☎775442; **Ta'Xbiex:** GS Cars, c/o Grand Hotel Les Lapins, ☎342551; **Żabbar:** Pitty's Rent-a-Car Ltd, 58 Sanctuary St, ☎828436; Qormi Garage, St Joseph St, ☎820843; St Joseph Garage, Convent St, ☎808253; **Żebbuġ:** Muscat's Garage, 16 Campis St, ☎460034; Reno & Joe's Garage, 340 Main St, ☎467431; Ron's Garage, Mdina Rd, ☎640200; **Żejtun:** Pyramid Car Rentals, A. Grima St, ☎803171.

GOZO: Sannat: Frank's Garage, Ċenċ St, ☎556814; **Victoria:** Gozo Garage, 5 Xagħra Rd, ☎551866; Gozo United Ltd, 31 Republic St, ☎556291; Maygo Rent-a-Car, 34 Republic St, ☎556678.

Of the purely Maltese firms, the larger ones such as Wembley's of St Andrews (the largest of the locals) and Billy's of Mellieħa, are open day and night and will collect you at the airport at 2am with no extra charge, but even the one-man-one-car business does its best to match this service.

The smaller firms are more inclined to offer you a cheaper rental but the car you get may be a year or two older: in fact, virtually all the cars for hire in Malta are past their showroom peak. You must expect a touch of rust, wear on the upholstery, a missing mirror or a dent in the bumper.

Import tax. The reason is obvious when you realise that there is an import duty of 65% on all cars from the EEC, and an 80% duty on cars from everywhere else, the tax based on valuation by Glass's Guide plus freight and insurance paid by the importer. As the Maltese standard of living is lower than that in western Europe, this makes ownership of a car expensive, and motorists do their best to keep their vehicle on the road for as many years as possible: you will see many British cars that were built in the 1950s and 1960s, and buses dating back to just after the Second World War: some of these have clocked up a million miles.

The absence of de-icing salt preserves the bodywork, but the rippled road surfaces damage the steering and suspension while doing little to reduce driver speed; and there's no annual roadworthiness check on cars although buses and lorries are tested.

Licence. You will need to show your national driving licence: an international one is not needed. A provisional licence for a learner driver is not acceptable.

Age limit. The minimum age for driving a car in Malta is 18, but some firms are reluctant to rent a vehicle to anybody younger than 25 or older than 70: if this applies to you, check first.

Cost. There is no mileage rate; all rentals are purely on a time basis and payable when you order or collect the car. Most small agencies quote a single price regardless of the make of vehicle: from 1 June to 14 October Lm6 a day, the remainder of the year Lm5 a day, based on a minimum of three days, including third party insurance and restricted vehicle insurance, the 'collision damage waiver' of other countries. The rates vary slightly, and you may get a reduction in midwinter. A nine-seat minibus costs around Lm10 a day in summer, Lm7 in winter.

The ceiling of Gozo Citadel's Cathedral is cleverly painted to give the impression of a dome – but there isn't one.

Usually you start with a full tank of fuel, and you return the car with a full tank, but you'll find it difficult to use a tankful with a week's hard driving in an Austin Metro.

Petrol. Gas stations have been closed on Sunday since 1979 but may open again when self-service pumps are introduced; they're open Mon-Sat 0600-1800, more or less. Petrol costs Lm1.20 a gallon, 44p per litre (DM1.30 per litre, US$3.15 per US gallon with the dollar at $1.95 to £1), both before and after Iraq invaded Kuwait. Four-star is the only grade available, with unleaded impracticable in view of the age of many vehicles.

Motoring laws. The speed limit is 64kph (40mph) on main roads out of towns and 40kph (25mph) in urban areas; it is not compulsory to wear **seat belts** and there is no legal limit to **alcohol** consumption, no breathalyser and no blood test. Driving-and-drinking becomes evident only after an accident, but the courts punish the drunken driver more severely.

Rule of the road. Malta drives on the **left,** a legacy of British colonialism, but when you hear Maltese drivers joke that they drive in the shade, don't laugh: they're probably serious. Roundabouts are a hazard for visitors as few Maltese motorists slow down when approaching them, and some actually accelerate.

Roads and signs. In 1987 the islands had 897 miles (1,444km) of tarred roads, carrying 86,298 cars, 21,339 commercial vehicles and 367 buses − 120 vehicles per mile of tarmac. Main roads are comfortably wide, but minor roads may be little more than 8ft (2.5m) across, and on the island of Malta there is a need for better signposting: you will get lost, no matter how well you follow the map. Signs on Gozo have been greatly improved since the appointment of a minister for the island.

Number plates. Hire cars across the islands are recognisable by their registration beginning with an X, on yellow plates. Y−numbers on red plates are for coaches and taxis catering for the tourist trade.

BUSES

Malta's buses, like those on the Rock of Gibraltar, are small, to negotiate the narrow streets in many of the island's villages. Most of them are also old: a few have driven the equivalent of round the equator at least ten times, but they are all lovingly maintained.

There is no bus timetable; the service starts around 0530 and finishes around 2300, with each vehicle setting off when it has an adequate payload. For a small country, Malta has an intricate network of 74 routes, many of them starting and finishing at the main bus station on the large roundabout outside Valletta city gate.

Fares. Fares are modest: Valletta to Senglea or to Żebbug is 8c (13.5p, 40pf) single.

Buses do not carry the name of their destination; if you are to avoid getting lost you *must* know the route numbers, which are the same for the outward and the return journey.

VALLETTA to:
1 Vittoriosa terminus via Verdala
2 Vittoriosa, Victory Sq.
3 Senglea
4 Kalkara
5 Paola
6 Vittoriosa
8 Gudja via Għaxaq
GUDJA to:
9 Cospicua via Għaxaq
VALLETTA to:
11 Birżebbuġa
12 Kalafrana
13 Ħal Far
14 Birżebbuġa via Qajjenza
15 Santa Luċia
18 Żabbar
19 Marsascala
ŻABBAR to:
20 Cospicua
VALLETTA to:
21 Xgħajra
COSPICUA to:
22 Marsascala
23 Xgħajra
VALLETTA to:
26 Żejtun
27 Marsaxlokk
MARSAXLOKK to:
28 Cospicua via Żejtun & Bulebel
VALLETTA to:
29 Żejtun via Bulebel
32 Żurrieq via Luqa & Airport
33 Żurrieq via Luqa, Karwija & Safi
34 Żurrieq via Luqa, Airport, Kirkop & Safi
35 Qrendi via Guardroom & Mqabba

36 Luqa **(Airport)**
37 Ħas Seħr
38 Wied iż-Żurrieq
40 Attard
41 Birkirkara via San Ġwann & Mrabet St, Sliema
43 Mellieħa
44 Għadira
45 Marfa **(Gozo ferry)**
46 Mġarr via Mosta
47 Għajn Tuffieħa via Mġarr
48 Marfa via Sliema **(Gozo ferry)**
49 Buġibba
50 Armier
51 Armier via Ħamrun
52 Għajn Tuffieħa via St Paul's Bay
53 Mosta
54 Naxxar
55 Għargħur
MOSTA to:
56 Naxxar
NAXXAR to:
57 St Julian's
VALLETTA to:
60 Sliema, Savoy
61 Sliema Ferry
62 Sliema, Spinola
63 Sliema 'C' via Ta'Xbiex
65 San Ġwann
66 Ta'Giorni
SLIEMA FERRY to:
67 Ta'Giorni via Dingli St.
VALLETTA to:
68 St Andrew's via Paceville
71 Birkirkara
72 Birkirkara, Brared
73 Ħamrun
74 Balżan, Corintha Palace Hotel
75 Gwardamanġa, St Luke's Hospital

TOUR OPERATORS

You want to see the islands on a luxury coach or mini-coach excursion? **Nova Tours** and its rival **Link Up Tours**, have a wide range of all-day, morning, afternoon, or evening tours, with almost all the islands' attractions on at least one schedule. The list includes

Malta's southernmost point, the cliffs by Hassan's Cave.

Mosta's church dome, a cruise around **St Paul's Islands,** Ġgantija, a limestone quarry, the Three Cities, Popeye Village, a Grand Harbour cruise, the Marsa races, the Casino, Calypso's Cave, a village *festa* in season and, in collaboration with Virtu Rapid Ferries, a visit to the rim of Mt Etna's crater.

Nova Tours is on ☎239076 and Link Up Tours is at Triq Il-Trunċiera, **Bugibba** ☎471966, 472262; Link Up has departures from Bugibba and Sliema.

TAXIS

Taxis meet all arriving planes at Luqa Airport, day and night, with a sample fare to Mellieħa, at the other end of the island, being Lm8 for the cab (not per passenger: clarify this point with your driver) at 2am; book your return at the same time and you'll expect to pay Lm12.

The daytime fare between Victoria and Mġarr on Gozo is around Lm1, *for all passengers.* Cabs are metered so the only possible disputes could be over the number of passengers, and the route taken.

You'll also find taxis at the Gozo ferry terminals, outside the major hotels, in the resorts, and at the south-west end of Republic St, Valletta.

KARROZZINI

Karrozzini are the elegant horse-drawn carriages introduced in 1856 and still found in Valletta, Sliema, St Julian's and Rabat. Each karrozzin is costly to maintain, and is usually pulled by a high-stepping fine-limbed horse that might be seen on the Marsa racecourse, but the carriage driver's return on his investment is very irregular and there are many days in a year when he doesn't earn anything.

There are no set fares. On a good day in high season a steady supply of customers may push the price to Lm8 per person per hour, but on a bad day you can bargain down a long way from an asking price of Lm6.50. Whatever happens, agree the price, the time and the route before you step aboard.

OTHER TRANSPORT

A few hotels and car hire agencies rent pedal cycles, but I can comment from personal experience that Malta is not a good place for the cyclist: in the conurbations the traffic is too dense for safety, and in the countryside the hills are steep, the weather hot, and punctures come a little too frequently.

For a softer option, try Peter's Scooter Shop at 175a D'Argens Rd, Ġzira, ☎335244, or Nova Tours on ☎239076 for motor-bike or cycle hire.

7: WHERE TO STAY

From hotels to hostels

THERE IS NO SHORTAGE OF ACCOMMODATION in the Maltese islands, from five-star hotels, through apart-hotels, privately-owned and company-owned self-catering flats, to guest houses and a few hostels. The government has adopted the internationally-accepted star-rating system in favour of its earlier unique grading and, in its policy to maintain standards, it inspects all premises and sets an upper limit to the tariffs charged in all but the five-star hotels.

Symbols. These symbols are used in the following charts, showing services available *in addition to* the specification for each star rating. Information supplied by the MNTO.

- ⋈ number of beds
- 📺 television in all rooms (tv lounge in guest houses)
- ❊ private beach
- ⌅ pool
- ⇘ scuba diving instruction available
- ♫ night club
- ✗ full restaurant services
- ⚲ tennis courts
- ♿ wheelchair visitors accepted

HOTELS

Five-star. All five-star hotels are fully air-conditioned, with bar, restaurant, pool, laundry, hairdresser, and day-and-night room service and reception; all rooms have en-suite bath *and* shower, telephone, radio and television.

Dragonara Palace, St Julian's, ✆336422 357⋈, ❊ ⇘ ♫ ⚲ ♿; **Hilton Inernational,** St Julian's, ✆336201 400⋈, ❊ ⇘ ♫ ⚲ ♿; **Holiday Inn,** Tigne St, Sliema, ✆341173 364⋈, ❊ ⇘ ♫ ⚲ ♿; **Phoenicia,** The Mall, Floriana, ✆225241 175⋈, ♿; **Ta'Ċenċ,** Sannat, Gozo, ✆556830 100⋈, ❊ ♫ ⚲.

Four-star. All four-star hotels have some air-conditioning, with bar, restaurant, pool, laundry, hairdresser; room service is from breakfast to 2400hrs; all rooms have en-suite bath *or* shower. Television is not standard in all rooms.

Atlas, St Andrew's Rd, St Andrew's, ✆332860 196🛏, ♿; **Cavalieri,** Spinola Rd, St Julian's , ✆336255 210🛏, ✿ ♪; **Comino,** Comino, ✆473051 188🛏, ✿ ⇲ ♪ ♾; **Corinthia,** De Paule Ave, Attard, ✆440301 310🛏, ✿ ⇲ ♪ ♾; **Eden Beach,** St George's Bay, St Julian's , ✆341191 203🛏, ⇲ ♪ ♾; **Fortina,** Tigne Seafront, Sliema, ✆330449 198🛏, ♿; **Grand Hotel Les Lapins,** Ta'Xbiex Seafront, Ta'Xbiex, ✆342551 377🛏, ⇲ ♪ ♾; **Grand Hotel Verdala,** Inguanez St, Rabat, ✆451700, 328🛏, ♪ ♿; **Jerma Palace,** Marsascala, ✆823222 688🛏, ✿ ⇲ ♿; **New Dolmen,** Qawra, St Paul's Bay, ✆473661 594🛏, ✿ ⇲ ♪ ♾; **Paradise Bay,** Cirkewwa, ✆473981 406🛏, ✿ ⇲ ♪ ♾; **Preluna,** 124 Tower Rd, Sliema, ✆334001 406🛏, ✿ ⇲ ♪ ♿; **Ramla Bay,** Marfa, ✆473522 220🛏, ✿ ⇲ ♾ ♿; **Selmun Palace,** Mellieha, ✆472455 296🛏, ♾.

Three-star. All three-star hotels have bar, restaurant and laundry; all rooms have en-suite bath or shower. Swim pool is not standard.

Adelphi, Victory St, Gzira, ✆335110 96🛏; **Alphonso,** Triq il-Qaghliet, Sliema, ✆330053 54🛏; **Ambassador,** Shipwreck Promenade, Xemxija, ✆473870 60🛏, ≈; **Ascot,** St Andrew's St, Sliema, ✆331736 124🛏, ≈; **Astra,** 127 Tower Rd, Sliema, ✆331081 70🛏; **Atlantis,** Qolla St, Marsalforn, Gozo, ✆554685 54🛏, ⇲ ♿; **Calypso,** Marsalforn, Gozo, ✆556131 244🛏, ≈ ⇲ ♪ ♾ ♿; **Capua Court,** Borg Olivier St, Sliema, ✆334081 116🛏; **Carlton,** Tower Rd, Sliema, ✆315764, 80🛏; **Castille,** Castille Sq, Valletta, ✆243677 75🛏 ♪; **Carolina,** St Anthony St, Bugibba, ✆471536 72🛏;**Charella,** Triq il-Konz, Bugibba, ✆471329 110🛏, ≈; **Concorde,** Pioneer Rd, Bugibba, ✆473831 84🛏, ≈; **Cornucopia,** Gniern Imrik, Xaghra, Gozo, ✆556486 80🛏, ≈ ♿; **Country,** Luqa, ✆284364 140🛏, ≈ ♾; **Day's Inn,** 75,76 Cathedral St, Sliema, ✆331162 160🛏, ≈ ♿; **Eden Rock,** 117 Tower Rd, Sliema, ✆335575 76🛏; **Europa,** Tower Rd, Sliema, ✆330080 108🛏, ♿; **Flora,** Pioneer Rd, Bugibba, ✆473880 105🛏, ≈; **Golden Sands,** Golden Bay, Ghajn Tuffieha, ✆473961 503🛏, ✿ ≈ ⇲ ♪ ♾; **Green Dolphin,** St George's Bay, St Julian's , ✆337221 88🛏, ✿; **Grosvenor,** Pope Alexander VII, Balzan, ✆496023 100🛏, ♿; **Hyperion,** Triq it–Turisti, Bugibba, ✆473641 356🛏, ≈ ⇲; **Imperial,** Rudolph St, Sliema, ✆330011 153🛏, ≈ ⇲; **Kappara,** Kappara Rd, Kappara, ✆334367 40🛏, ≈; **Kennedy Court,** 166 The Strand, Sliema, ✆334367 175🛏; **Liliana,** Triq G, Centurjun, Bugibba, ✆472330 126🛏, ♪ ♿; **Marina,** Tigne Seafront, Sliema, ✆336461 120🛏, ♿; **Mediterranea,** Bugibba Rd, Bugibba, ✆471461 122🛏, ≈ ⇲; **Mellieha Bay,** Mellieha Bay, Ghadira, ✆473844 600🛏, ✿ ≈ ⇲ ♪ ♾; **Metropole,** Adrian Dingli St, Sliema, ✆330188 230🛏; **Midas,** 45 Tigne St, Sliema, ✆337822 82🛏, ✿ ⇲; **Miramare,** Main St, Balluta Bay, St Julian's , ✆341163 118🛏, ≈ ♪; **Nigret,** 29 Labour Ave, Rabat, ✆455960 96🛏, ≈ ♪; **Osborne,** South St, Valletta, ✆243656 119🛏; **Panorama,** Valley Rd, Mellieha, ✆473511 42🛏; **Plaza,** Tower Rd, Sliema, ✆341295 220🛏; **Plevna,** Qui-Si-Sana, Sliema, ✆331031 165🛏, ✿ ≈ ⇲; **Promenade,** 121 Tower Rd, Sliema, ✆313242

92🛏; **Qawra Palace,** Qawra Point, Qawra, ✆471963 400🛏, ♨ ⌇; **Regent,** Milner St, Sliema, ✆318764 140🛏, ⌇; **Rokna,** Church St, Paceville, St Julian's , ✆311556 45🛏, ♫; **Sa Maison,** Marine St, Pietà, ✆240714 136🛏; **St Julien,** Dragonara Rd, Paceville, St Julian's , ✆336271 99🛏, ⌇; **San Pawl,** Blacktail St, St Paul's Bay, ✆471369 226🛏, ♨; **Seabreeze,** Pretty Bay, Birżebbuġa, ✆871256 117🛏, ♿; **Seaview,** Qawra Rd, Qawra, ✆473105 102🛏, ✿ ♿; **Sliema,** 59 The Strand, Sliema, ✆336314 100🛏, ⌇; **Tigne Court,** Qui-Si-Sana, Sliema, ✆332001 168🛏, ✿ ⌇ ♿; **Tower Palace,** Tower Rd, Sliema, ✆337271 90🛏.

Two-star. Two-star hotels do not have en-suite bath or shower as standard, and the restaurant need not provide full meals.

Angela, Antonio Sciortino St, Msida, ✆339541 40🛏, ♨ ✗; **Balluta,** Main St, St Julian's , ✆339107 60🛏, ♨ ✗; **British,** 267 St Ursula St, Valletta, ✆224730 87🛏 ✗; **Blu Mar,** Xemxija Hill, Xemxija, ✆473229 92🛏, ✗; **Caprice,** Muscat Azzopardi St, Sliema, ✆330524 32🛏, ✗; **Caledonia,** Qui-Si-Sana, Sliema, ✆334917 100🛏, ♫ ✗; **Carina,** Windsor Terrace, Sliema, ✆334301 32🛏, ✗; **Cartwheel,** St Anthony St, Buġibba, ✆471496 80🛏, ✗; **Cerviola,** Trik il-Qaliet, Marsascala, ✆283287 64🛏, ✗; **Central,** Independence Ave, Mosta, ✆448947 86🛏, ♨ ✗; **Continental,** St Louis St, Msida, ✆330046 93🛏, ♨ ✗; **Cove,** Bay Junction, St Julian's , ✆335062 83🛏, ♨ ♫ ✗; **Crown,** Tower Rd, Sliema, ✆331094 72🛏, ✗; **Crystal,** Qawra Rd, Buġibba, ✆473022 36🛏, ✗; **Cumberland,** 111 St John's St, Valletta, ✆237732 23🛏; **Debonair,** 102 Howard St, Sliema, ✆313764 31🛏, ✗; **Elba,** 52 New St, Sliema, ✆336418 24🛏, ✗ ♿; **Gemini,** 38 Borġ Olivier St, Sliema, ✆315131 32🛏, ✗; **Grand Harbour,** 47 Battery St, Valletta, ✆246003 44🛏, ✗; **Health Farm,** 62 Main St, Tarxien, ✆786477 26🛏, ♨ ✗ ☞; **Jolly Friar,** 24 St Dominic Sq, Rabat, ✆454889 24🛏, ♨ ✗; **Lancer,** Naxxar Rd, Salina, ✆473891 25🛏, ✗; **Lion Court,** 9 Nursing Sisters Rd, St Julian's, ✆336251 29🛏, ✗; **Mirage,** John Borġ St, Msida, ✆235680 33🛏, ✗; **Olympic,** Paceville Ave, Paceville, ✆331765 30🛏, ✗; **Patricia,** New Howard St, Sliema, ✆336285 65🛏, ✗; **Seacliff,** 225 Tower Rd, Sliema, ✆330313 31🛏, ✗; **Spinola,** Upper Ross St, St Julian's , ✆336266 44🛏, ✗; **Tropicana,** Ball St, Paceville, ✆341188 132🛏, ⌇ ♫ ✗; **Viking,** Spinola Rd, St Julian's, ✆340930 41🛏; **Villa Mare,** Bay Sq, Buġibba, ✆473824 24🛏, ✗; **Xara Palace,** St Paul's Sq, Mdina, ✆454002 38🛏, ✗; **Xemxija Bay,** Xemxija Hill, St Paul's Bay, ✆473454 42🛏, ✗.

One-star. One-star hotels have a bath and toilet on the premises and provide breakfast; all rooms have a washbasin.

Adelaide, 229-231 Tower Rd, Sliema, ✆330361 50🛏, ✗; **Astoria,** 46 Point St, Sliema, ✆332089 20🛏, ✗; **Binamar,** Bishop Caruana St, Msida, ✆317315 33🛏; **Duke of Edinburgh,** 85-89 Republic St, Victoria, Gozo, ✆556468 50🛏, ♨ ⌇ ♫ ✗; **Electra,** 12-13 Valley Rd, Marsalforn, Gozo, ✆556196 27🛏, ✗; **Helena,** 192 Marina St, Pietà, ✆336417 21🛏, ✗; **Isola Bella,** Clarence St, Msida, ✆239047 42🛏, ✗; **Kent,** 24 St Margaret St,

Sliema, $\mathcal{C}$330928 19, ✕; **Marsalforn,** Rabat Rd, Marsalforn, Gozo, $\mathcal{C}$556147 35, ✕; **Ritz,** 8-10 Xagħra Rd, Marsalforn, Gozo, $\mathcal{C}$556143 34, ✕; **St Patrick's,** Xlendi Bay, Gozo, $\mathcal{C}$556598 15, ✕; **Sport,** St George's Rd, St Julian's , $\mathcal{C}$312558 28, ✕; **Taormina,** 6-7 Ponsonby St, Gżira, $\mathcal{C}$316473 40, ✕; **Wignacourt,** Notabile Rd, Birkirkara, $\mathcal{C}$441346 28, ⇌ ✕.

Unclassified. Unclassified hotels provide the basic services of a shower and lavatory on the premises, but sometimes their specification has a few surprises.

Belmont, Mrabat St, St Julian's , $\mathcal{C}$313077 45, ✕; **Conway,** Ross St, St Julian's , $\mathcal{C}$339482 30, ✕; **Delphina,** Dragonara Rd, St Julian's , $\mathcal{C}$335621 60, ✕; **De la Mer,** Xemxija Hill, Xemxija, St Paul's Bay, $\mathcal{C}$473029 72, ✕; **Grand Hotel Excelsior,** Great Siege Rd, Floriana, $\mathcal{C}$243661, 376, ✿ ⇌ ⇥ ♫ ✕ ℺; **International,** Islets Promenade, Buġibba, $\mathcal{C}$473071 42, ✿ ♫ ✕; **Regina,** 107 Tower Rd, Sliema, $\mathcal{C}$330721 28, ✕; **Salina Bay,** Kennedy Dr, Salina Bay, $\mathcal{C}$473781 214, ⇌ ♫ ✕.

HOLIDAY VILLAGES and HOTEL APARTMENTS
First-class:
Alexandra Palace, Schreiber St, St Julian's, $\mathcal{C}$341159 255, ⇌ ♫ ✕; **Buġibba,** Buġibba, $\mathcal{C}$472685 230, ⇌ ♫ ✕ ♿; **The Galaxy,** Depiro St, Sliema, $\mathcal{C}$311439 637, ⇌ ♫ ✕; **Halland,** Tal-Ibragg Rd, St Andrew's, $\mathcal{C}$333510 146, ⇌ ✕; **Mellieħa Holiday Centre,** Mellieħa Bay, $\mathcal{C}$473900 600, ⇌ ✕; **Mistra Village,** Xemxija Hill, St Paul's Bay, $\mathcal{C}$473944 354, ▥ ✿ ⇥ ♫ ✕; **Pergola,** New Bridge St, Mellieħa, $\mathcal{C}$474052 86, ⇌ ✕; **Riza,** Qawra Bay, Qawra, $\mathcal{C}$472100 208, ⇌ ✕ ♿; **St George's Park,** Dragonara Rd, St Julian's, $\mathcal{C}$332312 864, ⇌ ⇥ ✕; **Suncrest,** Qawra Coast, Qawra, $\mathcal{C}$475470 909, ▥ ✿ ⇌ ⇥ ♫ ✕ ℺; **Sundown Court,** Triq Ir-Russett, Kappara, $\mathcal{C}$335325 472, ⇌ ✕ ℺; **Sunny Coast,** Qawra Coast, Qawra, $\mathcal{C}$472964 160, ✿ ⇌ ⇥ ✕ ℺ ♿; **Topaz,** Triq Iċ-Ċagħaq, Buġibba, $\mathcal{C}$472416 332, ⇌ ⇥ ♫ ✕ ℺ ♿; **Villa Rosa,** St George's Bay, St Julian's, $\mathcal{C}$342706 616, ✿ ⇌ ⇥ ✕ ℺.

Second-class:
Dean Court, Upper Ross St, St Julian's, $\mathcal{C}$314839 155, ⇌ ✕; **Edrichton,** Ta'Bulebel, Qawra, $\mathcal{C}$472291 368, ⇌ ✕; **Festaval,** Mellieħa Bay, Mellieħa, $\mathcal{C}$233111 184, ⇌ ✕; **Four Seasons,** Qawra Point, Qawra, $\mathcal{C}$471393 124, ⇌ ✕ ♿; **Ħal Ferh,** Għajn Tuffieħa, $\mathcal{C}$473882 594, ⇌ ♫ ✕ ℺; **Hampton Court,** Triq Il-Gifen, Buġibba, $\mathcal{C}$472072 80, ⇌ ✕; **Luna,** Marfa Rd, Mellieħa, $\mathcal{C}$472711 106, ⇌ ✕; **Marina San Ġorġ,** St George's Bay, St Julian's, $\mathcal{C}$333102 168, ⇌ ⇥; **Malteng Court,** Triq Il-Parilja, Birkirkara, $\mathcal{C}$441023 108, ⇌ ✕; **Mavina Court,** Triq Il-Fliegu, Qawra, $\mathcal{C}$472200 111, ⇌ ✕; **Medisle Village,** St Andrew's, $\mathcal{C}$333262 424, ⇌ ✕ ℺; **Sabina,** Triq Il-Gifen, Buġibba, $\mathcal{C}$474549 100, ⇌ ✕; **St Paul's Court,** Pioneer Rd, Buġibba,

✆471606 500🛏, 🛁 ✗; **Speranza,** off Transfiguration Ave, Lija, ✆491776 186🛏, 🛁 ♫ ✗ ♒; **Stanton Court,** Erba'Mwiezeb, St Paul's Bay, ✆473252 272🛏, 🛁 ✗; **The Strand,** The Strand, Ġzira, 🛏15030 100🛏, ✗.

Third-class:

Archidea, Naxxar Rd, San Ġwann, ✆317924 66🛏, 🛁; **Arizona,** Buġibba Bay, St Paul's Bay, ✆473331 44🛏, 🛁 ✗; **Buskett Forest,** Buskett Rd, Rabat, ✆454266 36🛏, 🛁 ✗; **Chantilly,** University St, Msida, ✆333105 80🛏, 🛁 ♫ ✗; **Chez Francis II,** Triq Il-Fliegu, Qawra, ✆473708 196🛏, 🛁 ✗; **Euro Club,** Triq Il-Fliegu, Qawra, ✆471372 394🛏, 🛁 ✗; **Garden View,** Triq Is-Sidra, Siġġiewi, ✆332412 136🛏, 🛁 ✗; **Golden Sun,** Triq Il-Kajjik, Marsaxlokk, ✆871762 70🛏, 🛁 ✗; **Hannibal,** Triq Il-Mulett, Qawra, ✆471664 78🛏, ✗; **Palm Court,** Rizzi St, Qawra, ✆427484 330🛏, 🛁 ✗; **Royal Lodge,** Triq Is-Sajjied, Qawra, ✆476958 64🛏; **Reuben,** Majjieri St, Qawra, ✆472450 180🛏, 🛁 ✗; **St Gallen Court,** Gifen St, Buġibba, ✆473307 50🛏, ✗; **Serena,** St Simon St, Xlendi, Gozo, ✆553719 28🛏, 🛁 ↘ ✗; **Solair,** Gwiebi St, Buġibba, ✆472151 238🛏, ✗; **Sunny Isle,** University Heights, Msida, ✆313216 110🛏, ↘ ✗; **Sunrise Park,** Ganu St, Naxxar Rd, Birkirkara, ✆444181 144🛏, 🛁 ♫ ✗; **Ta'Monita,** Marsascala, ✆827882 112🛏, 🛁 ✗; **Wentworth,** Triq St Andrija, San Ġwann, ✆331758 110🛏, 🛁; **White Rocks,** Bahar Iċ-Caghaq, ✆342520 394🛏, 🛁 ✗ ♒.

Unclassified:

Cycas, Triq It-Turisti, Buġibba, ✆475239 96🛏, 🛁 ✗; **Santa Maria,** Triq Ir-Ramel, St Paul's Bay, ✆476381 496🛏, 🛁 ✗; **Suncreek Aparthotel,** The Strand, Ġzira, ✆342325 48🛏.

GUEST HOUSES

Guest houses never have television sets in each bedroom, so in this section the symbol 🖵 indicates the presence of a television lounge. All other symbols are used whenever appropriate.

First-class:

Angelo's 29 Islet Promenade, Buġibba, ✆473419 12🛏, ✗; **At Alison's,** Vajrita St, Marsascala, ✆829814 14🛏, 🖵 🛁 ✗; **Benrikeville,** Annunciation St, Balżan, ✆442559 17🛏, 🖵 🛁 ✗; **Cape Inch,** Triq Il-Merlużż, Qawra, ✆472025 30🛏, 🖵 ✗; **Coral Reef,** 243 Tower Rd, Sliema, ✆334020 31🛏, 🖵; **Fawlty Towers,** 23 Triq Il-Iskal, Vista Bella, Marsascala, ✆823110 14🛏, 🖵 🛁; **Gala,** 58-59 St Margaret St, Sliema, ✆336265 15🛏, ↘ ✗; **Haven,** 193 The Strand, Gzira, ✆335862 12🛏, 🖵; **Lady Godiva,** Tarġa Gap, Mosta, ✆411353 12🛏, 🖵 ✗; **Lingo,** Upr Conversion St, Buġibba, ✆471733 21🛏, 🖵; **Palazzo Costanzo,** Villegaignon St, Mdina, ✆456301 15🛏, 🖵 ✗; **Pension San Ġorġ,** Ball St, Paceville, ✆336136 48🛏, 🖵; **Pinto,** Sacred Heart Ave, St Julian's, ✆313897 43🛏, 🖵; **Ramla Lodge,** St Thomas's Bay, Marsascala, ✆824933 36🛏, 🖵 🛁 ✗; **Reno's,** 1 St Patrick St, Birżebbuġa, ✆871165

20🛏, ✖; **Sefranda,** Triq Il-Qasab, San Gwann, ✆315761 20🛏, 🅿;
Soleado, 15 Għar Id-Dud St, Sliema, ✆334415 28🛏, ↘ ✖; **Some Place
Else,** 29 Cathedral St, Sliema, ✆318600 14🛏; **Splendid,** P.P.Magri St,
Mellieħa, ✆473769 20🛏, 🅿; **Stefanella,** 31 St Francis St, Sliema,
✆341063 30🛏, 🅿; **Three Hills,** Xagħra Rd, Victoria, Gozo, ✆551895
20🛏, 🅿 ✖; **Villa Juana,** Triq It-Tiben, St Andrew's, ✆332980 24🛏, 🅿
≋ ✖; **Xagħra Lodge,** Parisott St, Xagħra, Gozo, ✆553405 12🛏, 🅿 ≋
✖.

Second-class:

Alfredo, 5 Big Ben Towers, Tower St, Msida, ✆312380 10🛏, 🅿;
Akwador, Triq Is-Salini, Marsascala, ✆825369 10🛏, ✖; **Asti,** 18 St
Ursula St, Valletta, ✆239506 15🛏, 🅿; **Bladon,** Naxxar Rd, Salina,
✆472959 10🛏, 🅿 ✖; **Bonheur,** 18 Sappers St, Valletta, ✆238433 14🛏,
🅿 ♫ ✖; **Brighton,** 126 Tower Rd, Sliema, ✆312904 10🛏, ✿;
Bucaneers (*sic*), Triq Iċ-Ċenturjun, Buġibba, ✆471671 40🛏, 🅿 ✖;
Camilleri's, Gafar St, Sliema, ✆444481 30🛏, 🅿; **Charles,** Valley Rd,
Msida, ✆236641 48🛏, 🅿; **Coronation,** 10 M.A.Vassalli St, Valletta,
✆237652 20🛏, 🅿; **Cottoner,** Vjal Cottoner, Fgura, ✆781476 22🛏, 🅿
✖; **Elida,** 85 Depiro St, Sliema, ✆331957 10🛏, 🅿; **Eros,** 147 St Anthony
St, Buġibba, ✆471600 22🛏, ✖; **Grand,** 56 St Anthony St, Mġarr, Gozo,
✆556183 14🛏, 🅿 ✖; **Green Arches,** St George's St, St Paul's Bay,
✆473417 10🛏, 🅿; **Green Grove,** Coppins Place, St Andrew's, ✆334372
19🛏, 🅿 ✖; **Il-Gifen,** 560 Main St St Paul's Bay, ✆471092 25🛏, 🅿 ↘ ✖;
Lantern, Marsalforn, Gozo, ✆556285, 21🛏; **Leonardo,** Wilga St,

Valletta's Opera House was destroyed in 1942; the site is now a car park. (photo: National War Museum Association).

Paceville, ☎333294 16🛏, ✕; **Le Mans**, Luqa Briffa St, Gzira, ☎339540 16🛏, 📺; **Manoel**, 61 M'setto Rd, Valletta, ☎220613 13🛏; **Maltese Cross**, 70 St Anthony St, Buġibba, ☎473517 26🛏, ✕; **Melita**, San Anton Gdns, Balżan, ☎441074 12🛏, 📺 ✕; **Midland**, 255 St Ursula St, Valletta, ☎236024 24🛏, 📺 ✕; **Miranda**, 139 Tower Rd, Sliema, ☎331524 21🛏; **Mont Rose**, 22 M'Rosa Gdns, St Julian's, ☎311790 12🛏, ✕; **Pompei**, Ganu St, Birkirkara, ☎444048 8🛏; **Point de Vue**, 5 The Saqqajja, Rabat, ☎454117 13🛏, 📺 ✕; **Saqqajja View**, Saqqajja St, Rabat, ☎454262 12🛏, 📺; **Savoy**, 444 Rue d'Argens, Sliema, ☎337016 31🛏; **Sea Bank**, Marfa Rd, Mellieħa, ☎473116 17🛏, ⚓ ♫ ✕; **Sea Pebbles**, 89 The Strand, Sliema, ☎492125 20🛏; **Southend**, Birżebbuġa Sq, Birżebbuġa, ☎828441 50🛏; **Spinakker** (*sic*), 163 The Strand, Gzira, ☎331234 24🛏, 📺; **St Joseph**, 131 Conception St, Qala, Gozo, ☎556573 14🛏, 📺 ✕; **Tower Point Residentials**, 4 Point St, Sliema, ☎332051 28🛏, 📺; **Trafalgar**, 7 Howard St, Sliema, ☎336527 12🛏, 📺; **Vanessa**, Soss St, Sliema, ☎338467 19🛏, 📺; **Villa Santa Maria**, 85 Tower St, Sliema, ☎339657 15🛏, 📺; **Windsor**, Schreiber St, Paceville, ☎312232 16🛏.

HOSTELS
First-class:
Marsaxlokk, Żejtun Rd, Marsaxlokk, ☎871709 70🛏, 📺 ⚓ ✕ ⚲ ♿; **St Francis Ravelin**, St Francis Ravelin, Floriana, ☎224446 80🛏, 📺 ✕ ♿.

Second-class:
Paceville, 30b Gale, Triq Wilga, Paceville, ☎239361 8🛏; **Trafalgar**, 100 Triq Iċ-Ċenturjun, Buġibba, ☎460412 30🛏, 📺 ⚓; **Youth Travel Circle**, Buskett, Rabat, ☎233893 38🛏.

PRICES
Contact the Malta National Tourist Office for the latest maximum prices in each category, except five-star hotels which have no government-imposed maximum.

Hotels. At the time of writing the maximum *per person* for demi-pension in a four-star hotel is around Lm15, with bed and breakfast in a one-star at Lm6, and bed and breakfast in a third-class guest house at Lm3.50. Double rates are higher, but when divided by two are significantly lower than the figures above.

Apartments. The maximum in a Class A-1 high-season two-bed apartment is Lm62; the maximum in a Class B low-season two-bed apartment is Lm26. Moving to four beds, the high-season A-1 is Lm92; low-season B is Lm30. Eight beds? High-season A-1 is Lm134, low-season B is Lm38. These prices are *per apartment*, not per person.

Villas. The maximum for a Class A-1 high-season two-bed villa is Lm73; the maximum for a Class B low-season eight-bed villa is Lm48; again, prices are *per villa*.

Seasons. In the hotel and self-catering business, **high-season** is 16 June-30 September; **low-season** is 1 November-31 March; and **mid-season** is the remaining months in spring and autumn.

SELF-CATERING APARTMENTS

All self-catering apartments must be registered with the Hotels and Catering Establishments Board, Republic St, Valletta, which ensures standards do not go below a set minimum nor do prices exceed a set maximum: the government sees tourism as a major earner and intends to minimise the risk of dissatisfied customers.

The board has a list of all self-catering accommodation in the islands, totalling 1,703 apartments and 7,626 beds, but it does not arrange bookings. If this is your preferred type of holiday home you have several options: book a package which will take you to one of the 688 company-owned blocks, almost certainly in St Paul's Bay, Buġibba, St Julian's or Sliema; ask the tourist office for a list of privately-owned premises and make your own booking by phone or post (this will almost certainly restrict you to the above areas plus Mellieħa and Gozo); come with nothing booked and look around (but *not* in high season); get a recommendation from a friend who has already been to Malta (this is how many apartment owners get their business); study the adverts in the specialist press; or consult my list.

Privately-owned self-catering accommodation. This list gives *all* the privately-owned self-catering flats available in the islands, where

Marsamxett Harbour seen from Valletta. The barquentine 'Black Pearl,' at the head of Msida Creek, is now a smart restaurant.

the owner has a telephone number; short of going to the H&CE Board in Valletta, this is your only chance of having the full selection before you. As there are so many I am listing them under the village where the flat is, and supplying only the owner's name, address and phone number, and in brackets the number of beds; the owner seldom lives on these premises and occasionally lives in another village, which is shown in CAPITAL LETTERS.

Postal address. All addresses must be completed by adding the property-owner's village; either the name in capitals or the name at the head of the paragraph

The list does not include company-owned premises as they are in the package holiday business, nor the 59 premises owned by foreigners — mostly Britons — as they advertise in the British press. By the way, foreigners may rent out their Maltese properties only if they bought it before July 1974 and if they registered it with the H&CE Board before January 1991; the sole exception to the registration deadline is for villas with pools.

ATTARD
A medium-sized village at the western edge of the Birkirkara urban area, 2 miles to Ta'Qali craft centre.
Pace, Evelyn, Dolyn, off Qormi Rd, ☎440956 (6).

BAĦAR IĊ-ĊAGĦAQ
A tiny coastal village between Qawra and Paceville; small beach, and handy for the Splash Park.
Ciantar, Mr E, 184 Main St, St JULIAN'S (6).

BIRKIRKARA Bustling town of 20,000 2 miles (3km) west of Msida.
Gauci, Vincent, 'Haven of Truth,' St Andrews Rd, ☎342470 (5).

BIRŻEBBUĠA Medium-sized village on sheltered Marsaxlokk Bay. Beaches, shopping, but near Kalafrana docks. Under Luqa Airport flight path.
Abela, Mrs Censina, Villa Leonard, Brolli Rd, ☎871408 (4); **Balżan,** Nikola, 47 Birżebbuġa Rd, ☎871242, 871646 (1,7); **Berry,** Mary, Shalom, Birżebbuġa Rd, ☎871611 (5,7,7,10); **Camilleri,** Anthony, 35 St Andrew St, ☎828508 (6); **Camilleri,** Joseph, 15 Brolli Rd, ☎828504 (6); **Camilleri,** Joseph, 32a St Patrick St, ☎871191 (4); **Camilleri,** J, 28 Pretty Bay, ☎871226 (6); **Camilleri,** Leli & E, Casa Camilleri, St Catherine St, ☎682887 (4,4,4); **Camilleri,** Louis, 'Elizer,' Zurrieq Rd, ☎871444 (6); **Camilleri,** Paul, 22 Zurrieq Rd, ☎871347 (4); **Camilleri,** Rita & Carmen, St Paul, St Patrick St, ☎871295 (4,4); **Cassar,** Josephine, 'St Marc,' Our Lady of Mercy St, ZEJTUN ☎882017 (4); **Cutajar,** Carmel, 75 Ħal Saflieni St, PAOLA, ☎225782 (6,6,2); **Cutajar,** Maria, 60a St Michael St, ☎828485 (4); **Cutajar,** Peter, 3 New St, ☎871226 (4); **Debono,** Mario, 4 Pretty Bay, ☎871141 (8,8,8,8,8,8); **Dowdall,** Alfred, 'Carol,' ns off Zejtun Rd, ☎828672 (4);**Farrugia,** Joseph, Sunrays, Triq Il-Kartaginizi, ☎8828529 (6,6); **Farrugia,** Mary, Grace, St Francis St, ☎871946 (6);**Glivan,** Paul, 'St Lorenzo,' Triq Il-Ghodda, ☎871450 (4); **Mifsud,** C, 223 Sawmill St, MSIDA ☎332916 (5); **Mifsud,** Lorenzo, St Patrick St, ☎871991

(4); **Muscat,** Peter, Il-Girna, Triq G. Galizia, ☎682766 (4); **Schembri,** Anthony, 100 Luqa Briffa St, ZEJTUN, ☎878491 (2,6,6); **Schembri,** Fortunato, St Paul, St Rita St, ☎871900 (5,6); **Zammit,** John, 6 St Vincent St, ☎682730 (6); **Zammit,** Joseph, Santu Formosa St, ZURRIEQ ☎682411.

BUĠIBBA and QAWRA

Two parishes sharing a peninsula east of St Paul's Bay, with no through-traffic. Tourism is the main industry, with hotels, restaurants, and the largest concentration of self-catering apartments, either private or company-owned. Good beaches on St Paul's Bay. In this section the address is complete.

Abdilla, J, Emmanuel, Sir Aug. Bartolo St, Ta'Xbiex, ☎222525 (8); **Abela,** N, Hope, Wignacourt St, Birkirkara ☎440421 (6,6,6); **Agius,** C, Green Valley, Wied is-Sir St, Mosta ☎441191 (2,4); **Agius,** F, St Paul, New St, Burmarrad, ☎472215 (4,4); **Agius,** G, Helix, Cannon Rd, Sta. Venera ☎494717 (4); **Agius,** J, Joe Carmen, New St, Burmarrad ☎471603 (4,4); **Agius,** J, 8 Triq Il-Ħġejjeh Buġibba, ☎472383 (2,2); **Agius,** J, Ganin, ns off Hope St, Mosta ☎471603 (4,4); **Anastasi,** J, 121 St Anthony St, Buġibba, ☎473233 (6,6,); **Aquilina,** C, Rosedal, Triq Il-Kannizzata, Balżan ☎443214 (4); **Arrigo,** M, 440a St Paul's St, St Paul's Bay ☎473342 (4); **Attard,** C, Clover, Censu Busuttil St, Birkirkara ☎492087 (3,3,3); **Azzopardi,** A, Stelina, Elat Il-Qamar Rd, Siġġiewi☎607768 (6); **Azzopardi,** G, 2 Goch, Triq Il-Bronzar, Sta. Venera ☎226504 (4); **Azzopardi,** P, 20 Housing Est, Qrendi, ☎822833 (2,2,2,2); **Azzopardi,** R, 25 St John's St, Siġġiewi☎607146 (3,4,4,4,4,5,6,10); **Bisazza,** A, 23 Stella Maris St, Sliema ☎331132 (4); **Bonavia,** G, Arzella, 21st Sept Ave, Naxxar ☎474031 (2);**Bonello,** J, 7 Violets, Dr Zammit St, Siġġiewi☎641157 (4); **Bonello,** M, Sinclaire, Spring St, Siġġiewi☎607243 (4); **Bonett,** G, Chanel, Jasmin St, Fgura ☎816559 (4); **Borġ,** A, Rishenpa, Birkirkara Rd, Attard ☎488250 (6 at 2,4,4); **Borġ,** G, Georita, Liedna St, Fgura ☎882577 (6); **Borġ,** G, Triq Il-Kus, Qormi ☎486156 (2,2); **Borġ,** M, 201 Main St Birkirkara ☎442234 (4); **Bugeja,** C, 1 Ivory Flats, Mimosa St, Gwardamanġa ☎222612 (8); **Bugeja,** J, Astra, Qawra Coast Rd, Qawra ☎441248 (4); **Bugeja,** J, Petit Fleur, Danny Cremona St, Ħamrun ☎222551 (6,6,6); **Busuttil,** J, 215 Bwieraq St, Birkirkara ☎640197 (4,6); **Cachia,** F, 27 Narcissi St, Sta Lucia ☎816168 (4);

Across Msida Creek.

Xewkija's church, finished in 1971, had the third largest church dome in Europe.

Calleja, F, Lorelei, Main St, Mosta ☎483230 (6,6,6); **Callus**, L, Lenant, Kırcıppu St, Siġġiewi☎641002 (4,4,4); **Camenzuli**, J, 5, Erba'Mwieżeb, St Paul's Bay ☎471854 (4); **Camilleri**, E, Charmaine, Pioneer Corps St, Buġibba, ☎471311 (6,6); **Camilleri**, J, 1 Pioneer Corps Rd, Buġibba, ☎471993 (5,5); **Caruana**, A, Vicagos, Eucharistic Congress Rd, Mosta ☎441220 (6); **Cashar**, G, Carmen, Alexander St, Ħamrun ☎603848 (4); **Cassar**, J, Cipress, Buskett Rd, Rabat ☎674250 (4,4); **Chircop**, E, Orchidea, Luqqata St, Misrah Kola, Attard ☎336776 (3); **Chircop**, G, Emanuel, Gate Ave, Zebbuġ ☎644472 (4,4,6,6,6,6); **Ciantar**, J, La Maison, Nigret Rd, Rabat ☎454642 (4); **Ciappara**, A, California, Luqa Briffa St, Naxxar ☎412402 (6); **Ciappara**, P, 38 Main St, Attard ☎488192 (2,4,6,6); **Cilia**, V, Villa Patris, Triq Il-Mohriet, Attard ☎444431 (5); **Cordina**, V, Nazju Falzon St, Msida ☎314169 (5); **Cutajar**, A, 20 Vitale St, Ħamrun ☎447206 (4); **Debattista**, Golina, Crocus St, Attard ☎440961 (5,6); **Debono**, J & Galea, L, Casa Debono, Sqolba, l/o Mġarr ☎474824 (3,3,4,4); **Decelis**, J, Flat 3, Jean Marie Flats, Mazzola St, Buġibba, ☎474576 (4,6); **Demanuele**, A, 1 Triq It-Trunċiera, Buġibba, ☎471371 (2); **Demanuele**, E, 1 Triq It-Trunċieri, Qawra ☎471371 (2,2,2,2); **Demarco**, M, 140 Main St, Balżan ☎442574 (2); **Ellul**, A, 118b, Our Lady of Sorrows St, Pietà ☎221680 (6); **Ellul**, F, 42 Triq Pensieri, Santa Lucia ☎816093 (4,4); **Falzon**, A, Sagra Familia, Regional Rd, Msida ☎312608 (6); **Falzon**, C, 53 Naxxar Rd, Birkirkara ☎491026 (six at 4); **Falzon**, J, Fraulein, Sillar St, Sta. Venera ☎448143 (6); **Falzon**, J & Bonavia, J, Capricorn, Triq Il-Farinal, Mosta ☎443545 (six at 4); **Falzon**, S, Blue Edge, Eucharistic Congress Rd Mosta ☎441227 (6); **Farrugia**, C, Fatima, Grace St, Zebbuġ ☎680874 (4,6); **Farrugia**, S,

---

When writing to these addresses, add the name of the village; 'ns' means 'new street' and can be abbreviated.

---

26 Dock St, Msida, ☎825906 (4,4); **Fenech**, C, Ave Maria, Wileg St, St Paul's Bay ☎ 472278 (6); **Fenech**, D, 37 Eucharistic Congress St, Mosta ☎445638 (5); **Formosa**, P, St Mary Ho, Quarries St, Sta. Venera ☎221487 (4); **Frendo**, Dr P, Dar Il-Mithna, Mill St, Mosta ☎486272 (4); **Galea**, J, 136 Eucharistic Congress St, Mosta ☎487682 (2,2,4,4); **Gatt**, A, Haven, Old Railway Rd, Balżan ☎441666 (6,6,6); **Gatt**, C, 134 High St, Ħamrun ☎222318 (5); **Gatt**, D, Ta'Salvun, Ħal Far Rd, Birżebbuġia ☎473797 (six at 4); **Gatt**, J, Ziffa, Buġibba Rd, St Paul's Bay ☎471015 (6); **Gatt**, J, 68 Nicolo Isouard St, Mosta ☎412404 (4,4); **Gatt**, J & V, 4 St Andrew's Ct, Triq Il-Brankutli, ☎472552 (2); **Gatt**, S, Asphodel, Valley St, Mosta ☎443839 (6); **Gatt**, V, Villa Etoile, Hope St, Mosta ☎493769 (five at 6); **Gauci**, G, 44 Grognet St, Mosta ☎443241 (6); **Gauci**, P, Arcadia, Icillio Calleja St, Zebbuġ ☎816775 (4,4); **Gili**, M, 30 Rudolph Junct, ☎332030 (4); **Grech**, I, 45 Main St, Zebbuġ ☎646279 (4); **Grima**, J, Warda, G. Caruana St, Rabat, ☎674872 (6); **Grupetta**, J, 53 Grognet St, Mosta ☎443260 (6,6); **Harney**, J, 11 Old Mill St, Mosta ☎440267 (6); **Jones**, A, Albemar, Danny Cremona St, Ħamrun ☎606487 (five at 4); **Magro**, J, 17 Housing Est, Qrendi ☎822374 (2); **Magro** S, Casa Magro, St Mary St, Naxxar, ☎411233 (4,6); **Mallia**, J, Malbon, ns off Dr Zammit St, Siġġiewi☎605518 (4,4,4,4); **Mamo**, J, Casa Mamo, St Paul's St, Naxxar ☎223726 (2,4,4); **Marguerat**, J, 20 Zebbuġ Rd, Paola ☎823564 (6); **Micallef**, G, Lucky Ho, New St, Luqa ☎820681 (4,4); **Mifsud**, R, 220 Conception St, Msida ☎314047 (2,6); **Muscat**, A, 19 Tony Bajada St, St Paul's Bay ☎473459 (6); **Muscat**, A, 17 Constitution St, Mosta ☎441171 (5); **Muscat**, C, 16 Niccolo Isouard St, Mosta ☎445045 (5,5,5,5); **Muscat**, J, 4a Gherien Rd, St Paul's Bay ☎471312 (4); **Muscat**, J, Palms, Eucharistic Congress Rd Mosta ☎441171 (6); **Pace, A, Mumruffin,**

Ta'Pinu church stands on the spot where Carmela and Francesco heard the voice of God.

Hemel St, Swieqi, ☎313646 (4); **Pace**, P, Shalom, Notabile Rd, Siġġiewi☎645426 (4); **Pace**, R, 45 Cardinal Sciberras St, Qormi ☎487212 (6); **Pullicino**, J & M, Ramona, St John St, Gharghur ☎443619 (2,2,2,4); **Sammut**, C, 121 Eucharistic Congress Rd, Mosta ☎441220 (4); **Sammut**, E, Merhba, Sir Harry Luke St, Mġarr, ☎474704 (4); **Sammut**, V, Chondrillia, L-Iklin Rd, L-Ilkin, Lija, ☎445219 (6,6,8); **Scerri**, A, Austwin, St Gregory St, Gwardamanġa ☎335678 (four at 4, nine at 6); **Scerri**, M, 15 Sta Venera Sq, Sta. Venera ☎473817 (4,5); **Sciberras**, S, Sliem, Icilio Calleja St, Zebbuġ ☎646379 (4); **Scicluna**, A, St Rita, Brared St, Birkirkara ☎442795 (4); **Scicluna**, A, 17 Valletta Rd, Luqa ☎897975 (4); **Scicluna**, V, Frances, Debono St, Naxxar ☎412411 (2,4); **Sciriha**, J, Fiorellina, Wied Il-Gh asel St, Msida ☎493757 (seven at 4); **Spiteri**, E, 88 Eucharistic Congress St, Mosta ☎441192 (4,6); **Tanti**, C, Flat 2, ns off Grace St, Zebbuġ ☎644843 (6,6); **Tanti**, J, Ivy, Caruana Dingli St, Zebbuġ ☎644848 (6); **Trevisan**, M, 37, Serafin M Zarb St, Zurrieq ☎822261 (4,4); **Vassallo**, J, Roses, Sliema Bypass, Sliema ☎644725 (4); **Vassallo**, P, 125 Eucharistic Congress Rd Mosta ☎447577 (6); **Vella**, A, 11 Saliba Flats, Sacred Heart Ave, St Julian's ☎440623 (3); **Vella**, F, 62 Eucharistic Congress St, Mosta ☎441267 (4); **Vella**, J, 79 Gerolamo Cassar St, Mosta ☎441255 (4); **Vella**, J, 1 Anglu Gatt St, Mosta ☎474031 (4,4); **Vella**, J & M, 126 Lucy St, Naxxar ☎488574 (4,6); **Vella**, P, Mondello, Bontadini St, Mriehel ☎444286 (6,6); **Xerri**, V, 324 Main St, Mosta ☎440658 (3,3); **Xuereb**, S, 613 Mosta Rd, St Paul's Bay ☎471154 (2,4,5).

GWARDAMANĠIA

A very busy area on the road between Sliema and Valletta. Traffic is heavy, but Valletta and Sliema within walking distance.

Abela, Joseph, Green Cove, St Luke's Rd, ☎4225851 (4,5).

71

ĠZIRA South-west of Sliema, facing Manoel Island; a busy area at the centre of things, but with parking problems. **Aquilina,** Victor, Flat 1, Tower Gate St, MSIDA ☎313041 (6); **Azzopardi,** Dr A, 154 Triq Il-Kampanella, SAN GWANN ☎338993 (2); **Borġ,** Violet, 78 Parish Priest Manche St, ☎314594 (2); **Brincat,** Charles, Victory St, ☎331711 (4,6); **Buttiġieġ,** Henry, Flat 1, Cuschieri St, ☎313365 (4); **Cuschieri,** Emanuela, Flat 2, Cuschieri St, ☎332879 (5); **Cuschieri,** Joseph, 3 Stadium St, ☎314622 (6,6); **D'Anastasi,** E, 2 St Mary Flats, D'Argens Junction, ☎339540 (6,6,6,6); **Debono,** Jesmond & Doris, 15 Ponsonby St, ☎339947 (3,4); **Farrugia,** C, 39 St Throphimus St, SLIEMA, ☎332386 (6); **Flores,** Josephine, 42 St Mary St, SLIEMA, ☎313593 (3,3); **Frankalanza,** Edward, 16 St Gregory St, GWARDAMANGIA, ☎336122 (4); **Genius,** Leone, 88 Cameron St, ☎314615 (2); **Mamo,** Paul, 430 D'Argens Rd, ☎314549 (4,4);**Pillow,** Theresa, 42 St George's St, ☎334444 (3); **Pisani,** Charles, 48 Annunciation St, SLIEMA, ☎330115 (6); **Savona,** Victor, 5 Jay Gee Flats, Luqa Briffa St, ☎339757 (3,3); **Vella,** Paul, 40 West St, VALLETTA ☎226222 (2).

ĦAMRUNA busy town 2 miles (3km) south-west of Valletta. Heavy traffic.
Mansueto, Anthony, Unicorn, Triq Il-Barrien, MSIDA, ☎225649 (8).

KALKARA A quiet village of 2,000 overlooking Grand Harbour. Many historic associations.
Brincat, Manuel, 68 Depiro St, SLIEMA, ☎334963 (2).

MARSASCALA A small village at head of narrow inlet; picturesque and quiet.
Borġ, Lawrence, 22 Triq Il-Qalb Imqaddsa, ŻABBAR ☎804956 (4); **Borġ,** Paul, Palmar Ho, Luqa Rd, PAOLA, ☎897380 (2,2); **Buttiġieġ** Depiro, A & J, 92 Isouard St, SLIEMA ☎605264 (4,6); **Cachia,** Lawrence, Christus Rex, Clover Hill, ☎824989 (4); **Calleja,** Edwin, Edmarwin, Pope Alex. VIII Junct, BALZAN ☎442636 (4); **Calleja,** Ray, Inmajdra, ns off St Andrew's Rd, St ANDREW'S ☎441768 (6); **Chetcuti,** David, 21 Tower Promenade, Sta LUCIA, ☎816208 (6,6); **Chetcuti,** Rosalie, 146 Rudolphe St, SLIEMA ☎640831; **Cutajar,** Carmelo, 75 Ħal Salfieni St, PAOLA ☎225782 (4); **Dalli,** Carmen, 51 Zabbar Rd, ☎821357 (6,7,8); **Degray,** Edward, 80/6 Merchants St, VALLETTA ☎225794 (4); **Dougall,** Charles, 4 Malti Grima St, COSPICUA, ☎823471 (2,2); **Ellul,** Louise, 147 Triq Lanzalor, N'hood 11, Sta LUCIA, ☎820905 (4); **Grech,** Alfred,21 Zejtun Rd, Ghaxaq, ☎897744 (4,4); **Grech,** Saviour, Mizpah, Guzeppi Montebello St, TARXIEN, ☎882195 (4); **Lia,** Carmelo, Margherita, Lia St, ŻABBAR ☎821432 (6); **Micallef,** Mary, 20, Triq L-Iskola, ☎825753 (4); **Pulis,** Anthony, 9 St Michael St, PAOLA ☎829857 (6,6); **Scicluna,** Salvatore, Divine Providence, Xghira St, ŻABBAR, ☎820792 (4,6); **Vella,** Frank & Rose, Inchari, St Nicholas St, ☎820032 (4); **Zarb,** Paul, 31 Victory St, ŻABBAR ☎823174 (2).

MARSAXLOKK
Quiet fishing village of 2,500 at the head of Marsaxlokk Bay. Picturesque, but no beach.
Cauchi, Guza, 26 Zejtun St, ☎871617 (4).

MDINA
The charming walled city of 400 people that was the ancient capital. Splendid views.
Bologna, Dr Carmel, Casa Inguanez, Mesquita St, ☎674596 (2,6,6,6).

MELLIEĦA

Mellieħa is popular for self-catering visitors. The village is on high land, giving excellent views over the northern part of Malta, including Mellieħa Bay, and extending to Comino and Gozo; good if basic shopping centre, with restaurants, banks, car hire agencies, and a splendid church. Mellieħa Heights is on the east rim with the **Santa Maria Estate** to the south, the latter an area popular with British residents as well as visitors.

In this section, *MH* is Mellieħa Heights and *SME* is Santa Maria Estate, to be written in full.

Abela, Norbert, Hope, Wignacourt St, BIRKIRKARA, ☎440421 (3,6); **Attard,** Charles, 536 SME, ☎520113 (2,2,8,8,8); **Bartolo,** Dr Joseph, Villa Hene, Triq Sant Elena, ☎473537 (6,6); **Bartolo,** Nicolas, Nickgrace House, Qala St, ZABBAR ☎460456 (4); Joseph, 429 SME, ☎473006 (4,4,6,6,7); **Bonanno,** Victoria, Malvenn, Schreiber St, PAOLA, ☎896227 (4); **Bonello,** Anthony, Villa Menhir, Triq Is-Sirk, SIGGIEWI, ☎804126 (8); **Borġ,** Anthony, Block 2, Flat 6, Merchants St, VALLETTA ☎220925 (2,2,2,2,); ;**Borġ,** Charles, 90 MH, ☎472817 (7); **Borġ,** Emmanuel, 337 MH, ☎472896 (4,6); **Borġ,** Josephine, 5 Taormina, Vista Estate, ☎520273 (6); **Borġ,** Frank, 14 Vista Est, MH, ☎471511 (6); **Borġ,** Maria, 4 MH, ☎471932 (6,6); **Busuttil,** Anthony, 125 Parish Priest Magri St, ☎473951 (2); **Busuttil,** Carmel, Id-Dawra, Zejtun Rd, TARXIEN ☎803481 (6); **Camilleri,** John, Velleri, Barbara St, MGARR ☎473039 (6); **Caruana,** Victoria, 24 Triq Il-Kbira, ☎472757 (4); **Casaleto,** Carmel, 336 Triq Il-Plejju, MH ☎474262 (2);

St Julian's Bay is peaceful, but Paceville is one of Malta's busiest districts.

Cassar, Francis, 4 Parish St, SIGGIEWI, ☎605683 (4); **Cauchi,** Anthony, 469 SME, ☎472707 (4); **Debono,** John, 440 SME, ☎473279 (6); **Debono,** Joseph, 513B SME, ☎472982 (10); **Debono,** Margaret, 43 Sir Adrian Dingli St, SLIEMA, ☎332427 (6); **Debono,** Vincent, 513A, SME, ☎472982 (10); **Deguara,** Mary, 248 Triq Is-Sattar, ☎520279 (6); **Falżon,** Stephanie, Franstan, High St, SLIEMA, ☎334815 (8); **Farrugia,** Louis, 145 1 Għoljiet tal-Mellieħa, ☎474113 (6); **Fenech,** Carmel, 91 MH, ☎471184 (6,6); **Fenech,** Charles, 477 SME, ☎824717 (5); **Fenech,** Lydia, 32 North St, ☎471184 (4); **Fenech,** Mario, 6 St Francis, Cross St, ☎520435 (4); **Gatt,** Carmel, Nobile, Notary Zarb St, ATTARD, ☎442381 (7); **Gauci,** Emanuela, Antemma, Parish St, ☎473512 (4,4,4,4,4,6,6,6); **Gauci,** Joseph, 29 SME ☎473703 (6); **Grima,** Louis, Taj Mahal, Plot 55, Napuljun Caruana Dingli St, ☎472900 (4); **Grima,** Reno, Flat 2, Plot K, MH, ☎473324 (4); **Magro,** Anthony, 62 MH, ☎474911 (6); **Mallia,** Carmelo, 31 Stella Maris St, SLIEMA ☎331823 (6); **Mallia,** Margaret, 529 Main Rd, ☎471070 (6); **Mifsud,** Angelo, 31 Dun Franġisk Sciberras St, ☎473503 (4); **Muscat,** Charles, 10 SME, ☎474054 (4); **Muscat,** Joseph, Seaside Court, Flat E, Marfa Rd, GĦADIRA, ☎312539 (6,6); **Pace,** Edward, 28 MH, ☎472800 (5); **Psaila,** Alfred, 4 Vista Estate, ☎473528 (4); **Psaila,** Andrew, 288 SME, ☎520050 (4); **Schembri,** Joseph, 463 SME ☎473006 (4,4,4); **Tabona,** Michael, 3 Alley 3, Main St, NAXXAR, ☎338981; **Vassallo,** Carmelo, Oleander, Dr Chetcuti St, MOSTA, ☎413559 (4); **Vella,** Alfred, Amamavell, MH, ☎473498 (6); **Vella,** Anthony, 149 MH, ☎472809 (8); **Vella,** Anthony, 451 SME, ☎474312 (6); **Vella,** Emanuel, 9 Villa Basset, Vista Est, ☎520639 (2,8,8); **Vella,** Emanuel, 316 MH, ☎520286 (6); **Vella,** Carmel, 13 Snajjin St, ☎474255 (6,6,6,6,6,6,6,6,6); **Vella,** Henry, 33 North St, ☎473645 (3); **Vella,** Joe, Long View, Vista Est, ☎472684 (6); **Vella,** John, 46G Main St, ☎473073 (6); **Vella,** Josephine, 5 Tas-Salib Sq, ☎472587 (4); **Vella,** Lucia, Mater Dei, Snajjin St, ☎472675 (4,6,6,6); **Vella,** Mary, 317 MH, ☎472809 (8); **Vella,** Mary, 37A New Mill St, ☎471511 (2); **Xuereb,** Francis, 36 Franċis Zahra St, ☎474399 (4); **Zammit,** Carmelo, Grace House, MH, ☎473320 (4,6); **Zammit,** Vincenza, 80, Ta'Pannellu, ☎473512 (4).

MĠARRA small village in the north-west, convenient for Ġnejna Bay and ancient history. Good walking country.

Caruana, Michael, 1 Sir Harry Luke St, ☎473705 (5); **Sammut,** Pauline, 10 Jubilee Esplanade, ☎43235 (4).

MOSTAThe village is noted for its enormous church dome. Good communications by car to all parts.

Axiaq, Francis, 25 Eucharistic Congress Rd, ☎487492 (5); **Bugeja,** Francis, 73 Cassar St, ☎493877 (4); **Calleja,** Angelo & Carmelo, 54 Cassar St, ☎410751 (4,6); **Grech,** Carmelo, 83 Gafa St, ☎448835 (6);**Montalto,** Reno, 14a St Francis St, St PAUL'S BAY, ☎473165 (3); **Montebello,** Doris, 147 Constitution St, ☎411151 (2); **Vella,** John & Mary, 'St Anthony,' Bidnija, ☎410663 (6); **Vella,** Salvina, 42 Parish St, ☎411612 (6); **Zahra,** Rita, Georita Ho, Eucharistic Congress Rd, ☎493112 (6).

MSIDA

At the head of Msida Creek and in the main conurbation, Msida is between the Science College and the University.

Baldacchino, Louis, 27 St Anthony St, SLIEMA, ☎335274 (6); **Bonello,** George, St Helen Ho, Għarghur St, BIRKIRKARA, ☎442194 (2,2,2,4); **Galea,** Anthony, Elton, St Mary St, BIRKIRKARA, ☎443881 (6); **Galea,** Paul & Mary, 39 Antonio Bosio St, ☎330265 (4,4); **Galea,** Paul, Casa Eureka, Casolani La, ☎317186 (4); **Gauci,** Alfred, 105 St Anthony St, BALZAN, ☎442040 (8); **Vella,** Eileen, 'La Madonnina delle Lacrime,' Wejter St, BIRKIRKARA, ☎441721 (5,5,10,10)

NAXXAR An ancient village overlooking the lower lands of the north-west, convenient for Buġibba, Splash Park and Sliema.**Bonello,** Anthony, 6 Mirabelle Ho, Hughes Hallet St, SLIEMA, ☎336689 (8); **Fenech,** Victor, 'Xefaq Gdid,' St Paul's St, San Pawl Tat-Tarġa, ☎440587 (8); **McEwen,** Eric, 43 St George's Rd, St JULIAN'S, ☎336816 (8); **Zammit,** Victoria, 'Marie,' ns off 21st September Ave, ☎445377 (3).

PACEVILLE Pronounced *pah-chay-ville* from the Italian for 'peace;' a vibrant area containing the Palladium night club, Styx disco, and the casino. Plenty of shops, and traffic.
Attard, Marianne, 'Polly,' Parish St, NAXXAR, ☎497812 (4,4,4); **Bajona,** Edmond, Farry Ct 1, Salvu Privitera St, ☎317715 (4,4,4,4); **Bianchi,** Raphael, The Bungalow, Ta'Stronka, Madliena, ☎232241 (4,6); **Buttiġieġ,** Francis, Jasmin, Belvedere St, GZIRA, ☎334271 (4,5,5); **Camilleri,** Romeo, Villa Oasis, BAĦAR IC-CAGĦAQ, ☎340931 (4); **Cauchi,** Carmela, 4 Isouard St, St PAUL'S BAY, ☎473463 (4,8); **D'Agata,** Vincent, 13 Paceville Ave, ☎313161 (4); **Farrugia,** Adeodato, Dato, Mosta Rd, St PAUL'S BAY, ☎488573 (6,6,6); **Farrugia,** C, 39 St Throphimus St, SLIEMA, ☎332380 (4,4); **Farrugia,** Denis, 67 St Albert St, GZIRA, ☎339448 (6,6,8); **Farrugia Randon,** Dr R, 'Franstan,' Pope Alexander VII Jnct, BALZAN, ☎442542 (6,6); **Gauci,** Helen, 14a Haven Lo, St George's Jnct, St JULIAN'S, ☎342719 (4,4,4); **Laferla,** Joseph, 91 Howard St, SLIEMA, ☎331220 (4); **Lia,** Mary, 'M'Grazia,' Napuljun Caruana Dingli St, TARXIEN, ☎482487 (6); **Magro,** Pasquale, 3 St Paul's By The Sea St, St PAUL'S BAY, ☎473273 (5); **Meruzzi,** Francis, 69 Parades St, St PAUL'S BAY, ☎471040 (5,5); **Spiteri,** Catherine, Block L, Flat 3, Znuber St, Sta. LUCIA, ☎897142 (4,4); **Sollars,** Elizabeth, 'Grellars Yat,' Triq Il-Gallina, Kappara, SAN GWANN, ☎341277 (4); **Xuereb,** Irene, 8 Alley One, Mosta Rd, ATTARD, ☎440375 (6); **Zammit,** Dr E, Villa Charlotte, Villa Rosa Est, St. JULIAN'S, ☎311805 (2).

> When writing to these addresses, add the name of the village; 'ns' means 'new street' and can be abbreviated.

PAOLA A residential town of 12,000 1 mile from the head of Grand Harbour. Moderately quiet.
Camilleri, Nazzareno, 99 Queen St, ☎239733 (4,4).

PIETÀ A busy community at the head of Marsamxett Harbour, 2 miles (3km) from Valletta.
Borġ, Tancred, Villa Portofino, Joe Gasan St, BLAT L-BAJDA, ☎238858.

RABAT A historic town of 12,000 with a commanding view over most of the island.
Galea, Vincent, 33 Riebu Well St, ☎820024 (6); **Grima,** Joe, 'Themara,' Sawra St, ☎454071 (5); **Grima,** Victor, 'Belview,' Sawra St, ☎455152.

SAFI A small village between Luqa and Ħal Far airports, but convenient for the Blue Grotto.
Zammit, John, 'Sebh,' ns off Mary St, ☎823162 (6); **Zammit,** Louis, 'Andrea,' Zurrieq Rd, ☎823166 (6).

SENGLEA On a historic promontory pointing into Grand Harbour with panoramic view of Valetta. Surprisingly quiet.
Sarsero, Lawrence, 57 Victory St, ☎823717 (2).

St. JULIAN'S The busiest, glossiest part of Malta, convenient for the casino, Palladium night club, and Styx disco. Street parking is difficult.
Aquilina, Rita, 129 Birkirkara Hill, ☎336758 (4); Arrigo, Robert, 37/3 Tigné Sea Front, SLIEMA, ☎339336 (eight at 2, five at 4); Calascione, Alfred, 'Sardinella,' Lourdes La, ☎335504 (4); Camilleri, Romeo, 'The Oasis,' Baħar Iċ-Cagħac, ☎340931 (4); Colombo, Richard, 'Astoria,' Dun Mauro Inguanez St, BIRKIRKARA, ☎487765 (2,2,2,4,4,4,6,6); Fiteni, Joseph, 'Hilarious Ho,' Stefanotis St, SAN GWANN, ☎337126 (2); Formosa, Dr J, 5 Għar Il-Lembi St, SLIEMA, ☎335698 (2,3,3,4,4); Formosa, Saviour, 140 Birkirkara Rd, ☎334369 (eleven at 4); Galea, Alfred, 180 Rudolph St, SLIEMA, ☎334511 (6); Gatt, Anthony, 'Haven,' Old Railway Rd, BALZAN, ☎41666 (6); Gatt, Carmelo, 25 Old College St, ☎340814 (2); Licari, Edward, 5 Fleur de Lys Rd, BIRKIRKARA, ☎440323 (six at 4); Lowell, Godwin, 6 St George's Rd, ☎330571 (4); Micallef, Joseph, 15a St Angelo St, ☎340854 (4); Pace, Vincent, 'Lourdes,' St Elias St, ☎339861 (6); Said, Salvino, 100 Spinola Rd, ☎316701 (3,4,6); Schembri, Vincent, 2a St Elias St, ☎332531 (4); Vassallo, C, 22 Blance St, SLIEMA, ☎336749 (4); Zammit, Carmel, 'La Fleur,' St Paul St, ZURRIEQ, ☎822100 (2,4).

St. PAUL'S BAY
A pleasant village strung along the south side of St Paul's Bay; beaches, shops, restaurants. Bypassed, so quiet.
Abela, Norbert, Hope, Wigna Court, BIRKIRKARA, ☎440421 (6); Agius,, John, c/o Gannin Ho, ns off Hope St, MOSTA, ☎471603 (4,4); Agius, Oliver, Villa Carolette, Long St, San Anton, ATTARD, ☎444723 (2); Arrigo, Maria, 440a High St, ☎473342 (4,4); Azzopardi, Rita, 25 St John St, SIGGIEWI, ☎607146 (6); Bonnici, Manuel, Donna Mauna, Burmarrad Rd, BURMARRAD, ☎473267 (2); Borġ, Maria, 201 Main St, BIRKIRKARA, ☎442234 (4); Borġ, Paul, Brug Block, Flat 2, 1st May St, Fleur-de-lys, Sta VENERA, ☎474872 (4,4,4); Buttiġieġ, Joseph, St Paul's Ho, Mosta Rd, ☎471872 (6,6); Camilleri, Carmel, 42 Burmarrad Rd, ☎445095 (6); Camilleri, Joseph, 12 Għerien, ☎472541 (4); Camilleri, Michael, St George's St, ☎471247 (8); Carabott, Mrs C, Danube, Misraħ Kola, ATTARD, ☎443910 (6); Castles, Thomas, 14 Cathedral St, ☎471348 (2); Cauchi, C, 4 Isouard St, ☎47346 (4,6); Chetcuti, Paul, 51 St Publius St, ☎473278 (6,6); Chircop, Carmel, 199 Maria de Domenicus St, Sta LUCIA, ☎896332 (6); Ciappara, George, Vigo, Triq Iċ-Cagħaq, ☎472986 (2,4); Curmi, Anthony, 58 Main St, St JULIAN'S, ☎332310 (4); Falżon, John, Villino Sacra Famiglia, Esperanto St, MSIDA, ☎312608 (2); Fenech, Victoria, 12 Wileg Rd, ☎472278 (4); Fitzpatrick, Joseph, Cova da Iria, Vista Est, BIRKIRKARA, ☎440424 (2,4,4); Galea, Joseph, Rondeview, Flat 2, Manikata Rd, ☎441124 (4); Galea, Josephine, 105 New St, LUQA, ☎226572 (5); Gatt, Rev C, 296 Main St. ZEBBUG, ☎647850 (4); Gatt, Jimmy, 13/2 Eucharistic Congress Rd, MOSTA, ☎495278 (4,4,4,4,4,4,4,6,6); Gatt, Mary, 134 High St, ĦAMRUN, ☎222318 (2,2); Gauchi, Joseph, Starville, Wileg Rd, ☎472278 (4); Grech, Leo, 255 Constitution St, MOSTA, ☎443296 (2,2,4,4); Gretch, Paul, 8 Hospital St, RABAT, ☎454537 (2); Mifsud, Alf, Blk Q, Flat 3, Housing Est, ĦAMRUN, ☎223664 (6); Mifsud, Renato, Renyvon, Flat 3, Erba Mwiezeb, ☎471317 (5,5); Muscat, Anthony, Dembryl, Mellieħa Hts, MELLIEĦA, ☎473810 (4); Muscat, Spiro, Chateau Repos, ns off Valletta Rd, ATTARD, ☎491895 (4); Pace, Joseph, 17 Lower Victoria Tce, SLIEMA, ☎341489 (4); Pullicino, Mario, 8 St Nicholas St, SLIEMA, ☎330308

It's 19 minutes past 11. . .

(2,6,6); **Pulis**, Francis, 592/2 Main St, ☎471140 (6); **Sammut**, Joseph, Damaris, Lascaris St, QAWRA, ☎473234 (7); **Sammut**, Pascal, 587 St Paul's St, ☎473210 (3); **Sapienza**, Louis, Athena, ns off St Andrew's Rd, St. ANDREW'S, ☎337503 (6); **Scerri**, Michael, Villa Fiorita, Good Shepherd Ave, BALZAN, ☎487749 (4,4); **Schembri**, Joseph, 48 Isouard St, ☎471130 (4); **Stivala**, Frederick, Flat 3, 314 St Paul's St, ☎472181 (2,2); **Upton**, Michael, Colston, Dingli Rd, RABAT, ☎454391 (6); **Vella**, Anthony, 12 Parish St, MELLIEĦA, ☎473498 (6,6); **Vella**, E, 34 Hospital St, RABAT, ☎454349 (4); **Vella**, John & Mary, St Anthony, Bidnija L/o, MOSTA, ☎444663 (4); **Vella**, Marianne, 34 Hospital St, RABAT, ☎456573 (5); **von der Velden**, Pauline, 3 Għajn Tuffieħa Rd, Zebbieġ, MGARR, ☎474956 (6); **Xuereb**, Salvu, 613 Mosta Rd, ☎471154 (6).

SLIEMA A bustling town of 14,000; the main shopping centre, with restaurants, cinema, and Captain Morgan cruises.

Aloisio, Anne, 109 Howard St, ☎335343 (4); **Aquilina**, Henry, 286 Manuel Dimech St, ☎311424 (10); **Aquilina**, Lina, 97 Lapsi St, St. JULIAN'S, ☎331846 (6); **Aquilina**, William, 14 Melita St, ☎338582 (2,4); **Baldacchino**, C. G. 6 Locker St, ☎331202 (6); **Baldacchino**, Raymond, 34 Mrabet St, ☎341908 (7); **Binett**, Gulia, 263 Triq Manuel Dimech, ☎334829 (3,6); **Bonello**, Joseph, 35 Falżon St, ☎337180 (4); **Bonnici**, George, 43A Valletta St, PAOLA, ☎805729 (4); **Bons**, John, 1 Depiro St, ☎336958 (2); **Borġ**, Beatrice, 13 Luzio St, ☎336144 (2); **Borġ**, Mary, 52 Tigne Seafront, ☎313638 (4); **Brincat**, Emle, 68 Depiro St, ☎334963 (4); **Bugeja**, Dr Joseph, 45 Main St, RABAT, ☎454567 (6); **Busuttil**, Mary, 47/6 Neptune Ct, Balluta Bay, St. JULIAN'S, ☎331825 (4); **Camilleri**, Larry, Topaze, Garden St, The Gardens, St. JULIAN'S, ☎334619 (4); **Camilleri**, Maria & Edwige, 60 St Vincent St, ☎330909 (2,4,4,4,4,4); **Camilleri**, Peter, Campster, Gwann Mamo St, MSIDA, ☎238553 (4); **Camilleri**, Peter, Sylla, Upper Gdns, St. JULIAN'S, ☎336509 (4); **Coppini**, Lawrence, 48A Borġ Olivier St, ☎331705 (8); **Cordina**, Charles, 30-31, St Charles St, ☎330699 (7); **Demajo**, Thomas, Belair, Valletta Rd, RABAT,

. . . on 5 May, at Mosta.

☎454563 (4); **Doublet,** William, 60 Triq Manuel Dimech, ☎313656 (5); **Farrugia,** Saviour, 26 Dock St, MSIDA, ☎825906 (4); **Fenech,** Martin, 189/1 Tower Rd, ☎331523 (3); **Formosa,** Francis, 168/5 Tower Rd, ☎334049 (4,6,6); **Formosa,** Lawrence, 9 Ghar Il-Lembi St, ☎335735 (2,4,4,4,4,4); **Formosa,** Saviour, 140 Birkirkara Rd, St. JULIAN'S, ☎334369 (4,4,4,4,4,4); **Formosa,** Saviour, Ninfea, Triq Il-Marbat, The Gardens, St. JULIAN'S, ☎314766 (2,4,4,4,4); **Galea,** Theresa, 73 Moroni St, GZIRA ☎313403 (6); **Garrone,** M'Rose, 44/3 Tigne Mansions, ☎334188 (5); **Gatt,** Conrad, Caprice, Triq Il-Harag, BALZAN, ☎442910 (4); **Giacchino,** Joseph & Paul, Casa Nel Sol, Valley Rd, MSIDA, ☎443472 (4,4); **Holland,** Lilian, 6 Holland Ct, Bisazza St, ☎330038 (2,4); **Lupi,** Valentino, The Lupins, N'Hood II, SAN GWANN, ☎332609 (4); **Maistre,** Winifred, 118 Old College St, ☎334718 (4); **Marguerat,** Josephine, 4/3 Tigne Terrace, ☎331171 (6,6,6); **Micallef,** Carmelo, 208 St Helen St, ☎311093 (6); **Micallef,** Ernest, 12 St Trophimus St, ☎331193 (2); **Micallef,** Joseph, Lucciola, Triq Il-Qiegha, Misrah Kola, ATTARD, ☎445093 (4); **Mizzi,** Francis, 6 Bisazza La, ☎312935 (6); **Pace,** Francis, 250 Tower Rd, ☎331986 (4); **Papgiorcopolo,** Joseph, Joshir, Triq l'Istrefanotis, SAN GWANN, ☎332519 (4); **Podesta,** Arthur, 2C St Paul's Mansions, Ta'Xbiex Seafront, TA'XBIEX, ☎331437 (6,6); **Polidano,** Bernadette, 3 St Ignatius Junc, St. JULIAN'S, ☎312052 (4); **Smith,** Mary, 10/2 Tigne Terrace, ☎334025 (2); **Tabona,** Dr J, 68 Main St, St. JULIAN'S, ☎331388 (4,4,4,6,6,6,6,6); **Tabona,** Mary & Evelyn, Harper, Harper La, FLORIANA, ☎223871 (4,4); **Tabone,** Marion, 108 Howard St, ☎335343 (4,4); **Tabone,** Tancred, 108 Howard St, ☎330098, 330432 (4,4,4,6); **Tufigno,** Virginia, 192, Old Bakery St, VALLETTA, ☎330449 (6); **Vassallo,** Carmela, 22 Blanc St, ☎336749 (2); **Vella,** John, 82/2 Tigne St, ☎339234 (4); **Zammit,** Paul, 69 Cassar St, MOSTA, ☎443194 (4).

SWIEQI

Also known as Is-Swieqi, this is the Maltese part of St Andew's Barracks. Moderately quiet.

Abela, Mrs Gemma, 8/8 Ghar Il-Lembi St, SLIEMA, ☎338469 (five at 2).

TA'XBIEX

At the centre of Malta's yacht moorings; picturesque.
Stilton, Rudolphe, Miramar, Ta'Xbiex Tce, ☎332778 (4).

VITTORIOSA One of the 'three cities' on the quieter side of Grand Harbour; splendid views.
Grixti, Anthony, 1 Alley One, St Anthony St, MOSTA, ☎493517.

ŻEJTUN A quiet town of 12,000 in the south-east corner.
Gatt, Joseph, 23 Sacred Heart St, ☎878444 (8).

GOZO

Gozo is peaceful, rustic, and its landscape is more scenic than mainland Malta's; its cliffs and coasts are particularly beautiful.

Addresses. When writing to these addresses, add 'Gozo, Malta,' after the village, except for Francis Debrincat, owner of property in Xlendì, who does not live on Gozo.

Għarb.
Azzopardi, Joe, L'Orangerie, Rock St, ☎556100 (6).
Għajnsielem.
Azzopardi, Carmel, Dar Tgħaliem, St Coronation St, NADUR, ☎553033 (6); **Borġ,** Carmen, 24 St Anthony St, ☎556116 (4,4); **Debrincat,** John, The Haven, Cordina St, ☎553212 (6); **Grech,** Anthony, 19 St Anthony St, ☎556543 (6); **Gretch,** N, Triq Il-Baħħara, ☎556050 (6); **Grech,** Patrick, 21 St Anthony St, ☎551549 (4,6).
Kerċem.
D'Anastasi, Silvia, Casa d'Ansavell, Borġ Geritu St, VICTORIA, ☎551274 (4).
Marsalforn.
Attard, Anthony, 13 St Domenica St, VICTORIA, ☎551198 (4,4); **Attard,** Anthony, San Antonio, Gilju St, VICTORIA, ☎556948 (6); **Axiak,** Victor, Morning Star, Rabat Rd, ☎551093 (4); **Azzopardi,** Marlene, 193 Main St, SANNAT, ☎554529 (5); **Borġ,** Charles, 146 St Gregory St, KERCEM, ☎555425 (4); **Borġ,** Emanuel, 4 Xuxija St, KERCEM, ☎554892 (4); **Camilleri,** Victor, Maria Victoria, Sacred Heart St, ☎551209 (4); **Cassar,** Anthony, 93 Hospital St, VICTORIA, ☎556753 (5); **Cassar,** Joseph, Alcazar, 8th December St, VICTORIA, ☎551681 (4,4); **Cutajar,** Joseph, 8 Garden St, GĦASRI ☎551455 (6); **Farrugia,** George, 2 Sump St, VICTORIA, ☎554685 (4,4); **Galea,** Francis, 51 Charity St, VICTORIA, ☎556143 (4); **Gretch,** Joseph, 63 Għar Qawqla St, ☎551173; **Hili,** Alfred, 23 Marsalforn St, XAGĦRA, ☎551478 (4); **Magro,** John, 158 St Ursola St, VICTORIA, ☎551170 (4,4,6,6); **Mizzi,** John, 14 Republic St, VICTORIA, ☎556048 (3); **Said,** Victoria, 56 Srug St, XAGĦRA, ☎553282 (4); **Scicluna,** Franco, Wied Seqer St, VICTORIA, ☎556640 (2); **Vella,** Gregory, Casalgo, Kerċem Rd, VICTORIA, ☎551274 (4); **Vella,** Salvu, Rabat Rd, ☎556147 (4); **Xuereb,** M'Anne & Maria, George Flats, Xagħra Rd, ☎556754 (4,6).
Qbajjar.
Mintoff, Rose, 11A Square St, GĦASRI, ☎556224 (4,4).
San Lawrence.
Vella, Lawrence, 167 Church St, GĦARB, ☎552091 (6).
Sannat.
Bugeja, Joseph, 19 By The Bastions Rd, VICTORIA, ☎556825 (6).

Xagħra.
Buttiġieġ, George, Dar Buttiġieġ, 8th September Ave, ☎556494 (6); **Said,** Gemma, 43 January St, ☎556621 (7).
Xlendi.
Attard, Jane, Janeph Estate, Sannat Rd, VICTORIA, ☎553566 (4); **Bigeni,** Pino, Holy Mary, St Elizabeth St, XEWKIJA, ☎556941 (4); **Borġ,** Joe, Springvale, Għajn Tuta St, KERĊEM, ☎554843 (4,4); **Bugeja,** Joseph, *see Sannat,* (2,2,2); **Calleja,** Charles, 79 Munxar St, MUNXAR, ☎554610 (4); **Caruana,** Salvina, Morpheus, St John St, VICTORIA, ☎553765 (4); **Cassar,** Anthony, Villa Pepprina, Ulysses Village, ☎551616 (4,5); **Debrincat,** Francis, 43 St Philip St, VITTORIOSA, MALTA, ☎807544 (4,4); **Galea,** George, 8 Terraced Hse, Sannat Rd, VICTORIA, ☎551175 (4); **Galea,** Joseph, Block 1 Door A Flat 5, G.H.E. Sannat Rd, VICTORIA, ☎556878 (6); **Grech,** George & Anna, Canadiana, Mġarr Rd, Għajnsielem, ☎551532 (4,4,4,6); **Mercieca,** Carmen, La Hacienda, Manwel Dimech St, VICTORIA, ☎551252 (5); **Mizzi,** Gino & Rev C. Borġ, c'o 11A St Peter & St Paul St, KERĊEM, ☎551365 (4); **Sacco,** Maria, 55 Charity St, VICTORIA, ☎553835 (4); **Said,** Carmela, 8 Xlendi Rd, ☎551583 (8); **Said,** Maria, 54 Pompei St, VICTORIA, ☎551312 (4); **Spiteri,** Maria, In God We Trust, Cocco Palmier St, SANNAT, ☎554505 (4); **Vella,** Joseph, Solaria, St Lucy St, KERĊEM, ☎551514 (4,6); **Xerri,** Carmel, 10 Sannat Rd, VICTORIA, ☎553654 (6); **Zammit,** Maria & Michael, Mike-Mary Hse, Mġarr Rd, GĦAJNSIELEM, ☎551532 (4,4,4).

Maximum prices. The H&CE Board fixes maximum prices for all licensed self-catering accommodation: a sample of the 1990 figures gives these **high season** prices for **apartments:** two-bed: class A1, Lm62; A, Lm52; B1, LM46; B,Lm42. Four-bed: Lm92, Lm78, Lm67, Lm62. Eight-bed: Lm134, Lm113, Lm98, Lm91.

Mid season: two-bed: Lm50, Lm42, Lm36, Lm31. Four-bed: Lm76, Lm62, Lm54, Lm50.

Low season: two-bed: Lm37, Lm32, Lm29, Lm26. Four-bed: Lm50, Lm38, Lm32, Lm30.

High season is 16 June–30 September; low season is 1 November–31 March. Villas are approximately 10% dearer.

Some apartment owners quote higher prices to overseas telephone enquirers. This is an offence punishable by a stiff fine, so ring off and try somebody else. There are plenty of flats on the market.

High summer at Għajn Tuffieħa Bay.

Landfall at Mġarr, Gozo, amid the churches.

Inside the dome of Mosta church.

St Paul's Co-Cathedral dominates Mdina.

8: **EATING OUT and ENTERTAINMENT**

Feeding body and mind

YOU CAN DINE OUT in Malta aboard a Swedish barquentine built in 1909; aboard a Constellation aircraft that was impounded when its crew abandoned it at Luqa Airport; in several forts and castles built by the Order of St John; or, if you're privileged, in the 500-ft-long great ward of a 16th-cent hospital. There are, of course, many other more conventional restaurants: the Hotel and Catering Establishments Board licenses 278, plus a greater number of snack bars.

Night life? Il-Qaliet and Paceville are the places for after-dark activity, with the Palladium night-club, the Eden Super Bowl and Styx disco in the same street, and the Dragonara Palace Casino a few minutes' walk away. Elsewhere, the leading hotels put on their own entertainment, there are pubs and clubs and lesser discos — and there are still a few cinemas left.

RESTAURANTS

Here's a list of the island-republic's first-class restaurants:

L'Ambjent has 70 covers at its premises at Xemxija Hill, Gozo; ☎573223.

Anni Venti, 11 The Strand, Sliema, ☎517289, seating 50.

Auberge Ta'Frenċ, Marsalforn Rd, Xagħra, ☎553888, one of the two top places on Gozo and with seating for 60.

Arches, behind a splended arched fa0ade at 113 Main St, Mellieħa; 100 covers, ☎573436.

Barracuda is a 50-cover place at 194 Main St, St Julian's, ☎331817.

Bellevue, in Main St, Mellieħa, seating 80; ☎573723.

The **Belluga,** at Ramla Rd, Marsascala, with 100 covers; ☎829460.

Bologna, serving Italian cuisine at 50 Republic St, Valletta; ☎626149, seating 80.

The 80-seat **B.J.'s** is at Paceville Court, St Julian's, at the heart of things.

The **Carriage,** on Sliema's Strand, has just 30 covers, making it the smallest restaurant among the greats. ☎334584.

The **China House** is one of two Chinese-food specialist in the top class; 70 covers, ☎335021, and it's at 8 Spinola Rd, St Julian's.

La Dolce Vita is at 159 St George's Rd, St Julian's; 70 covers, ☎337036.

Giannini, at 23 Windmill St, is one of two first-class restaurants in Valletta city; ☎237121.

Gillieru, at Church St, St Paul's Bay, with seating for 200, is the largest top-class restaurant; ☎573480.

Kyoto is the Japanese restaurant, at 131 Spinola Rd, St Julian's; ☎334398.

La Loggia, a 60-seat restaurant at 39 Mrabat St, Sliema; ☎513476.

Luzzu, named from the Maltese fishing-boats, specialises in fish dishes at Salina Bay, Qawra; 60 covers, ☎573925.

Madliena Cottage at Caf-Caf Lane, Madliena, Mosta, has seating for 50; ☎515782.

The **Marco Polo** on Dragonara Rd, St Julian's, ☎331995, serves Chinese food.

The **Medina** at 7, Holy Cross St, Mdina, is in a Norman building in the heart of the Silent City; call quietly on ☎674004.

On St Paul's St, in St Paul's Bay, the **Palazzo Pescatore** has a colonnaded façade and seating for 120; ☎573182.

Paul's Punch Bowl is at St George's Rd, St Julian's; ☎447644.

The **Portobello** at St Luke St is the smartest restaurant in bustling Buġibba; ☎471661 for one of its 56 places.

Make a **Rendezvous** at 56 Dingli St, Sliema; ☎337468.

St Thomas's Tower is in a clifftop fortress east of Marsascala, the most easterly restaurant in the islands. ☎821369.

San Guiliano, at 3 St Joseph's St, St Julian's, seats 84; ☎231553.

There's no surf at Tower Rd, Sliema, but there is **The Surfside,** seating 48. ☎333125.

Indian food? Try the **Taj Mahal** at 122 The Strand, Ġzira; 60 covers, ☎339246.

Whisper, at Eucharistic Congress Rd, is near Mosta's giant church; ☎441122.

The **Winston,** at 16 High St, Sliema, specialises in fish; 150 covers, ☎334584.

Black Pearl. Among the restaurants which offer the most unusual setting is the Black Pearl, (class two, 100 places ☎310989, Ta'Xbiex

Marina), built in Pukavik, Sweden, in 1909 as the brigantine *Black Opal*. (A brigantine has square-rigged sails on the foremast and fore-and-aft rig on the main.) She was 112ft (34m) long and 26.5ft (8m) wide, built with two skins of solid oak to withstand the Baltic ice, and for 59 years she navigated by sail, carrying basic cargoes around Sweden.

In 1969 she had a fore-and-aft-rigged mizen mast added during a refit at Ramsgate, Kent, making her a barquentine. Renamed *Aeolus*, she sailed for Australia in 1974. Coming back in 1976, her engine-room caught fire in the Suez Canal and the boat's crew and owners abandoned her in Marsamxett Harbour, where she sank.

Salvaged in 1979 and repaired, she was used in the 1980 film *Popeye*, shot in Malta — and sank again, in Anchor Bay. Refloated, she was towed to Ta'Xbiex on Marsa Creek, brought ashore, and converted into a restaurant. Diners now enter through a doorway cut into her hull just above the water line, for she'll never float again.

Super Constellation. The Super Constellation Restaurant on the south side of the tunnel under Luqa runway, seats 40 diners in the main fuselage, with the kitchens in an annexe on stilts. The aircraft was carrying guns when it made an emergency landing at Malta in 1968; the crew jumped bail while awaiting trial, and in 1973 the plane was sold, towed off the airfield, and converted to its present use. It's a class-four restaurant, ☎822429.

Gillieru. Gillieru's Restaurant in St Paul's Bay began in 1920 as a place where the village peasantry could buy simple fish meals, cooked by the great-grandmother of the present owner, Paul Cremona. It became the Harbour Hotel and Restaurant in World War Two, its popularity with British officers putting it on the road to success. Expansion began in the 1950s, and at completion in 1965, Prime Minister Borġ Olivier and future president (and poet) Anton Buttiġieġ, were guests. Gillieru's has also served Maltese historian Ernle Bradford, and actors Roger Moore, Lee Marvin and Oliver Reed.

The neighbouring **Church of St Paul's Shipwreck** replaces one destroyed in the war.

Il-Fortizza. On Tower Rd, Sliema, Il-Fortizza Restaurant (class two, ☎336908) occupies a fortress built by the British between 1872 and '76 as the Sliema Point Battery, with granite walls facing the sea and limestone for the landward side; it was a searchlight base during the Second World War, and became a restaurant in 1974. Having seating for 200, it shares with Gillieru the role of the largest restaurant on the island of Malta; the **Cupid** on Republic St, Victoria, Gozo, also has 200 covers, but the republic's largest restaurant is the **Ulysses Lodge** at Ramla Bay, Gozo, with 400 places.

Exotic dishes. There are very few restaurants specialising in the more exotic cuisines of the Orient and India.

THE MENU

This menu takes sample dishes from the Black Pearl and Il-Fortizza:

Cold hors d'oeuvres:
    Stuffed cuttlefish with rose island sauce Lm2.80
    Poached cherna with lemon sauce Lm2.50

Hot hors d'oeuvres:
    Escargots Lm2.30
    Fried shrimp in garlic and rice Lm1.95
    Baked mussels with herb butter Lm1.85

Pasta:
    Noodles and seafood Lm2.60
    Spaghetti with octopus and tomato sauce Lm2.25
    Macaroni in foil with shellfish and brandy Lm1.75
    Noodles with salmon and caviar Lm1.95

Main dish:
    Char-grilled tenderloin steak Lm3.35
    Pork fillet casserole with peas and onions Lm2.95
    Grilled swordfish Lm4.25
    Pan-fried lamb fillet Lm4.10
    King prawns sauté'd in white wine Lm4.35

Desserts:
    Cheese board (or ice cream) . . . . 65c.

Tax. There is a 10% tax on all restaurant meals.

MALTESE CUISINE

Maltese cuisine is a product of the island's climate and its history, with main ingredients being fish, rabbit, cheese, fruit and vegetables, and with main culinary influence coming from Italy and Spain, with a soupçon of British influence.

Soups. You should recognise **minestra** as a thick vegetable soup, but **soppa ta'l-armla** is 'widow's soup,' a popular dish for Lent and containing cheese, eggs and mixed vegetables.

Pies. The basic recipe for many dishes is a mixture of all the vegetables in season and baked in a pie, the essential difference and flavour coming from the meat or fish which give the dish its name.

Thus **timpana,** the most popular pie, has minced beef or mutton and a liberal helping of macaroni mixed with the core ingredients; **lampuka** pie adds the lampuka fish, **braġoli** adds minced beef, ham or bacon, **qarnita** adds squid or octopus, and **rabbit** pie, the national dish, is self-explanatory. Rabbits are the largest mammals to be found in the wild in Malta, mostly confined to St Paul's Islands, but when the

Order of St John ruled, rabbits were so numerous that some grand masters ordered the peasants to catch and eat them. The custom has persisted, but today's rabbit meat is reared in captivity.

Other dishes. The Italian influence has created a liking for **pasta** in all its forms, and **ravjul** is on many menus. Of the island cheeses, **ġbejna,** made from goats' milk, is the favourite.

Wines. Malta produces a good range of wines, which are cheap by northern European standards as they are not taxed. Most common are *Lachryma Vitis,* the 'tears of life,' and the *Marsovin* range, with *Verdala* and Gozitan wines in lesser quantities. Farson's Blue Label and Hopleaf are the brand leaders among the island's lagers.

Fish. Among Maltese fish, the **lampuka** ('lampuki' in the plural) is the most legendary as it breeds somewhere near the Nile delta then swims past Malta from August to December, the times varying each year, to an unknown destination which, some people suggest, could be the Caribbean. Line fishermen float large lumps of cork at sea-level, anchored to the sea bed; they thrust palm leaves into the cork to give shelter to passing lampuki, then entice them out by baited hooks. Recently the lampuka shoals have been dwindling: could it be because the Aswan Dam in Upper Egypt is trapping the Nile sediment and so starving the delta of nutrient?

Other fish and sea creatures in traditional Maltese cooking include the swordfish, tunny or tuna, octopus, squid, and several whose name has yet to be translated out of Malti.

Bread. One of the delights of Malta is its bread – *ħobz*. For generations it has been baked in the true Mediterranean style, once found from Spain to Cyprus, producing a crusty round loaf full of temptingly soft crumb that must be eaten within the day. It still is baked that way, but at the end of the 1980s the bakers started adding preservatives; you can now keep the bread for several days but it has lost that mouthwatering flavour.

NIGHTLIFE

The high spot of Maltese nightlife is the **Eden Palladium Night Club** at St George's Bay which bills itself as 'featuring the most spectacular laser show in all of Europe' every Tues-Fri from 2030, and on Sat from 2200. Opening for business in October 1989 with seating for 650 and standing space for 2,000 in air-conditioned comfort, the Palladium certainly sets a very high standard and flies in English-speaking comedians, cabaret artists and singers for the summer season; in its first year it featured David Copperfield and Jerry Harris. Call ☎341191 for reservations. Tickets cost Lm7 for the show and the buffet, or Lm4.50 for the show, and dress is semi-formal with jeans not allowed.

By day the auditorium and its deep stage are available for

conferences, product launches, and any other special event, with the parent company's four-star Eden Beach Hotel nearby, available for guests.

Next door is the **Eden Super Bowl,** first opened in November 1988 and now open daily from 1000 until the early hours for ten-pin bowling; admission 85c for adults until closing time, and 55c adults until 1900 and for juniors (up to 14 years, 1000-1800 Mon-Sat only); shoe hire is 25c. ☎319888, or 341196 for high-season reservations as this is a popular sport with the Maltese; membership of the bowling association rose from 30 to 400 in early 1989. There are 20 lanes, 20 leagues, and prizes include tickets to Walt Disney World in Florida.

The **Eden Roller Rink** on the top floor is open daily in summer, from 1200 at weekends and from 1800 Mon-Fri; in winter it's open only Fri-Sun. Admission is 30c, plus hire of skates (75c booted, 50c unbooted) for the session.

Across the road but still within the Eden Leisure Group is **Styx II Disco,** the island's liveliest. It's under the Eden Beach Hotel — but is soundproofed.

Other discos. Styx doesn't have the monopoly of the disco world. **Axis** is a strong rival within earshot in St George's Rd, ☎318079; **Dewdrops** is at Ball St, Paceville, just a short walk away, ☎311747; **Guanpula** is near Racecourse St, Rabat, catering for nightlife in the west, ☎237350; and **Vibes** is at the Tal-Balal crossroads in Birkirkara, ☎315220. On Gozo there is the **Platinum Disco** at the Hotel Calypso in Marsalforn, ☎556131, and **La Grotta** in Xlendi, ☎551149, with a restaurant attached.

And look for the ♪ symbol in the hotel index.

Casino. Right on the tip of Dragonara Point, Il-Qaliet, the elegant 19th-cent palace of the Marquis Emmanuel Scicluna with its 76 Ionic columns, is now the Dragonara Palace Casino. Open daily (except Christmas, Maundy Thursday, Good Friday and Our Lady of Sorrows, in July) from 2030 to 0300, or even 0430, admission is Lm2. Gambling, of course, costs extra: the minimum stake on roulette is 50c, the maximum Lm10; the range on blackjack is Lm1 to Lm50; and Lm20 starts chemin de fer, with no ceiling. Passports *must* be shown on entry, to prove your age; minimum for foreigners is 18 years, for Maltese 25. If you're not a gambler, come in and look around at the elegant interiors, carved mantelpieces, and works of art including a Constable copy.

Since the casino opened in July 1964 it has seen guests make and lose fortunes; it hit financial trouble itself when its first gaming manager was convicted of embezzling Lm12,556 in 1964, and again in the 1984 tourism slump when the bank called in its overdraft. The casino is now run by a new company, with a lease on Scicluna's old palace.

9: THE SPORTING SCENE

On land, at sea, in the air

THE MALTESE NATIONAL SPORT is **football,** as spectator or player. The Ta'Qali National Stadium near the centre of the island is the main arena for league matches, creating major interest during the September-to-May season. The sport is so popular that Malta competes internationally, and Ta'Qali is sometimes the neutral ground for other international tournaments. Even the larger hotels have their own teams, ready to give tourists a thrashing at any time. The Malta Football Association is at 280 St Paul St, Valletta, ☎222697.

Next in popularity is **horseracing,** with events held at the race track in Marsa every Sunday from October to May. The card usually has seven or eight trotting races and one on the flat. Contact the Marsa Racing Club at Racecourse St, Marsa, ☎224800.

Visitors can join in all other sports, be they on land or in the water. The Marsa Sports Club ☎603809, has the island's only **golf** course, an 18-hole green; a **cricket** pitch, **mini-golf, archery,** (contact the Malta Archery Federation at 'Saggitarius,' Triq il-Wizna, St Andrew's, ☎244351), five **squash** courts (☎240842), a swim pool and 18 **tennis** courts; tennis is also available at many of the larger hotels, for guests' use only, or contact the Vittoriosa Lawn Tennis Club at PO Box 476, Valletta.

Badminton comes under the Badminton Association of Malta at Chesyill, Windmill St, Birkirkara, ☎491545; **ten-pin bowling** is on offer every day at the Eden Bowl (see 'nightlife'); and at Enrico Mizzi St, Msida ☎332323.

The Shooting Association at PO Box 340, Valletta, ☎444747 or 445566, controls **clay pigeon shooting** which is gaining in popularity and holds shoots every Sunday: one can hope this will ease the pressure on the killing of migratory birds. **Horse riding** is available at several schools near the Marsa race track, and at some of the hotels.

The Malta Amateur Athletics Association holds a marathon and a women's half-marathon in the cool of February, as well as organising road and cross-country races, and a series of track and field events leading to the championships at the Marsa Stadium in May. You may also contact the Malta Marathon Organising Committee at 56 Autumn St, Mosta.

You can join the locals in a game of bowls in most villages; this is like the French *pétanque* and has nothing in common with the Britsh game played on immaculate lawns. Just ask for a game of *bocci*. **Basketball** fixtures and details are available from the Basketball Association, 5 Sunvalley Flats, Msida Valley Rd, Birkirkara, ☎499481, and for details on basketball, cycling, hockey, the martial arts, table tennis and wrestling, ask the MNTO office in Valletta, ☎224444.

Water sports. The most popular water sport for islanders and for visitors is **windsurfing,** available at almost every popular beach, with Mellieħa Bay the busiest. The Sicily-Malta Windsurfing Race is held each May, and there are international championships in September. Malta frequently has breezes strong enough to make the sport really exhilarating. A useful contact is Wishbone Windsurfing Promotions at 193 St Albert St, Ġzira, ☎314956.

The Valletta Yacht Club at Manoel Island, ☎331131 or 333109 is your contact for anything to do with **yachting and small-boat sailing,** including the main events in the racing calendar, the Comino Regatta in June, the Malta-Syracuse Race for keelboats in July, and the Rimini-Malta-Rimini Yacht Race in August. The club is also an agent for the charter of locally-based yachts.

The Yacht Marina at Ta'Xbiex (pronounced 'tash-baysh') has stern-on mooring for up to 272 yachts, with connections for water, electricity and sewage disposal, plus a weather office, MF and VHF radio station, chart shop and chandlery.

Virtu Rapid Ferries claims its 'Santa Maria' to be the world's fastest passenger ferry. (photo: Virtu Rapid Ferries)

Diving. Diving has plunged to new depths in the Maltese archipelago in the past few years and has become a year-round activity with sea temperatures in winter bottoming out at 55°F (13°C) from their summer maximum of 73°F (23°C). The sport is under strict government control for the safety of everybody who dives, with safety for the diver and the preservation of the underwater habitat being of paramount importance: if you find any archaeological treasure, leave it but report it.

Nobody may dive without a permit, the C-card available from the Department of Health in Merchants St, Valletta, ☎224071, for Lm1, on production of your log book, two photos, and a medical certificate; it's easier to apply through a diving school before you reach Malta. But if you plan to dive independently you will also need to show the CMAS (*Confédération Mondiale des Activités Subaquatiques*) 2-star certificate as minimum qualification. Unlicensed spearfishing is justifiably punished by a heavy fine, and there are certain no-go areas of archaeological importance.

The beginner *must* attend a diving school to qualify for his CMAS or PADI (Professional Association of Diving Instructors) certificate, which is valid worldwide. A five-day course for the British Sub Aqua Club Novice certificate costs around Lm80 including equipment hire, and the BSAC Sports Diver certificate costs around Lm115 with six days of training. A PADI Open Water Diver certificate, the first step, costs Lm100 and takes five days – but you must be able to swim before starting any course.

Diving conditions off the Maltese islands are ideal. The water is crystal clear – you can see up to 100ft (30m) – with no currents in summer and only a few in winter, plus a tidal range that's no more than a handspan. While you will not find the splendour of Red Sea marine life, you will meet a fascinating variety of fish, molluscs, and the occasional octopus up to an arm's length. You won't meet dolphin, tuna, or shark, but you should see grouper, sting ray, damsel fish, the occasional nudibranch and, preferably on a night dive, moray eel. A surprising resident is the flying fish, found in large numbers around the islands and sometimes even seen by passengers on the Gozo ferry.

Where to dive. Diving is possible in all weathers except storm, as there's always one coastline in the lee of the land. Favourite diving spots, listed clockwise from Valletta: Bengħajsa Point, south-east of Birżebbuġa; the Blue Grotto for its splendid caves; Wied iż-Żurrieq for an underwater cave and crabs by night; Għar Lapsi for underwater caves; Anchor Bay for a large cave; Ċirkewwa for its underwater caves and arch, and its steep drop to 100ft (30m); Aħrax Point for marine life and a large cave, but you must use a marker buoy as the nearby channel is busy with small boats; Santa Marija Caves on

Comino for a shallow dive; Qawra Point for sponges and a cave; Merkanti Reef off St Julian's Bay; Ta'Ċenċ on Gozo, with access from the private beach of the Ta'Ċenċ Hotel; Dwejra Point for underwater access to the Inland Sea and dramatic scenery; and Irqieqa Point on Comino for a meeting with enormous grouper.

Contacts. You can find BSAC at 16 Upper Woburn Pl, London, WC1H 0QU, ☎071.387.9302; CMAS is at Rue du Colisée 34, 75008 Paris; the Federation of Underwater Activities (Malta), affiliated to CMAS, is at PO Box 29, Ġzira; and the Association of Professional Diving Schools is at Msida Court, 61-62 Sea Front, Msida. Call the Palace Control Tower, ☎225961, for the weather forecast.

Diving schools, listed alphabetically, are: Calypso Diving and Aquatic Centre, Calypso Hotel, Marsalforn, Gozo, ☎556132–4; Cresta Diving Centre, St George's Bay, St Julian's, ☎310743; Dive Systems, 48 Ġzira Rd, Ġzira, ☎317137; Divewise Services Ltd, Dragonara Hotel, St Julian's, ☎336441; Expo, 20 St John's St, Valletta, ☎223586; Frankie's Gozo Diving Centre, Mġarr Rd, Xewkija, Gozo, ☎551315; Jerma Palace Hotel, Marsascala, ☎823222; Lilywhites Sports Shop, St George's Rd St Julian's; Maltaqua, Mosta Rd, St Paul's Bay, ☎471873; Strand Diving, Gillieru Restaurant, St Paul's Bay, ☎473480; Tauchschule, Paradise Bay Hotel, Ċirkewwa, ☎470384; Tony's Diving, Comino Hotel, Comino, ☎473051.

Emergencies. There's a recompression chamber at St Luke's Hospital, Gwardamanġa, ☎234765; the Armed Forces of Malta rescue helicopter is on ☎284371; and the AFM patrol boats are on ☎238797.

In the air. Paragliding is no longer purely a water sport when you can take off and land from the deck of a boat or a dockside. It's on offer at Golden Bay, Qawra, Mellieħa Bay, St George's Bay and St Julian's.

The **International Air Rally** brings light aircraft from Europe and occasionally from the USA for this event in June, which began in the late 1960s. The Air Rally Organising Committee is at Rally House, Granary Square, Floriana, ☎622860.

10: MOVING IN

Your holiday or retirement home

MALTA WELCOMES FOREIGNERS WANTING TO BUY a holiday or retirement home in the islands, despite having one of the highest population densities in the world. Property is much cheaper than in Britain and northern Europe, approximately equal to values in an average midwest American city; personal taxes are less, property tax is non-existent — but water was considered expensive relative to Britain until the late 1980s when British water soared in cost.

Almost all the expatriates living in Malta are British, and Britons are the most welcome, probably due to historic links which have survived the occasional disagreements since independence.

RESIDENCE STATUS.

The foreigner wanting to buy property in Malta can do so as a *non-resident*, a *temporary resident*, or a *permanent resident*.

Non-resident. Non-resident status is the same as tourist: you are allowed to stay for up to three months at a time. Non-residents who buy property are exempt from all local taxes.

Temporary resident. A temporary resident may stay for an unlimited time, but does not have the inalienable right of residence. He or she is liable for Maltese taxes only if his stay exceeds six months, when tax on income from abroad is levied for the entire stay at the standard rate. A temporary resident must have a permit from the Principal Immigration Officer, with the main qualification being an income of at least Lm4,000 a year originating from abroad; this money must be brought into Malta on a pro-rata system — a six-month stay must be financed by bringing in the equivalent of Lm2,000.

Permanent resident. A permanent resident has a permit issued by the Office of the Prime Minister at the Auberge de Castille, for which he has proved *either* an annual income equal to Lm10,000 (£17,330 or DM45,000 at the rate of exchange used in this edition), *or* proven capital of Lm150,000, which can be in property or investments and need not be brought to Malta. A permanent resident must bring into the islands a minimum of Lm6,000 per year plus Lm1,000 for each dependent; thus a married couple must have an income of Lm7,000 a year.

Taxation. The income tax levied on all remittances for foreign residents is 15%, after the deduction of the married couple's allowance of Lm1,730, but permanent residents pay a minimum annual tax bill of Lm1,000. Value Added Tax, *taxe valeur additionelle*, *Mehrwertsteuer* is not levied in Malta, but Death Duties (taxation on the value of a dead person's estate) *is* levied on the assets held on the island. This taxation level is seen as a major inducement for foreigners to take up residence in the islands.

Double taxation agreements exist with almost every country in western Europe, plus the United States, Canada and Australia.

Jobs or businesses. The granting of a residence permit does not carry an automatic right to look for a job. Work permits are granted only if there is no islander qualified or available for a particular job, and government permission is needed before a foreigner sets himself up in business.

BUYING PROPERTY.

Property is cheap but, to avoid pricing the islanders out of the market, a foreigner of no matter what status may not buy a house for less than Lm30,000 or an apartment for less than Lm20,000, or lease anything for less than Lm1,200 a year. The limit is one property per person, and funds for the purchase must come from abroad. There is no capital gains tax on any profit made on resale, and all the proceeds, including profit, may be exported.

The property is for the sole use of the owner, his family, and immediate friends: it may not be rented out for profit.

The purchase. Chosen your property? Before you commit yourself, make certain it has a telephone installed and working — the waiting list for connection has been up to two years — and that it has mains water and electricity, and an undisputed right of access.

Now you need a permit to purchase, an AIP, 'Application for Immovable Property,' which costs Lm100 from the Ministry of Finance and which gives the address of the home you want.

The first document for you to sign is a Preliminary Agreement, drawn up by your notary public (lawyer or solicitor) and signed by all parties involved in the transaction; if you can't be there in person you may give power of attorney to your nominee. The agreement details the conditions of the sale and when it is signed the deposit of 10% is due. Malti is the language of the law courts, but your deeds are written in English.

Shipping your car? Three to six months may pass before completion, giving you the chance to arrange to ship out your furniture and car. But wait! If you're a non-resident, don't bring your car as after six months you'll be required to pay import duty on it at the rate of 65% (80% if you come from outside the EEC) — and the car is worth more in Malta than it would be in Britain. A resident may import

Toy soldier? No, just a visitor to the Valletta Carnival.

one used car duty-free.

Completion − the costs. The costs, in addition to the AIP, are 1% of the property value for the notary's fee, 0.05% for your receipt, and 3.65% for stamp duty. When you sell, you incur the estate agent's fee instead of the AIP and stamp duty.

Household items. There are no problems with your furniture, and no customs duty on it provided it is in the republic within six months of your taking up residence in your new home. It's cheaper to move the furniture overland, using the car ferry from Sicily, than to freight it through the Strait of Gibraltar, with the cost of transporting the contents of the average three-bedroom house being around £3,000.

Your pet cat or dog will spend its first three weeks in Malta in quarantine, at your expense.

Financing the purchase. Mortgages are not normally available in Malta for foreigners, but if you plan to buy a large property you can arrange for a bank in your home country to guarantee the loan. Several British building societies offer a mortgage on your British home to allow you to buy property in Malta.

Domestic bills. There are no property taxes at all, nor any substitute for them such as Britain's controversial 'Poll Tax', but you will need to budget for Lm50 to Lm75 a year in ground rent (few properties are sold freehold), and your combined electricity and water bill will be from Lm25 to Lm45 for three months, with liquid propane gas in large cylinders costing Lm2.50 each. Your annual television license is Lm12 for a colour set, and you must allow Lm24 for your car tax, including the tax for parking in Valletta. Two people can feed themselves comfortably on Lm20 a week, including meat.

ESTATE AGENTS in Malta:

Alexander Gretch, 14 The Strand, Sliema, ☎336663; **Belair Travel Bureau,** 12 High St, Sliema, ☎336159; **Building Services,** 107c Rudolph St, Sliema, ☎334164; **Cassar & Cooper,** St Anne Court, Bisazza St, Sliema, ☎336348; **Choice Properties,** 239c Tower Rd, Sliema, ☎331186; **Dhalia Investments,** Testaferrata St, Msida, ☎316670; **Frank Salt Real Estate,** 2 Paceville Ave, St Julian's, ☎337373; **Godwin Lowell Estates,** 3 Ross St, St Julian's ☎311766; **Grosvenor Estates,** 3d 2nd floor, Tagliaferro Centre, Cathedral St, Sliema, ☎312282; **Landmark,** 4a Karm Galea St, Sliema, ☎310744; **M Properties,** 24 Kingsway Palace, Republic St, Valletta, ☎231492; **Perry,** 86 Tigné St, Sliema, ☎316880; **Property Consultants,** 7 The Whispers, Ross St, Paceville, ☎333334; **A. Pullicino & Co,** Flat 4, San Juan, St George's Rd, Sliema, ☎332529; **Standards Properties,** 10 St Julian's Hill, St Julian's, ☎317117; **William Cobbett Estates,** 18 Tagliaferro Centre, Cathedral St, Sliema, ☎337967.

St Helen's Gate leads through the Margherita Lines into Cospicua.

Żabbar Gate, in the Cotonera Lines, now stands on a traffic island.

Ġgantiga, on Gozo, a gigantic temple that proves Neolithic Man must have developed an orderly society.

The Cave of Darkness: the camera's flashlight reveals the interior of Għar Dalam.

Fungus Rock framed on an ancient beach, Gozo.
It's Carnival time! Valletta's Carnival is in February.

The imposing front to Gozo's cathedral.

Captain Morgan moors in Comino's Blue Lagoon.

MALTA THROUGH THE AGES

11: PREHISTORIC

From the Cave of Darkness

HOMO SAPIENS CAME TO MALTA around 5,000BC, almost certainly on a primitive boat from Sicily and bringing a few domestic animals and grain for planting.

These original settlers colonised a tiny island that had none of the minerals which were to help mankind build its civilizations, but it did have dense forest, an abundant rainfall (though the summers were already probably drying out), and some of the larger wild animals, including bear and boar. The island's dwarf hippopotamus and elephant, and the red deer, marooned with the other mammals by the rising of the sea level after the Ice Age, had already become extinct.

Neolithic Man. The culture these first human inhabitants brought with them is now known as the Neolithic or New Stone Age, covering the millennium to 4,000BC and divided into the **Ghar Dalam, Grey Skorba** and **Red Skorba** eras.

GHAR DALAM

Maybe 170,000 years before that first primitive boat landed on Malta's shores, a rushing stream carved a hole in a limestone hill in the south of the island. As the last Ice Age ended and the sea level rose, the climate of Malta changed as southern Europe's dense forests yielded to open woodland, and northern Africa's savannahs and woods gave way to the desert of the Sahara.

The stream failed, the forests shrivelled, and animals that once roamed across post-glacial Europe became trapped in the limestone cavern to add their bones and teeth to a growing mass on the floor of the cave, building up to 3ft (1m) deep on a layer of virgin clay of the same depth. Water dripping through the limestone roof welded the mortal remains of these hippos and elephants into a solid, calcified mass. Then, when these creatures had died out on the island, the antlers and bones of red deer built up another layer 4ft 6in (1.5m) thick.

Man appears. And then came New Stone Age man. Homo sapiens found this cave, which extends back into the hillside for 700ft (215m), and colonised it. Near the entrance, where daylight could still penetrate, Neolithic man let his own rubbish accumulate on the cave's floor, building to a maximum of 1ft 3in (38cm) and containing many fragmnents of his pottery, distinguished by its grey or brown clay and by the thumb- and tool-marks used as decoration — almost identical to the pots fired in southern Sicily at the same period and so providing a clue to the origins of these first Maltese.

The Stone Age inhabitants probably used the Għar Dalam cave for living and sleeping, as well as burying their dead in its floor, while they cultivated patches of soil in the valley now called the Wied Dalam. Eventually they moved away and the cave was unoccupied until the Bronze Age of 2,000 to 3,000BC, when a more advanced band of early farmers took up residence, treading another layer of rubbish into the cave's floor and so into the scant records of prehistory.

Għar Dalam today. Għar Dalam, the 'Cave of Darkness,' is half a mile (700m) north of Birżebbuġa, on the left of the road to Valletta, with a convenient car park. The **Għar Dalam Museum,** open 0745-1400 daily in summer and 0815-1700 Mon-Sat, 0845-1615 Sun, in winter, for 15c (& only to the museum), holds a vast array of teeth, tusks and bones from several thousand animals whose remains were found in the cave when excavations began in 1865, including some from the rare giant tortoise. While we now associate the elephant and hippo

Storm clouds gather over the Skorba Temples at Żebbieh.

with Africa, those creatures which lived on Malta were of the same sub-species which roamed Europe, and so give us strong evidence that the island is truly European rather than African.

A flight of concrete steps leads down to the entrance to the Cave of Darkness, whose rugged rocky floor makes normal walking impossible; large sheets of rock which seem to be on the point of collapse from the roof, though they have hung there for thousands of years, deter the average visitor from going more than 50ft (15m) in, though you could easily penetrate to 200ft (60m). The cave is unique for its size as well as for being the earliest known human habitation on the islands, and is worth a visit.

SKORBA TEMPLES

While those first inhabitants were still living in Għar Dalam, later Neolithic peoples developed another community at Skorba, by Żebbieħ. The Skorba Temples are in truth the remains of just one above-ground structure consisting of three circular huts, like a clover leaf. The walls had heavy stones for a base, probably with wattle-and-daub (twigs plastered with mud) or mud-brick for their upper parts, but only those base stones remain.

The excavation between 1961 and '63 yielded clay models of oversexed females, as well as goat skulls, dated by radio-carbon analysis to the New Stone Age, plus some human bones of the Bronze Age, 4,000BC. On this scant evidence the Skorba remains became known as temples, but their main feature of interest is that they outdate Stonehenge and the Great Pyramid at Giza.

The pottery found here, and to a lesser extent in other places, was made from a distinctive grey clay, later giving way to red; from this the archaeological world has named the Grey and Red Skorba periods.

Skorba's inhabitants were primitve farmers, proved by the discovery of domestic animals' bones, the burned remnants of cereal and lentil seeds, and a hand-mill for grinding them.

Ancient wall. Nearby is the base of a wall, 15ft 6in (4.8m) long and built in a straight line. It s purpose remains a mystery but, in an age when all buildings were round, it is the oldest man-made straight line on Malta.

The Skorba Temples today. To most people the Skorba Temples are nothing more than a few stones, overgrown with grass and protected by a chain link fence; you need your imagination to re-create living conditions of 6,000 years ago. To find them take the Għajn Tuffieħa road from Żebbieħ; 100m on the left a sign on a house wall point to the temples. The key to the gate is in the Museum of Archaeology in Valletta, but for normal purposes you can see everything through the fence.

THE COPPER AGE

Copper Age man buried his dead in tombs hewn from the rock in several places on the islands, but notably at Żebbuġ where, around 3,000BC, he put up a menhir or standing stone (the word comes from the Breton *men*, 'long' and *hir*, 'stone'). Other tombs are on the hillside above Xemxija, the little village at the head of St Paul's Bay, but are difficult to locate and are not outstanding for the casual visitor, though their kidney shape has caused speculation that they were an attempt to return the dead to the womb in the hope of rebirth.

The Copper Age on Malta never saw the use of copper. This soft, non-rusting metal that was so common on Cyprus (see *Discover Cyprus* in this series), was unknown on Malta and never even reached the island through the course of trade, although obsidian (a natural glass-like substance) from Pantelleria and the Lipari Islands was brought here. Archaeologists refer to the Copper Age only to identify the period when early man was working in copper elsewhere in the Mediterranean. Indeed, the Iron Age never made an impact here, either.

Miscellaneous Temples. Despite this absence of metals, Copper Age man on Malta managed to hew, dress and move limestone and granite. The **Ta'Ħaġrat Temples** (ta-*hhag*-rat) in their enclosure at Mġarr (Malta, not Gozo) are a larger version of the Skorba Temples. Access? Ta'Ħagrat is on the south of the village down a road labelled for eastbound traffic only. The site is dominated by one large standing stone and is easily seen despite its wall, but the key is also in the Archaeology Museum in Valletta.

The **Kordin Temple III** at Corodino, a district near Valletta which came into prominence during the Great Siege, stands in the grounds of a technical college — the key is at the Archaeology Museum in Valletta — and is better preserved, but the temples which arouse the greatest admiration, even from people to whom ancient ruins are just heaps of rocks, are at **Ħaġar Qim** (ajar |eem) and **Mnajdra** (im-*nye*-dra) on Malta, and **Ġgantija** (zhig-*ant*-ia) on Gozo.

Radio carbon dating puts Ġgantija at 2800 BC with the others at 2600 BC, though dendrochronology, the fixing of dates by analysing the growth rings in long-dead trees associated with the sites in question, hints that Ġgantija may be as old as 3300 to 3800BC.

HAĠAR QIM

Ħaġar Qim, on the south-west coast of Malta beyond Qrendi, is built of the soft globigerina limestone that has gone into many of the houses on the islands, and though it has eroded badly over the millennia it still justifies its Malti name of 'standing stone.'

The temple complex is around 200ft by 100ft (60m x 30m), occupying a prime position on a slope with a view across to the little island of Filfla. The land around cannot be tilled profitably, and presumably couldn't when the temple was built — so was a secluded site chosen to add to the mystique, since we know there were animal sacrifices and fertility rites carried out here?

Social order. Imagine the effort involved in digging up these stones, moving them to the site, standing them upright, and then covering the entire site with earth — without metal tools or the wheel. Now imagine the social order that was necessary before any such work could begin: there had to be a group leader; food and water had to be plentiful enough to allow for spare time for such activities; and there had to be a rudimentary religion as motive for the work. In other words, Malta was already civilized.

The excavations, beginning in 1839, yielded several oversexed feminine figures carved in stone, one of which is known as the Venus of Malta. There were seven statues called 'sitting woman,' for want of a better description, the most impressive of which is in the Museum of Archaeology in the Auberge de Provence, Valletta.

Mushrooms or priests' stools? Among the features peculiar to Maltese Copper Age temples are the flat—topped stone mushrooms which may have served as display tables for gods or fertility figures, or could have been simply the priests' seats. Additionally, many of the massive building stones are meticulously pitted to give an effect similar to that found on patterned glass of the 1920s, and there are several large flat slabs mounted vertically and with square openings

Ħaġar Qim is a Copper Age temple built without the use of any metals.

Mnajdra – a marvellous achievement for people working without the wheel and lifting tackle.

carved in them. Archaeologists believe that a fortune-teller or oracle may have sat behind a leather drape covering such an opening, rather like a Catholic priest in a modern confessional.

The tallest of Ħaġar Qim's standing stones rises to more than 21ft (6.5m) above present ground level, adding to the majesty of the site and equalling with a stone at Ġgantija for the record of the island's largest quarried block. Despite this majesty, we are merely looking at the skeleton of the temple that Copper Age Man knew: the builders covered all their megaliths with earth so they resembled the burial mounds of northern European culture, the resulting gloom inside doing nothing to dispel the air of mystery. The dome of Ħaġar Qim remained an enigma for more than 4,000 years until a Maltese farmer, attempting to work this unyielding soil, struck one of the roof stones with his plough and decided to investigate.

Ħaġar Qim today. Admission is 15c for adults (usually interpreted as older than 10), daily in summer 0745-1400, and in winter Mon-Sat 0815-1700, Sun 0815-1615, &; toilet (restroom) on site.

MNAJDRA.

Five hundred yards down the slope along a concrete path are the twin temples of Mnajdra, of the same age and created in the same image as Ħaġar Qim, though with subtle differences. The Mnajdra complex, for example, is the only one of these three giants to have two oracle rooms and two temples. The temple on the left, the south, is oval and around 44ft (13m) long, with both its oracle rooms at the right end; they're uncomfortably tiny recesses. The right or northern temple has less to offer and was possibly added later.

Mnajdra's excavation in 1840 revealed a great wealth of pottery fragments, including some decorated in the same pitted pattern as the stonework; it's as if the potter pushed his fingertips into the wet clay and the stonemason tried to achieve the same effect. As Mnajdra is built in harder corraline limestone than Haġar Qim, hewn from the Dingli cliffs, the masonry is better preserved.

Misq Reservoirs North-west of Mnajdra lie the seven Misq reservoirs which the temple builders cut from the solid rock. Presumably the water had its uses in washing the sacrificial altar, but it could also be the oldest evidence of irrigation in the islands.

Mnajdra today. Mnajdra is unfenced, so there are no admission fees or hours of opening; access is along a footpath 500m from Haġar Qim's car park making ♿ access more of an effort, particularly on the uphill return.

ĠGANTIJA

The third giant temple is also a giant by name. Ġgantija, near the Gozitan village of Xagħra, is again two semi-detached premises in the same block. The southern one has a ground plan like a leaf made of five distinct segments all leading off the central stem, while the northern temple is down to four segments.

Excavation began at Ġgantija in 1827, with further work more than a century later in 1936, but the earth infilling has been left between the inner walls of the temple chambers and the outer stone circle, giving a better idea of how the place must have looked in 2800BC. The temple has several small altar niches, but the offerings and graven images they contained are now in safe keeping in the Victoria Museum.

Ġgantija today. The Ġgantija temple is the best-preserved of the trio, open Mon-Sat 1 Oct-31 Mar 0830-1630; Mon-Sat 16 Jun-15 Sep 0830-1900, and the rest of the year 0830-1830. Sun, year round, 0830-1500. Fee 15c adults; ♿ with care.

HYPOGEUM

These above-ground buildings went out of favour around 2400BC (or as early as 3000BC according to dendrochronology) when Copper Age Man decided to carve his next temple from the living rock. The Hypogeum (the word means underground chamber) of Ħal Saflieni at Burials Street, Paola, is the result, with a complex of many chambers carved out of the soft globigerina limestone – again without the use of any metal tools.

What was the true Copper Age in other parts of the Mediterranean was really the 'limestone' or Chalcolithic Age on Malta as the island

The Hypogeum is a temple that went underground.

craftsmen had yet to learn how to work in metal, although they must have come into contact with iron and copper carried by the traders who were already sailing the length of the Mediterranean. The Glass Museum in Bodrum, Turkey, holds copper, bronze, tin and gold salvaged in the 1980s from a ship that was wrecked nearby in the 14th cent BC, and the Cyprus Museum in Nicosia has exhibits showing the use on that island of copper around 3900BC, and of bronze by 2500BC. It is strange that Maltese man never learned how to use this vital material.

Pick-work. The Hypogeum's builders carved away tons of limestone using nothing more than picks made of bone and scrapers chipped from flint, while working in the subdued light of oil lamps. Their masterpiece still has the oracle rooms of the earlier temples, and the red ochre decorations on the ceilings have survived down the centuries despite the ravages of 1902 when men digging foundations for houses cut into the cavern. They kept their discovery secret, probably from fear of losing their jobs if work ceased on the construction. Still in secret they built brick walls in the Hypogeum to carry the extra weight above, and even dumped much of their rubble in the once-sacred chambers.

Three years later the secret was out, and Sir Thermistocle Zammit, the father of Maltese archaeology, excavated the cave, finding between 6,000 and 7,000 human corpses buried in tons of red earth, plus a number of oversexed female statues which have joined the others in the Archaeological Museum in Valletta.

The lowest level of the Hypogeum, protected by seven uneven steps and an unguarded drop, looks more as if it has been built up, as at Ggantija, rather than carved out, and may have been used as a reservoir and a granary, the bread and water of life protected by the spirits of the dead on the upper floor.

The Hypogeum today. Admission times are daily in summer, 0745-1400, and in winter, Mon-Sat 0815-1700, Sun 0815-1615, for 15c. There's no ♿ access.

TARXIEN TEMPLES

Nearby are the three above-ground temples of Tarxien (tar-*shen*), dating from 2000 to 2400BC, or back to 3300BC on tree-ring evidence, but these are indisputably the most recent and the most lavishly decorated of Copper Age works on the islands; they could even be considered as the cathedral of megalithic culture in Europe.

The Tarxien Temples improved on everything the Copper Age had done so far, except for sheer scale. The masons dressed their stones with greater precision, almost achieving the perfection found among the Mayas of the Americas. Their bas-relief carvings were done with geometric accuracy, and if we may judge by the fire staining at the base of many of the stones, their sacrificial fires were much hotter.

This hints that the inhabitants of Malta not only had a well-developed society but had one with rigid beliefs in the nature of death, though from the evidence available modern man cannot decide whether these ancestors feared or revered the afterlife.

At this time in the development of civilization, certainly before individual deities were invented, it appears that mankind was in tune with nature and the spirit world; the presence of oracles infers clairvoyant or clairaudient ability, and the discovery of clay models of human limbs hints that spiritual healers may also have practised here.

Three temples. Tarxien has three temples, with access through an impressive doorway into the third, the western, temple. Here, a fire-stained floorstone, on which domestic animals were sacrificed, lies in front of an altar decorated with spiral motifs. Charred bones of cows, pigs, sheep and goats, as well as simple carvings of the animals, were evidence of the activities here at Tarxien; a sacrificial knife made from stone was also found lying on a stone slab, as if ready for the next animal victim. The third temple also held remains of humans who had been burned, presumably an act of cremation after death rather than execution by fire, and there were several funeral offerings in the same locations.

The second temple is smaller, accessible from the first through a small opening beside another altar; in the roofed-over temple of 3,000 years ago, lit by smoking fires, venturing into this inner sanctum may

The lower part of a fertility goddess still adorns the Tarxien Temples in Paola.

have been like going deep into the bowels of the earth. Undoubtedly the most spectacuar find, which is still on site, was the **goddess of fertility,** an ugly and disproportioned effigy of a human from the waist down.

Oracles. Several small oracle-cells were built into the Tarxien Temples, accessible from outside but offering communication to the people inside through tiny openings. Clay models of men dressed only in skirts, but with good facial detail, may represent not only the oracles in general but perhaps some specific prophets as well. And we can speculate that the shattered remains of thousands of simple earthenware pots, found in all the temples, may indicate a ceremony in which the drinking vessel was deliberately destroyed.

The first temple, at the east of the complex, was the original structure, replacing a smaller temple built around the time of Ġgantija.

Demise. We don't know what happened to destroy this spiritually-alert society, but we do know that their culture died suddenly around 1800BC (2500BC according to the tree-rings), and with it the Copper Age passed into prehistory leaving the islands uninhabited for 200 years.

THE BRONZE AGE.

Bronze Age Man came to Malta bringing the first metal to be seen in the islands — not bronze but iron and copper, found as daggers and

Clapham Junction: who carved these ruts in the rugged limestone, and why?

axes in the cremation cemetery on the Tarxien site yet not belonging to the temple's builders.

Tarxien Cemetery. These later arrivals had either covered much of the temples' floors with several feet of sand, or maybe they had failed to clear away the sand which had blown onto the site; either way, they burned their dead on the sand, leaving bits of bone and cloth to go with the ashes, and traces of sand, into their funerary urns. Around 200 urns have been found in 20th-cent excavations, but there is little else available to show what kind of peoples now inhabited the islands; they had copper axes and obsidian arrow-heads, but did that infer they were more warlike, or was it that they had greater need to defend themselves from invasion?

Borġ-in-Nadur. There is little of charm in the Bronze Age culture, which left us the ruins of a small temple in an otherwise large settlement near Borġ-in-Nadur, excavated in the 1920s. This community found the need to build on a point of land protected on two sides by *wieds* – streams – which in those times may have carried water for much of the year, and on the third by a massive wall. The first piece of bronze to be discovered on the Maltese islands was found here at Borġ-in-Nadur but the site is not open to the public.

The Bronze Age also bequeathed to Malta a scattering of dolmens of which the most impressive is now the centrepiece of the gardens of the **Dolmen Hotel** in Buġibba – and the mysterious cart-ruts.

Clapham Junction. The ruts are found in several places on the islands, notably on the Dingli cliffs south of the Buskett Gardens; on the western prominence of Ras ir-Raħeb; and north of Mġarr (Malta). Man had yet to invent the wheel, and what could not be carried on his own or his animals' backs, was presumably dragged along on sleds much as American Indians were doing when Europeans arrived. It is argued that during the thousand years the Bronze Age endured, these sleds wore distinct tracks in the exposed rock, looking so much like railway lines converging, diverging and crossing that the maze of ruts at Dingli is called Clapham Junction. The tracks seem to go nowhere, or to disappear over the edge of the cliff, which may be an indication of the state to which Maltese society had fallen.

I am not a trained archaeologist, but I cannot understand how the ruts could have been worn so perfectly smooth, sometimes 6in (15cm) deep, while the rock between them is still jagged. What of the human feet or animal hooves which would have been needed to pull the sleds? But I have no better explanation.

Weavers. The Bronze Age peoples had some redeeming points. They were adept weavers, and they carved many smallish pits in the bare rock, probably for storage of wheat or water − remarkably, cisterns of similar type were in the main square of Floriana until after the Second World War.

Baħrija. The last of the Bronze Age colonists settled near the western headland of Ras Ir-Raħeb, where the remains of their village have been given the modern name of Baħrija. By now, mankind had mastered the art of navigation on this inland sea, and the inhabitants of islands as small as Malta needed to be forever vigilant against attack and invasion. The first historically-recorded incursion was by the Phoenicians, and from this time onward the peoples of Malta were to enter a long period of subjugation from outside, which ended only with independence in 1964.

12: PHOENICIAN

The honeyed isles

THE PHOENICIANS CAME SLOWLY, infiltrating their culture along the shores of the Mediterranean. Their homeland was the insignificant stretch of coast north from Acre, now in Israel, to somewhere on the shores of modern Syria, but their culture was pervasive and far-reaching, eventually extending beyond the Pillars of Hercules to reach Cornwall in the north, and west Africa in the south.

They formed a colony at Carthage on the northern tip of modern Tunisia and implanted their Semitic language, based on Hebrew, and their religion, based on the god Baal and his goddess Astarte. Around the 6th cent BC, as navigators gradually learned the shape of the inland sea and knew where to take short cuts, the Carthaginians realised the significance of Malta as a mid-sea refuge from storm or attack, and seized it.

Malti language. The Maltese people now had the beginnings of what was to become their unique language, Malti, the only Semitic tongue to use the Latin alphabet.

Malta's name. They also had a name. *Malta* may have come from the Phoenician *malat,* 'harbour,' as the maritime-minded Phoenicians were quick to realise the importance of Grand Harbour — but it could have come from the Greek μελι, *meli*, signifying the honey for which the islands already had a reputation. The Phoenicians called Gozo *gol,*a broad-beamed merchant vessel, which sounds more plausible than the suggestion that the name might have come from the *Ogygia* of Homer, the place where Calypso lived when she lured Ulysses.

Greek culture was already sailing on Phoenician vessels, and the National Museum of Archaeology shows a tomb offering, probably from Tas Silġ, which carries an inscription in both Greek and Phoenician and so provided the first clue into the deciphering of the Punic language.

Tas Silġ. St Angelo may have been the site of a Phoenician temple dedicated to Astarte, goddess of love; she was certainly revered at Tas Silġ near Marsaxlokk in what may have been the **Temple of Juno** mentioned by Cicero. The Tas Silġ temple, which is not presented for the tourist industry, was built on the remains of a Copper Age structure and in a small storechamber were the bones of sacrificed animals as well as fragments of pottery carrying dedications to the goddesses Astarte and Tanit. Astarte is associated with Ashtoreth of the Old Testament:

For Solomon went after Ashtoreth, the goddess of the Zidonians . . . and the Lord was angry with Solomon. (I Kings 11, v 5, 9) and:
And the high places . . . on the mount of corruption, which Solomon the king of Israel had builded for Ashtoreth, the abomination of the Zidonians . . . (II Kings 23, v 13.)

The cult of Astarte later merged with that of Aphrodite, the Greek goddess of love who, mythology claims, was born in the sea-foam off Cyprus (see *Discover Cyprus*). And Tanit was Astarte or Ashtoreth – or even Aphrodite – under another identity. She was principally the protector of Carthage from the 5th cent BC, and her symbol is still widely used in Tunisia.

Punic sanctuary. The Phoenicians also carved the unusual Punic sanctuary at Wardija Point on the south-western tip of Gozo, not easily accessible.

Punic settlers. Some Phoenicians settled on Malta, but their burials were little different from those of the Bronze Age peoples in graves hacked out of the solid rock, circular at first but gradually becoming rectangular. There is no firm evidence to support earlier beliefs that a purely Greek colony was established around the 6th cent BC, nor do we know how well the new islanders mingled with the originals.

But the Phoenicians and their Greek travelling companions were responsible for the beginning of the deforestation of Malta, using the wood to build their rowing and sailing galleys, which still influence the design of the modern Maltese *dgħajsa* (day-sa).

Carthaginian conquest. The Carthaginians, who had some degree of independence from their Phoenician ancestors once they controlled what are now the Tunisian and Libyan coasts, plus Sicily, saw Malta and Gozo as vital to protect the area from further influence from the Greeks. The Punic hand of authority rested lightly on the Maltese people, most of whom were of Punic descent, allowing them to trade freely with all comers, a form of licence which was to be repeated in later centuries.

Phoenician demise. The Phoenicians lost Malta to the Romans in 257BC, during the First Punic War, but although Attilius Regulus held the islands for only two years, it was long enough for him to rape and plunder. Carthage recaptured the honeyed isles and held them until the Second Punic War when, in 218BC, they passed permanently into the Roman empire.

13: ROMAN

St Paul's Islands

THE MALTESE PEOPLE were tired of the demands made on them from Carthage, and they saw the Second Punic War as a salvation. The facts are that the Carthaginian general Hamilcar surrendered the islands to the Roman consul **Titus Sempronius** in 218BC, that Titus came in friendship, and that he quickly took this new territory out of the control of the Roman province of Sicily and gave the islands of Malta and Gozo each the status of a *municipium*, a town, with the right to mint its own coinage, send its own ambassador to Rome, and control its internal affairs: in effect, Malta was still enjoying the kind of liberties it had had under the Phoenicians.

If we compare this treatment with that imposed on other nations that Rome ruled, the conclusion is that the Maltese people had invited Titus to invade.

Semitic survival. As the Semitic nature of the Maltese language survived the 654 years of Roman and Byzantine rule, as well as the strong Greek influence early in that epoch, we can assume that these new masters left the islanders to manage their own affairs, and there was little colonisation from the north. This is another unusual aspect of Roman rule, as Latin replaced the local speech from Lisbon to the Black Sea, giving us the present languages of Portuguese, Spanish, Catalan, French, Italian and Romanian. In north Africa, too, the Berbers kept their own language although they accepted Christianity from Rome.

Roman remains. Malta has surprisingly few relics of these six centuries under Roman rule. Cremation was still popular, and burials used the old Punic tombs with the original corpses pushed to the back. By the 4th cent, the islanders were burying their dead in catacombs under the Roman capital city of Melita (now Mdina) much in the style of the Hypogeum at Paola, but these were merely Maltese workings in the Roman era, not truly Roman.

The Romans extended the **Sanctuary of Juno** at Tas Silġ and continued using the Punic sanctuary at Wardija Point on Gozo, but the only classical remains they left us were of a town house at Rabat (it's now much restored and houses the Roman Villa Museum); at

Burmarrad; and near Għar Dalam.

Roman baths. The most impressive Roman relic is the baths complex with its open-air communal lavatory, just off the road to Għajn Tuffieħa.

Dwejra Line. On the military front, the Romans found that the north of Malta, with its deep bays and gently sloping shores, was prone to sudden attack from any passing pirate, and they built rudimentary defence positions, now called the Dwejra Line, across the island so that the north-western part could be abandoned temporarily; there was no permanent settlement in northern Malta between prehistoric times and the Middle Ages. Over the centuries the Arabs and the Normans, and even the British, were to find increasing need to reinforce these defences, and the walls, bastions and counterguards built by the British are, not surprisingly, known as the **Victoria Lines.** Two lookout towers also survive from Roman times, at Misraħ Ħlantun and at Il-Miżieb, both between Żurrieq and the Ħal Far airfield.

St Paul's shipwreck. The most important event in the Roman era was unquestionably the shipwreck of Paul the Apostle in 60AD. Paul, who has been called the second founder of Christianity, was on his way from Alexandria to Rome, where he was to write many of his Epistles and eventually become a martyr and a saint.

The legendary site of the wreck is on St Paul's Islands at the northern entrance to St Paul's Bay, where an impressive statue of the saint now stands at the highest point on the twin islands, and Paul wrote of the Maltese who befriended him:

And so it came to pass that they escaped all safe to land.

And when they were escaped, then they knew that the island was called Melita. _____

St Paul's Islands on the northern shore; legend claims the saint was shipwrecked here.

The cathedral in Victoria's Citadel was completed in 1711.

And the barbarous people showed us no little kindness; for they kindled a fire, and received us every one, because of the present rain and because of the cold. (Acts, 27, 44 and 28, 1 and 2).

St Paul's Cave. Local legend, not the Bible, claims that Paul was 'received' in a cave at Mellieħa, but there is no trace of such a cave today, nor any folk memory claiming to know where it may have been.

Dubrovnik? There are other theorists who claim Paul was wrecked off the island of Meleda (Mljet) near Dubrovnik, Yugoslavia, an argument that's difficult to sustain in view of the fact that the Roman governor of Malta, Publius, is historically recorded as having converted to Christianity in 60AD, and who but Paul could have engineered it? The Mljet school of thought fails on another issue: why would Paul have sailed from Egypt to Rome via the Adriatic?

Publius. We can therefore say the apostle arrived in Malta in February and stayed for three months as Publius's guest. The assumption was that Publius lived in Mdina, where there is the site of a Roman town house — it's not a 'villa' despite being called one — but excavations on the site of the 17th-cent church of **San Pawl Milqi**, 'St Paul Welcomed,' at Burmarrad on the main road south from St Paul's Bay, have established that a Roman villa was here as well, and by the 7th cent the spot had its own church and was the focus of a pilgrimage in honour of St Paul.

More legends. Despite the evidence of the villa by St Paul Milqi, legend claims that Rabat cathedral, which is in the enclave city of Mdina, stands on the site of Publius's house, and that in this town Paul performed the miracle of removing snake poison from his own body after being bitten; Acts 28 verses 3 to 11 gives the Biblical account of the snakebite and mentions Publius by name, yet another argument against the Mljet theory — but it doesn't locate the exact site of the miracle. A further legend adds unkindly that Paul put the snake poison on the tongues of Maltese women but, for the record, there are four species of snake on the islands and the only one that's poisonous hasn't enough venom to kill a human adult.

The pity for Paul was that he could not prevent a relief ship — 'a ship of Alexandria' — taking him on to Rome and his eventual execution.

First European Christian community. Publius, however, was to become the first Bishop of Malta, and later of Athens, and eventually the patron saint of several Maltese churches, while the Maltese people were the first in Europe and its offshore islands to accept Christianity, the faith they have held onto staunchly, even when they were overrun by Arabs.

14: ARAB

Interlude in Islam

THE ARABS CAPTURED the Maltese islands in 870 after laying a year-long siege to the Byzantine garrison, but in their stay of 220 years they left even less physical evidence than the Romans, despite the vast gulf between the two cultures.

The Byzantine Empire at its greatest stretched from the Algarve to the Crimea and down to Aswan in Egypt, but it had been crumbling for several centuries. In 711 Islam erputed from Africa on a surge that took the followers of the Prophet from their landing point at Gibraltar to the middle of France. The tide had turned against Christianity, and in 827 the Aghlabid Emirate in what is today's Tunisia and Libya, seized a toehold in Sicily.

Malta falls. Historians don't know why they waited a further 43 years before taking Malta, but we could speculate that the Maltese were already tiring of Byzantium and had allowed the emirate's sailors to use their harbours: or, to put it another way — would they have dared refuse? But once Islam was in control the Maltese willingly helped their new masters to defend the islands against reprisal attacks from Byzantium, and they crewed the emirate's galleys on slave-raids to other shores.

Perhaps as a reward for this co-operation the Arab rulers treated the Maltese with respect — most of the time. Certainly they tolerated Christianity in a world where the Cross and the Crescent were perpetually at war, although this was by no means unique; Jewish communities have been allowed to live in Moslem lands since the spread of Islam, even if as second-class citizens.

No mosques. Is that tolerance the reason why there are no mosques in Malta today, barring the elegant one built in Paola in 1980? Is that also why there is no Arab influence in Maltese art or architecture? The facts are there but the reasons elude us.

Irrigation. The Arabs were more advanced culturally and scientifi-cally than the Europeans. For example, the Crusaders had seen their first windmills in the Arab lands and had taken the idea back to Europe; now the Arabs brought irrigation to Malta, which was already a barren sunbaked rock for six months of every year. They also

St Paul's Shipwrecked Church stands tall in St Paul's Street.

116

divided the island into parishes, each still called a *casal* from the Arabic 'rahal,' a village. Yet Malta's main legacy from its Afro-Asian masters was a slight darkening of the skin of its peoples, and a major contribution to the island language, Malti.

If you count in Malti most of the words are understandable to a person speaking Arabic – or, for that matter, Swahili or Hebrew. Malti also borrowed two sounds from Arabic, the glottal stop, and the rasping sound now represented by that peculiar letter Ħ. The letter itself is a modern invention and has nothing to do with Arabic.

The Notabile Gate into Mdina has some wonderful carvings, but see how the limestone erodes. The Malta Railway ran under the bridge in the foreground.

Place names. The Arabs also left a number of place-names in the Maltese islands, notably Żebbuġ, Żurrieq, and the startlingly obvious one, Mdina, the city they made their capital after reducing its size and so leaving the Roman town house outside its walls. These Arabic names were to live on, even after the Norman Conquest of Malta, 24 years after William the Conqueror led the Norman Conquest of England.

117

Malta attracts artists, even on a November day in Victoria.

A one-horse-power karrozzin is a popular way of seeing Malta — but don't expect to use one on the hills.

15: NORMAN and SPANISH

A promise broken

WILLIAM THE CONQUEROR ruled his new domains in England with an iron fist leaving no scope for other ambitious knights. Lesser Normans seeking new lands of their own looked in envy at the success of one of their number, Robert Guiscard who, in 20 years, had conquered Byzantine Italy, the southern half of the modern country, then turned on the Moslems in Sicily.

By 1090 Roger de Hauteville, also known as Roger the Norman and Count Roger I of Sicily, was seeking his own lands beyond the realms of Guiscard, and he chose Malta.

Dingli Cliffs. Roger introduced strategy to his campaign by feinting an open attack with a few vessels on St Paul's Bay and so drawing the Arab army to the north of the island, while his main forces landed on the inhospitable south-west coast of Malta and scaled the Dingli cliffs; the actual spot is believed to be Miġra Ferħa near Mtaħleb. It was a strategy worthy of this son of the great Tancred de Hauteville who was to be one of the leaders of the People's Crusade six years later.

Maltese flag. Legend credits Roger with ripping off part of his red personal standard and giving it to the Maltese people as their own; the islanders added a white section to bring the standard up to a suitable size, and so the Maltese flag was created. The motif in the upper canton was added in 1942 and is the George Cross, not the Maltese Cross.

Roger allowed Christianity to flourish once more, along with the cathedral in Mdina, where a Mass is still said for him every November 4 as the 'deliverer of Malta and founder of the table of the Cathedral, the Bishop, and the Canons.' His successor, Roger II, who ruled from 1095 to 1154, created the Kingdom of Sicily stretching from Malta to Pescara on the Adriatic coast, and gave all his peoples a new sense of law and government. Constance, the wife of the German Emperor, held the Kingdom of Sicily until 1194 when it passed into the hands of the German dynasty of Hohenstaufen, taking Malta with it.

Sicilian Vespers. Malta was to be involved in European affairs for some years to come, and was part of the prize that Charles of Anjou gained when he seized the Kingdom of Sicily from the Hohenstaufens. But Charles was unpopular and the Sicilians rioted in 1282 in the event known as the Sicilian Vespers; they then invited King Pedro I of Aragon to finish the job, and he defeated Charles in a naval battle in Grand Harbour.

Corsairs. The Maltese people found their new masters in Iberia just as intolerant as their earlier ones had been. Corsairs from north Africa continually raided the islands and after a particularly hard reprisal from Aragon the pirates sailed out and sacked Malta and Gozo.

Università. When the Maltese were not subject to overt harrass-ment from Africa they had to tolerate covert exploitation from their Aragonese overlords. In response they organised the *Università*, which we could understand as being a medieval mix of trade union, trade guild, political party, town council and farm co-operative.

Alfonso the Magnanimous. The Aragonese king Alfonso V, the 'Magnanimous,' mortgaged the islands with a nobleman to raise funds, but the Maltese people found this even more objectionable than direct rule from Aragon, so in 1428 the Università managed to induce Alfonso to come to Malta, when they gave him 30,000 florins so that he could redeem the islands. In return the Università extracted a signed pledge that the Aragonese crown would never again give the islands to any other power: this document is one of the prize exhibits in the Valletta Museum.

While it was no fun being ruled by Aragon, later to become incorporated into Spain, it would be even less fun to be the vassals of some of the other states bordering the Mediterranean. But events in Bodrum, in south-western Turkey, dictated that that was to be a distinct possibility in the very near future.

16: ORDER OF ST JOHN

The elected monarchy

POPE GREGORY THE GREAT had established the Order of Knights Hospitaller near the end of the 6th cent, shortly after the rise of the Prophet Mahomet, to give protection to Christian pilgrims in the Holy Land. The cavaliers moved to Jerusalem in 1099 when the Crusaders captured the Holy City; soon they were calling themselves the Order of the Knights of St John of Jerusalem, in honour of St John the Baptist; at other times they were just plain Jerusalemists. In 1191 Richard I of England, better known as **Richard the Lionheart**, who had just seized Cyprus for England, moved the Order to Acco (Acra or Acre) where it stayed exactly a century before pulling back to Cyprus.

Knights Templar. Meanwhile, a party of French knights had founded the Order of the Knights Templar in 1118, again with the motive of protecting pilgrims from Arab attack. The 'templar' connection was the Temple of Kuvat es Sahra, near the Temple of Solomon (Temple Mount) and the Wailing Wall (Western Wall) on the southern edge of the walled city of Jerusalem, which the Christian King Baldwin II of Palestine had given to them.

In 1128 the Templars drew up their constitution, giving their elected leader the title of Grand Commander and a status equal to that of prince; 20 years later the Pope granted them their own cross, with four bars of equal length, each of which opened out at its end like a swallowtail, to reveal two sharp points; it was identical to the Crusaders' cross except that theirs had a longer vertical bar. The bars signified Prudence, Temperance, Fortitude and Justice, and the eight points represented the Beatitudes.

It was in 1252 that Pope Innocent IV granted the Knights Hospitaller the right to use the title of Grand Commander, and to carry an eight-pointed cross: the same title and the same cross for both orders. Over the centuries this has become known as the Maltese Cross and today it is still the emblem of the Order of St John of Jerusalem, better known for its public work in the St John Ambulance Brigade.

The Knights Templar became wealthy and powerful, owning large castles and vast estates across Europe. Soon they became bankers for Christian pilgrims, and they even made a loan to a king of France. When the Arabs took Acco, the Knights Templar, like the Knights Hospitaller, moved to Cyprus (see *Discover Cyprus*).

Templars' downfall. The Templars grew too powerful on this small island and in May 1310 Pope Clement V put them on trial. Three years later he ordered their disbandment; he even imprisoned several knights in the castle at Kyrenia, now Girne in North Cyprus. The Knights Hospitaller had seen the danger signs and in 1310 transferred to Rhodes which one of their number, Fulke de Villaret, had taken after a four-year siege. Surprisingly, the knights established a satellite outpost in Bodrum on the Turkish mainland (see *Discover Turkey*), even though Asia Minor was under the control of Islam.

And at Bodrum castle the Grand Master met the deposed caliph Çem who asked for protection from his brother Bayezid, ruler of Turkey. Çem made an offer: if the Knights would put him back on his throne, he would guarantee peace between Christians and Muslims. The Knights of St John refused, imprisoned Çem in Rhodes, and so allowed the holy war to continue.

Gradually the knights built a powerful fleet, establishing themselves as seamen first, hospitallers second. They inherited part of the Templars' estates by courtesy of Pope Clement V, and they managed to hold onto their second island home despite being besieged in 1444 and 1480.

Homeless knights. But they couldn't withstand the six-month siege of 1522 and on Christmas Eve of that year they were forced to surrender Rhodes to Süleiman the Magnificent. Allowed to depart the island in peace, on the first day of 1523 Grand Master Villiers de l'Isle Adam and his 180 followers began a nine-year search for somewhere to call home.

Maltese falcon. Finally, in 1530, the Holy Roman Emperor, Carlos V of Aragon, broke the agreement made between his ancestor Alfonso the Magnanimous and the Università of Malta – and gave the islands of Malta and Gozo to the Order of St John of Jerusalem. The agreement was signed on 24 March 1530, with the actual document now preserved in the Maltese archives.

Carlos had seen the homeless, errant knights as a possible barrier between himself in the western Mediterranean and the raging Turks in the eastern part. The knights hadn't been keen to accept the offer as Malta looked so barren and forbidding, but they knew they had no choice and in return they agreed to give the Viceroy of Sicily an annual tribute of a Maltese falcon.

Soon the Order of St John had established itself, beginning the slow process of integration with the native Maltese and their few Sicilian overlords, and preparing the island's defences, for the threat of a Turkish invasion was never far away. The seagoing knights showed their strength by helping Felipe II of Spain seize the tiny, barren rock of Peñon de Velez de la Gomera, lying just off the Moroccan coast. Strangely, Spain holds those rocks to this day (see *Discover Morocco*).

Henry VIII of England. Just ten years into their occupation of Malta, the Order lost its English Langue (sector) when Henry VIII overthrew the monasteries of England and deprived the knights of their financial backing. On Malta the knights lived in vain hope of the eventual English return, and later named some of the defences of Valletta city from their departed fellows: the English Curtain.

Fort St Angelo. In 1530, when the knights arrived, Fort St Angelo at the tip of Birgù had been the island's only defence, armed with three small cannon and a few mortars. The old Arab capital of Mdina was mostly uninhabited, the island had no permanent running water, and the 17,000 Maltese and Gozitans, still speaking their strange language, scratched a subsistence living from the land.

Grand Master Villiers de l'Isle Adam strengthened the fort and the old capital, but only as much as was necessary for immediate repairs as he still had dreams of returning to Rhodes; his successor Juan de Homedes, with growing interest in the island's defence, built Fort St Michael at L'Isla (it was renamed Senglea in honour of Grand Master Claude de la Sèngle who took office in 1553) overlooking Grand Harbour, and Fort St Elmo on the tip of the bare and rocky Mount Sciber-Ras, whose Malti name means 'light on the peninsula.'

De la Valette. Then came the Frenchman Jean de la Valette, elected Grand Master in 1557. He had spent the year 1541 as a Turkish galley slave and had no desire to repeat the experience. He knew that his little island was all that stood between the Turks and Christendom; he knew that an attack would come at some time – and he knew the price of failure. He brought earth from Sicily to strengthen St Elmo, the main fortress defencing the headland where the city of Valletta would rise, and he reinforced the 2.5-mile (4km) long curtain wall of Birgù, the new capital of the islands.

Warning. In October 1564 a Venetian merchant warned the Order that Süleiman the Magnificent, the man who had driven the knights from Rhodes, was assembling a fleet in Constantinople to sail against them early the next year. Valette sent an urgent message to the Viceroy of Sicily, Don García de Toledo, for forwarding to all the knights of Europe, urging them to come to Malta's aid by the spring of 1565.

But there were problems in Europe. The knights came from several lands, each one represented in Malta by its own *langue,* or language. France couldn't help the Order because it had a non–aggression treaty with Süleiman; the German states had border problems with the Turk and didn't want to disturb the hornets' nest; and England under Good Queen Bess was Protestant and not inclined to become involved in what appeared to be Catholic affairs, though when Her Majesty reminded herself there was a solitary English knight still on Malta – Sir Oliver Starkey – she ordered prayers to be said in all

English churches thrice weekly for six weeks. It was the least she could do; it was also the most she ever did.

The combatants. War was inevitable. On the one hand we had Süleiman, the 70-year-old Sultan of the Ottomans, who was totally lacking in humility; among the dozen grandiose extra titles he had claimed for himself were King of Believers and Unbelievers, Allah's Deputy on Earth, and Refuge of all the People in the World. For brevity the Turks called him Süleiman the Lawgiver, and the Europeans, in awe, agreed he was Süleiman the Magnificent.

And on the other hand we had Jean Parisot de la Valette, born in Provence, France, and a lifelong believer in service and humility, particularly in his daily prayers. De la Valette was also 70, had been in the Order of St John of Jerusalem for half a century, and was currently its Grand Master, a status equal to monarch of a small nation.

Invasion fleet. Süleiman's fleet sailed from Constantinople in April, with 130 galleys, 30 galleases each with 1,000 men, and a few smaller ships. There were up to 40,000 troops, including the Iayalars, religious kamikaze fanatics, and the formidable Spahis from central Turkey. In addition there were 6,300 Janissaries, the *yeni cheri* or 'new soldiers,' stolen from Christian homes as infants and brainwashed to become Islam's suicide squad.

They had 80,000 shot, 7.5 tons of powder, plus horses, tents, and enough food and water to take them through the siege, which they saw as lasting just a few weeks.

Piali and Mustapha. The fleet was under Admiral Piali Pasha, born a Christian but brought up a Moslem, while the merciless Mustapha Pasha controlled the army ('pasha,' spelled paşa in modern Turkish, was the title given to generals and provincial governors). And in that divided command lay the seeds of the Turkish downfall.

Behind all this there were the inevitable bargain-hunters who hoped to pick up a few spoils when the fighting was over.

Valette had a mere seven galleys, all oar-driven shallow-draft vessels around 180ft by 20ft wide (55m by 6m) and similar to the modern *dgħajsa*. He had sent two to Sicily with further pleas for help, moored three in Galley Creek, today's Dockyard Creek, and sunk the other two, to be raised as required.

Garrison. As the Turks drew nearer, Valette garrisoned St Elmo with 52 knights and 800 men, including 200 from Spain, all that came of the promised 1,000; the cavalry and a few other troops took station in Mdina. He stretched a 600-ft iron chain across the entrance to Galley Creek, supporting it on rafts, then told his men: "If Heaven requires the sacrifice of our lives, there can be no better occasion."

Mustapha, on the high seas, told his troops: "When we meet the unbelievers, turn not your back on them."

The Great Siege begins. On 18 May, a Friday and thus the holy day, the Turkish fleet was in sight. It anchored at dusk off Għajn Tuffieħa Bay but after sunset rowed down to Marsaxlokk Bay, and on Saturday morning the Turks landed and attacked Żejtun, capturing the knight Adrien de la Rivière, whom they tortured and killed. By the end of the day the Turks had occupied the southern half of Malta without meeting opposition.

They made a skirmish on Birgù, and Valette saw that the Janissaries were excellent marksmen but slow to reload. Twenty-one Christians were killed, but several hundred Turks also died.

Now the divided command began to help the defenders. Mustapha wanted to occupy all the open land, including Gozo, then pick off Mdina, Birgù and L'Isla, while the fleet blockaded.

Plan of campaign. But Piali wanted his fleet safe in harbour, and decided the harbour had better be Marsamxett, protected from any errant storm from Africa. And that meant St Elmo had to be taken.

Valette was pleased when his spies brought the news; he had more time to strengthen the forts of St Angelo and St Michael. But he sent 200 men and 64 volunteer knights across Grand Harbour in darkness to help the garrison at St Elmo. Already he could guess they were going to their death.

Mustapha brought up siege guns from the transport galleys moored in Marsaxlokk, pulled by slaves and the cattle which the Turks would later eat. He added two 60-lb and ten 80-lb cannon, and a basilisk (catapult) capable of throwing 160lb (70kg) a time. And he dragged up thousands of sacks of earth to build a dyke across the rocky ridge of Sciber-Ras, probably where Great Siege Square stands today.

St Elmo's siege begins. On 24 May the bombardment began, concentrating on selected areas of St Elmo's curtain wall, and within hours the soft globigerina limestone began crumbling. Valette sent a small boat to Sicily with the simple message 'help!' but it crossed with the answer to his earlier appeal. That letter urged him to hold on; there were so many Turks that Don García needed more soldiers. And he would need Valette's galleys to move them.

The Grand Master knew what Don García really meant. There would be no help.

Valette mounted two cannon on St Angelo to fire on Mount Sciber-Ras, while the cavalry from Mdina harassed the Turkish water parties; this was to be a continual problem for the besiegers.

On Sciber-Ras the Turks' slaves strengthened their earth rampart, building their dead into it. And St Elmo's walls crumbled so badly that the knights rebuilt them from inside, so reducing the area they were defending.

Defeat looming. The Turks couldn't storm St Elmo from the sea because the approaches were too steep, but both armies could see the fort wouldn't hold out for long; the commander sent a message

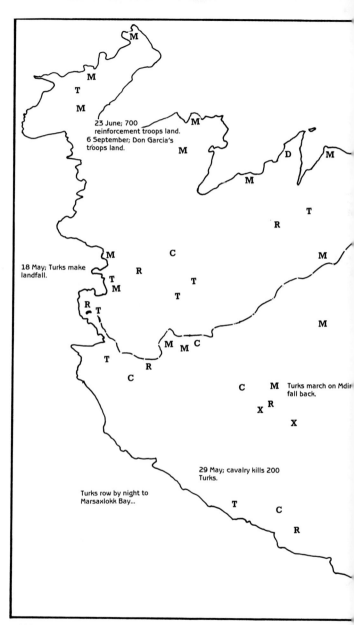

23 June; 700 reinforcement troops land.
6 September; Don Garcia's troops land.

18 May; Turks make landfall.

Turks march on Mdir fall back.

29 May; cavalry kills 200 Turks.

Turks row by night to Marsaxlokk Bay...

MALTA IN HISTORY

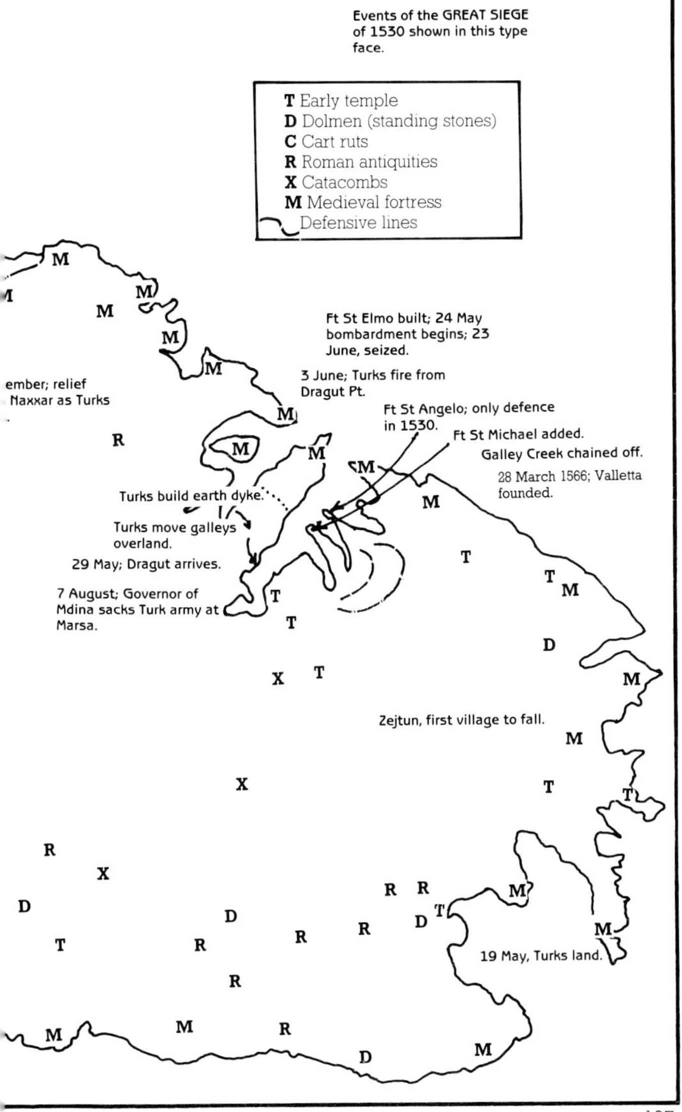

Events of the GREAT SIEGE
of 1530 shown in this type
face.

T Early temple
D Dolmen (standing stones)
C Cart ruts
R Roman antiquities
X Catacombs
M Medieval fortress
⌒ Defensive lines

M

M

M M

M

M

M

Ft St Elmo built; 24 May
bombardment begins; 23
June, seized.

3 June; Turks fire from
Dragut Pt.

ember; relief
Naxxar as Turks

R

M

M

M

Ft St Angelo; only defence
in 1530.

Ft St Michael added.
Galley Creek chained off.

28 March 1566; Valletta
founded.

Turks build earth dyke.

Turks move galleys
overland.

29 May; Dragut arrives.

7 August; Governor of
Mdina sacks Turk army at
Marsa.

M

M

T

T M

T

T

T

D

M

X T

Zejtun, first village to fall.

M

X

T M

T

R

X

D

T

D

R

R

D

R

R

R

R

R

D T

M

19 May, Turks land.

M

M

M

M

D

M

127

back to Valette predicting defeat within eight days.

Valette vowed he'd go over in person, but the Chevalier de Medran and 200 Spanish soldiers called his bluff and went instead.

Meanwhile, the Turks' slaves began another earthwork closer to St Elmo, allowing the Janissaries to snipe at individual defenders. And the Chevalier St Aubin, who had been raiding the Barbary Coast in a galley, could hear the gunfire from miles out to sea. St Aubin went on to Sicily to plead again with Don García.

Christians attack. On the night of 28-29 May the Christians struck back, running a sortie from St Elmo and destroying the Turkish earthworks. Mustapha replied by calling in the Janissaries who seized the outer defences of St Elmo. The siege was just ten days old, the bombardment beginning its fifth day, and already the knights were reeling.

St Elmo's fire. Later on the 29th Piali paraded 80 galleys past St Elmo and fired on it, but many shot went over the fort and landed among the Turkish troops. The knights retaliated and St Elmo's fire claimed one galley. That other St Elmo's Fire, the static electricity around the masts of sailing ships, was long believed to be a sign that Elmo, Ermo, or Erasmus, the Mediterranean sailors' patron saint, had taken the ship into his care.

On that same day, 29 May, cavalry from Mdina and Birgù caught 400 Turkish infantrymen by the Dingli cliffs and killed half of them.

The corsair Dragut. Also on that same day, Dragut arrived from Africa. Dragut, known as Turgut Reis to the Turks, the 'drawn sword of Islam,' had been Governor of Tripoli since he captured it from the Order in 1551. He had raided Malta six times over the years and

The Hundred-Ton Gun never fired in anger. Behind it, to the right, is the Mediterranean Film Studio's special effects tank.

although he was 80 he was still the greatest Moslem seaman of his time. And he brought with him 15 galleys and 1,500 picked men.

He had Süleiman's blessing, and supported Mustapha's policy of seizing the islands and starving out the garrisons, but he decided to continue with Piali's plan now it had begun. He added 50 guns to Sciber-Ras and put four others on the headland commanding access to Marsamxett Harbour; it's called Dragut Point to this day.

And on that first night Dragut inspected the Turks' defences, then refused a silk-lined tent at Marsa in order to sleep in the trenches of Sciber-ras with his troops.

On 30 May another message came from Sicily urging the Order to hold on as, claimed Garcia, there was difficulty in raising the reief forces. The next day Valette told his Grand Council: "It is upon God and our own swords that we may rely. It is better to know the truth of one's situation than to wait on false hopes."

Fungus Rock. Dragut's guns on Dragut Point (later also known as Tigné Point) opened fire on St Elmo on 3 June. Inappropriately, it was St Elmo's Day. While the fort now needed the help of all the saints in Christendom, Valette, knowing he could rely only on mortal men, sent in reinforcements under cover of darkness. The same small boats brought back the injured, whose wounds the hospitaller knights treated with the fungus already collected from Fungus Rock in Gozo. The green mould, still seen on the rock today, had been known for many years for its ability to stop bleeding.

Four beautifully-carved columns by the gateway are all that's worth seeing of Fort Ricasoli, once the largest fort in the British Empire.

Two mornings later the Turk scouts saw a breach in St Elmo's outer defences and the guards behind it asleep. At once the Janissaries surged in, seized part of the wall and a linking bridge, and were able to put scaling ladders to the walls of the main fortress.

Wildfire. The Christians replied with the most fearsome weapon they had, the dreaded wildfire. A mixture of sulphur, tar, potassium nitrate, ammonia salts, turpentine and wood resin, poured into thin clay pots and armed with four lighted tapers, wildfire was the ancient version of the Molotov cocktail and napalm combined. It wrought havoc on the Janissaries' flowing white robes as they fell back in disarray. Then came the firework hoops, soaked in brandy and oil, dipped in gunpowder, and dropped, blazing, over the enemy troops' heads with devastating effect. In this skirmish ten knights and 70 soldiers died, but the Turks lost 3,000 men.

Before dawn on 4 June the knight Raffael Salvago slipped into St Elmo by boat, saw the terrifying conditions in which the men lived, ate, defecated and died where they stood, and he carried a message of gloom back to the Grand Master.

Meanwhile, the Viceroy Don García promised men by 20 June, but only if Valette would collect them in his three galleys. Don García now expected to see Malta fall and knew Sicily would be the next target: he was preparing his escape clauses and strengthening his own garrison.

St Elmo crumbles. On the seventh, a Thursday, the Turks resumed their barrage with up to 7,000 shots a day pouring into St Elmo. The Janissaries attacked again and were driven back, but the fort was crumbling by the hour. Its turcopilier (commanding officer; the word came from *turcos expellere,* 'drive out the Turks') begged for withdrawal but Valette ordered him and his men to fight to the death. "When we joined the Order we swore on vows of chivalry that our lives would be sacrificed when and where the call might come."

The call had now come for St Elmo.

Eighth of June: a daylong attack. Sentries shot within minutes of taking their post. The central square is a killing ground and the stone visibly crumbling. Some soldiers preparing to swim to safety, others to sally forth and die.

That night: Chevalier Castriola raises 600 volunteers in Birgù to go to St Elmo but Valette thinks it's too many. Sends a scathing letter on the night of 9-10: "A volunteer force is coming. Return to Birgù where you will be safe. I shall be confident knowing the fort (of St Elmo) is held by trustworthy men."

Tenth of June: shamed, the defenders fight on. Five hundred troops come in two galleys from Sicily but Piali's forces drive them away. Piali decides to station 100 galleys north of Gozo to intercept any further replacements. And Dragut rebuilds the gun emplacement on

Gallows Point, later to be called Ricasoli Point as well.

Night attack. On the night of 10-11 June, Mustapha ordered the first attack by darkness. Janissaries hurled firebombs which stuck to the armour of the knights, who jumped into barrels of water to avoid roasting alive. The Janissaries were driven back with 1,500 losses for a mere 60 Christian dead.

On the night of 14-15 June, Mustapha remembered Rhodes and offered any knight free passage from Malta if he would surrender. None did — on that occasion. In fact, during the siege, several knights and Christian soldiers deserted to the Turks, but not a single Maltese joined the enemy: after all, *they* were fighting for their homeland, whereas the defending soldiers were mercenaries or unwilling conscripts.

Arquebusier. On 16 June, 4,000 arquebusiers lined across Sciber-Ras with their weapons, which were guns hooked onto tripods and named from the German *Hackenbüsse*, 'hook gun.' Piali's fleet ringed St Elmo and the circling fire was thus complete.

Then the Iayalars went in for the first time, crazy with hashish, an earlier form of cannabis resin, and were driven back. The Dervishes attacked; they too were repelled. Then the Janissaries tried, but as dusk fell they withdrew leaving St Elmo still in Christian hands. The Turks lost 1,000 men in the day, the knights just 150.

That night Valette asked for the last volunteers to offer their lives for St Elmo. Thirty knights and 300 men, including Maltese, crossed in darkness to their certain deaths.

Dragut hit. The next day a splinter of rock caught Dragut on the head and he was carried off unconscious. Moments later the Ağa (leader) of the Janissaries was killed on the same spot, and on the 19th Mustapha's second in command died in action. With three Turkish commanders out of the battle and Piali and Mustapha still failing to agree on tactics, Valette could begin to believe that his prayers were being answered.

Corpus Christi. On 21 June, the Feast of Corpus Christi, the knights dressed in their formal robes of the Order of St John and paraded through the streets of Birgù as was their custom on this day.

But that night the Janissaries and the arquebusiers attacked yet again, and in the morning the knights, in armour, fought hand to hand with the fanatics, killing 2,000 Janissaries for the loss of 200 Christians.

St Elmo falls. On the night of 22-23 the last volunteers, including two Jews, tried to reach St Elmo by boat but were driven back. The fort was now ready to die, and at dawn on the 23rd the knights buried their precious relics in the chapel floor, burned all else, and rang the chapel bell. Turkish galleys came into Marsamxett Harbour to fire on them, and the entire Turkish army massed on Mount Sciber-Ras for the final attack. Yet the last 100 men held onto St Elmo for a further hour before Mustapha's troops surged through to victory.

St Elmo had held out for 31 days, costing the Turks almost a quarter of their army. The Order of St John lost 1,500 men and 127 knights, including nine who were captured: five Spaniards, three Italians, and a Frenchman, five of whom were never heard of again. The other four came back to Birgù the following night — headless, heartless and strapped to crosses on which they floated over Grand Harbour. In retaliation Valette ordered every Turkish prisoner to be decapitated and his head fired back at Sciber-Ras as a cannonball.

Last stand. On the day that St Elmo capitulated, the first real relief forces landed on the north of Malta. Forty-two knights, 20 gentlemen volunteers, 56 gunners and 600 Spanish soldiers had sailed over from Messina but their leader, Captain Don Juan, had orders to return if St Elmo had fallen. "Has it?" he asked.

The scouting party of this *piccolo soccorso*, the 'little relief,' lied to him, then the entire party crossed Malta by night in a *scirocco* mist and sneaked in through the gates of Birgù, the defenders waiting for them.

Surrender offer. Mustapha heard of the new arrivals as he began moving his guns from Sciber-Ras to the base of St Michael's in L'Isla (Senglea). He sent a Greek slave with the offer of free passage but Valette sent the slave back offering just the defensive ditches — for Mustapha to fill with the bodies of his Janissaries.

Furious, Mustapha vowed he would wipe the island clean of

The British were here, too: the Ta'Qali Craft Centre still uses wartime Nissen huts.

Christians. Piali still couldn't row his galleys past St Angelo so Mustapha ordered his troops to drag the vessels overland, from the head of Marsamxett Harbour to the head of Grand Harbour. It meant the south-west flank of L'Isla would be open then to naval attack.

Deserter's warning. A deserter from the Turkish forces brought the Grand Master grave news: the knights must reinforce that flank at once. They did so, taking nine nights to drive in wooden stakes at sea level along today's French Creek. Mustapha sent swimmers to destroy them but Maltese swimmers drove them off; the Maltese were becoming even more determined than the Order of St John to drive out these Turks. At worst, the knights could pull out and save their skins, but the Maltese would become slaves in their own land.

Holy War. The fifteenth of July brought the next Turkish onslaught, by three galleys from their Marsa moorings with imams proclaiming a *jihad* or holy war, and backed by cannon from Sciber-Ras, Corradino (Kordin), and from outside the walls of St Michael's.

Bridge of boats. The galleys tasted success when a lucky shot blew up a powder magazine in L'Isla, bringing down a large chunk of wall. The Turks flooded in, but Christian troops from Birgù hurried across a bridge of boats that linked the two forts and drove the invaders out.

Mustapha threw a five-hour barrage against the walls of St Michael but the knights' counterfire cost him 3,000 soldiers against the 250 the Order lost — though among them was the son of the Viceroy of Sicily.

In desperation Mustapha sent ten galleys of Janissaries from Marsa Creek to seize the tip of L'Isla, but again he met defeat. The knights had hidden a five-gun battery at the base of St Angelo which sank nine of the galleys with chain shot, drowning 800 Janissaries. Those who swam ashore were slaughtered.

In the searing heat of mid-July the knights continued to fight in their 100lb (45kg) suits of armour, still with their leather jerkins next to the skin, and many chose to sleep in their armour as well. They were on strict and unpalatable rations while the Turks, who wore loose robes and little armour, went back to their tents at night and dined well.

September deadline. Yet the Turks knew things were going badly for them. Mustapha had planned on conquering the entire islands long before now and he was already aware of the September deadline. If he hadn't defeated Valette by then, he never would, for the galleys had to be back in Constantinople before the autumn storms set in.

The merciless Mustapha Paşa tried in desperation to bribe the Maltese to turn against the knights, but they told him they'd rather be slaves of St John than companions of the Grand Turk.

As July drew to a close Mustapha hurled a day-and-night barrage at Birgù, shattering half the houses in town. Valette ordered the few remaining Turkish slaves to use the rubble and build walls across the streets during the bombardment. Reluctant slaves lost their ears while those who refused lost their head, and during that awful day 500 of them died.

Mustapha threw yet another major attack with every gun firing, and the six-hour barrage was heard at Catania in Sicily, 100 miles (60km) away.

The Turks made five attempts to break into St Michael with scaling ladders but were repulsed each time. Mustapha vowed he would have a five-day barrage as reprisal, yet during that barrage a small boat managed to slip out with one more cry for help to Don García.

Collapse. On the sixth morning, 7th August, with the barrage over, the Turks thought that Allah was at last on their side. There were breaches in both fortress walls and the Turks poured through in their hordes. They packed themselves so solid in the Birgù breach that the Christians were able to slaughter them in their hundreds, but those who penetrated L'Isla surged into the town. House by house the knights were retreating, with total collapse a possibility, when the Turks suddenly withdrew, while success was within their grasp for the only time in the siege.

Recovery. Caballero Mesquita, Governor of Mdina, had noted the five-day barrage and on that sixth morning had made his counter-attack on the Moslem troops at Marsa. He surprised them so well that Mustapha thought more reinforcements had arrived, and he ordered the retreat from L'Isla.

Mustapha's vow. His reserve and resting troops at Marsa had been crushed. Stores and tents were burned, horses and men slaughtered. Mustapha vowed that if Allah were to grant him victory he would kill every Christian on Malta — except the Grand Master, who would go in chains to Süleiman the Magnificent.

Meanwhile, the Grand Master was reading the latest letter from Sicily. Don García was promising 16,000 men by the end of August — but that was more than two weeks away, and Valette told his Grand Council yet again that there was no hope of relief. The knights prepared to sell their lives as dearly as possible.

The tide turns. Nobody on Malta realised that this time the Viceroy was telling the truth. He had at last accepted that Malta stood a chance of resisting the Turks and therefore the attack on Sicily would not come. But for Malta to survive, the Order of St John needed urgent help — and only Don García could give it.

There are many ways to win a war, and Mustapha now tried the medieval trick of undermining his enemy's defences; his sappers were tunnelling under the Castile ramparts of Birgù's outer defences. Work was slow but by 18 August the mine was in position by the town gate. Mustapha then threw heavy cannon fire at L'Isla, hoping to persuade the knights to rush across the bridge of boats from Birgù and so reduce its defenders. It never happened, and when the mine brought down the front wall of Castile the knights were ready with their counter-attack. Once more the Turks fell back.

Siege machine. The next day was the worst so far for the Christians, in a siege which was already among the worst in history. On that 19th of August, 1565, the Turks brought up a siege machine, a huge wooden tower, and stationed it by the undamaged part of Birgù's Castile wall. For hours the knights had no answer to this monster which could almost peer over their ramparts, then they tunnelled through the undamaged base of their own curtain wall and fired chain-shot at the legs of the tower until it collapsed.

The Turks replied by hurling an 'infernal machine' — a time-bomb in our language — over the wall, but the fuse was too long, the knights hurled it back, and it exploded amid the Turkish troops.

Disease and despair. Despair was now infiltrating through the army of Islam as the deaths mounted, disease spread, and the deadline for departure grew nearer. There were three clear weeks after which, Mustapha urged, the army must commit itself to stay on the island until the spring.

Piali disagreed. "My fleet goes at the first sign of winter." He also pointed out that Christian ships were harrassing his galleys bringing food and water from Tripoli, and he had suffered uncomfortably high losses.

The knights never knew of the despondency among their enemy as the Grand Council urged Valette to pull back from the ruined walls of Castile and abandon the town of Birgù.

No retreat. Valette refused. "We cannot hold all the people of Birgù in St Angelo, and we will not abandon them to the Turks." He reminded them that Maltese women were now fighting on the ramparts and running the hospital, while their children were carrying ammunition. "If we retreat the Turks could fire on both flanks of L'Isla and attack St Angelo from the landward." To add weight to his argument he blew up the drawbridge connecting town and fort.

Both sides were now worn out, exhausted, punch-drunk, and prone to make errors of judgement. Sancak Çeder, an old Turkish warrior, made such an error when he vowed death or glory, put on his bright clothes and turban, and led 8,000 weary Turkish troops into battle. His reward was death.

Storeship seized. And Piali suffered a major defeat when Christian mercenaries patrolling the waters south of Malta seized a large storeship bringing food from Tripoli. Supplies in the Turkish camp were now down to a bare reserve of 25 days, and it would take the invaders at least 30 days to row back to Constantinople.

The admiral ordered immediate withdrawal, but Mustapha was

more afraid of the wrath of Süleiman the Lawgiver than he was of the Order of St John. In a desperate gamble he decided to seize the fortress of Mdina.

Change of tactic. It was another error of judgement. The change of plan demoralised his troops as they pulled cannon from the crumbling but undefeated Castile to attack an undamaged fortress half an island away.

Furthermore, Don Mesquita, the Governor of Mdina, was fresh in body and vibrant with ideas. He alone knew he couldn't hold out for long, but he took the townspeople, men and women alike, and dressed them as soldiers. He stationed them all, with every gun at his disposal, on the Turks' obvious approach, the east wall. And long before the enemy was within range he ordered his troops to open fire with cannon and musket. The message was plain: Mdina had plenty of powder and its troops were hungry for battle.

Mustapha rode forward alone, looked at the defenders lining the battlements, and withdrew.

It was almost the end of the Great Siege. As the Turkish troops trundled back to L'Isla and Birgù they convinced themselves that even after victory here, there was another major battle to be fought at Mdina. And the defenders of the two battle-weary towns asked themselves: if Mustapha daren't attack weak Mdina, what hope had he here?

Don García's fleet. Over in Sicily, Don García put to sea on 25 August with 10,000 men in a fleet of 28 sailing ships and oared galleys. They made first for the island of Linosa where Maltese had left messages giving the state of the war, but a storm drove them back to Sicily before they could reach the tiny isle. This was the weather that Piali feared and it was already troubling the low-freeboarded galleys on the short crossing from Sicily; the Turks would fare much worse on their long voyage back to Constantinople. Don García's fleet reached the mailbox on 4 September, found the latest report, and landed at Mellieha Bay two days later.

Valette's spies told him the news and he released a Turkish slave primed with the information that 16,000 troops had landed and Mustapha may as well go home.

Turkish evacuation. Mustapha agreed. On the night of 7-8 September, while the first of the new troops were camped at Naxxar, he ordered a mass evacuation. As the dawn of 8 September broke over Malta the knights and the Maltese people found the battlefield deserted, and scouts reported the Turks were already rowing out of Marsamxett Harbour.

This day had long been celebrated as the Feast of the Birth of the Virgin Mary, and now Grand Master Valette called for extra prayers of thanksgiving for deliverance from Islam.

Xlendi and its bay, in western Gozo.

But as the enemy fleet reached the open sea Mustapha learned the true size of the relief force and he ordered: *stop the evacuation!* Piali took half the fleet to St Paul's Bay while Mustapha ordered the other half back to Marsamxett.

Final rout. It was another tactical blunder. The troops at Naxxar fell on Mustapha's men, backed by the garrison from Mdina and the Maltese themselves, while the soldiers freshly landed at Mellieħa routed Piali's men.

Mustapha thus managed to commit the unpardonable sin of sacrificing a further 3,000 of his men on the day after he had lifted the siege, a tenth of his total losses over the 107 days since the bombardment began.

Death roll. The knights lost almost 250 of their number, and most of the survivors were crippled. Seven thousand Christians died, many of them Maltese civilians, and at the end of hostilities only 600 of the defenders were able to carry arms.

Mustapha and Piali crept back into Constantinople by night and Süleiman spared their lives. He vowed to lead the next attack on Malta in person, but he died on 5 September 1566.

Don García was relieved as Viceroy of Sicily and died in Naples, forgotten.

World's hero. But Jean Parisot de la Valette was the Christian world's hero. Among the many kings to honour him was Felipe II of Spain who sent him a jewelled sword with the Latin inscription *plus* *quam valor valet Valette.* Funds poured in from all over Europe for the rebuilding of Malta, of a Birgù now named Vittoriosa (Victorious) and a L'Isla named Invitta (Invincible). Felipe II urged the Order of St John to rename Mdina and so it became Città Notabile.

The knights decided they would have a new capital, the smartest in the world, and they would build it on the old ridge of Sciber-Ras — Sciberras in modern spelling — but they never allowed themselves enough time to level the site.

Valletta founded. On 28 March 1566, Grand Master de la Valette laid the foundation stone of the city called *Humillima Civitas Vallettae,* the 'most humble city of Valletta.' Twenty-nine months later, on 21 August 1568, Valette died of a heart attack and is now buried in his cathedral in the capital city that has taken his name, an honour that few other men can share.

The old Order changeth. The Order of St John of Jerusalem stayed in Malta a further 233 years, but historically its rule was to become an empty stage looking for a sequel fit to follow the opening performance.

By 1571 the city of Valletta — usually spelled with *ll* as opposed to Jean Parisot de la Valetta who had just the single *l* — was ready to accept the Convent, the central body of the Order, on its move from the old capital at Birgù; the next year there were 2,000 houses built, and by the end of the century Valletta was completed.

Knights' new forts. The knights were understandably obsessed with defence for the remainder of their time in Malta, and while Valletta was still under construction they rebuilt the Castile wall, and had a fort provided for them at Ricasoli Point (pronounced ri-*ka*-soli), the old Gallows Point at the entrance to Grand Harbour where smugglers had been hanged.

They added Fort Manoel on the island protecting Marsamxett Harbour, reinforced the Dwejra Lines with forts at Binġemma, Mosta and Madliena, built Pembroke and Spinola forts near St Julian's, forts Lucian and Delimara overlooking Marsaxlokk Bay, and Fort Chambray guarding Mġarr in Gozo. Finally, in 1793, five years before they left Malta, they added Fort Tigné on Dragut Point.

Margherita Lines. Grand Master Jean Lascaris Castellar began the Margherita Lines in 1639, a defensive wall which 97 years later was to stretch across the landward approaches to Birgù and which had long ago been renamed Senglea.

Cotonera Lines. Grand Master Nicolas Cotoner began the even more impressive Cotonera Lines in 1670, sweeping further inland than the Margherita Lines and enclosing sufficient open countryside to hold all the Maltese peasantry and their livestock.

Meanwhile, in 1658, Grand Master Martin de Redin completed a chain of 13 towers sretching from the Qawra in western Gozo to the

Qawra in Buġibba, and on to Wardija in southern Malta, located so that each could be seen from its neighbours, and if Malta were ever threatened again, towertop fires would summon the people to action within hours.

Many of the towers still retain official associations, with the police in occupation at Wied-iż-Żurrieq near the Blue Grotto, and the Armed Forces of Malta controlling the Red and the White towers on the Marfa peninsula.

Earthquake. An earthquake shook Malta in 1693 but failed to shake the Order of St John from the sense of complacency into which it was gradually sliding. In the second half of their occupation the knights were more concerned with a show of opulence than with defence, and their castles became palaces such as those that line the banks of the River Loire in France.

Maltese palaces. Onorato Visconti of Milan, the Inquisitor of Malta from 1625 to 1627, built the Inquisitor's Palace as his summer house near the large Verdala Palace which Hughes de Loubenx de Verdalle had already built during his period as the most opulent Grand Master of them all, from 1582 to 1595. Grand Master Antoine de Paule, 1623-1636, built the Palace of San Anton between Attard and Balżan; it's now the official residence of the President. In the same mould come the Żammitello Palace near Mġarr (Malta), the Għemieri near Nadur, and the Selmun near Mellieħa, built as a poorer replica of Verdalle's palace and recently converted into an excellent hotel.

Inquisitor. It was Jean de la Cassière who introduced the office of Inquisitor to Malta during his grand mastership from 1572 to 1581, but when the bishops, the Inquisitor and Cassière found each was eroding the others' authority, a perpetual power struggle began. The inquisitors were plainly too dominant, as Fabio Chigi demonstrated by rising from that post to become Pope Alexander VIII, setting the career course for Pope Innocent XII who was the other of Malta's inquisitors to reach the top.

Snake pit. The inquisitors had a second palace in Vittoriosa equipped with a snake pit and an execution yard, forming a complete contrast to the work of the Mallorcan brothers, Rafael and Nicolas Cotoner who had had the interests of the average Maltese peasant at heart: Nicolas is remembered for his Cotonera Lines but both men created the *Sacra Infermeria* which drew patients from all over Europe.

Colonial power. In 1653 Malta became a colonial power in its own right when Grand Master Lascaris paid Louis XIV of France 123,000 livres for the West Indian islands of St Croix, St Barthélemy, St Martin (Sint Maarten), part of St Christopher (St Kitts), and Tortuga. Like most colonial purchases it was a bad investment, for the isles' last owners were, respectively, the USA, France, the Netherlands, Britain and

Haiti.

Decadence. Over the decades as social change worked through Europe, Maltese society was stagnated in what was becoming an anachronistic, self-perpetuating hierarchy composed of affluent foreigners living off the labours of a peasantry which increasingly saw itself as downtrodden. It did not help that Jean Lascaris Castellar became Grand Master at the age of 75 and reigned a further 22 years.

Twenty-eight grand masters ruled the islands in all, twelve coming from France, eight from Spain, four from Italy, three from Portugal, and the last of them all, Ferdinand von Hompesch, from Germany.

Last Grand Master. Hompesch's predecessor, Emmanuel de Rohan, had introduced the *Codex Justinian* which was to form the basis of Maltese common law. Rohan was aware of the social revolution developing in his native France, and he allowed the first women into the Order's receptions. A staunch royalist nonetheless, he sent silver plate to Louis to help finance his escape from Paris. Napoleon Bonaparte found out and called the Order of St John 'an institution to support in idleness the younger sons of privileged families.'

Hompesch knew the end was in sight before he moved into high office in 1797. The French peasantry had stormed the Bastille and wiped out the aristocracy, including any further recruits to the Order. He tried to reduce the mystique of majesty and bend towards the peasantry, and succeeded to a degree: he was the only grand master to speak Malti, and he gave his name to Siġġiewi as Città Ferdinando, to Żabbar as Città Hompesch, and to Żejtun as Città Beland (Bylandt), his mother's maiden name. Żebbuġ had already become Città Rohan and Qormi Città Pinto – and though Mdina had long been Città Notabile the knights always spoke of it as Città Vecchia, the 'Old City.'

Hompesch Arch. None of these names was to endure, and Hompesch's main testimonial is the Hompesch Arch he built over the road into Żabbar. It was a symbolic welcome to the crowned heads of Europe, but Napoleon Bonaparte, the self-appointed, uncrowned head of an egalitarian France, came in through the back door.

17: FRENCH

Pillage and plunder

THE PARIS MOB STORMED THE BASTILLE and so began the chain of events which would bring about the fall of Louis XVII in 1793. In 1791 the Tiers État, the people's "Third Estate," issued a decree stripping the French knights of the Order of St John of Jerusalem of their nationality and their possessions, and the following year the Order suffered similar blows from Germany, Naples, Portugal, Sicily and Spain.

The knights of Malta had enjoyed an income from overseas of 3,000,000 livres in 1788, which was down by two thirds in 1797. Grand Master Ferdinand von Hompesch saw the signs of a military attack following the economic one, but his confidence had been undermined so that he lacked the resolution of Jean de la Valette. The Order was in serious trouble.

Russian intervention. Czar Paul of Russia had followed events and had courted Grand Master Emmanuel de Rohan (1775-97), offering money to found a langue for Russian nobles. Britain, which had recently held on to Gibraltar after a three-year siege, didn't like the idea of Russia seeking bases in the Mediterranean under any guise, and offered Rohan help.

Rohan took Russia's offer, but to sweeten British opinion he awarded the Maltese Cross to Lady Hamilton, wife of the British Ambassador in Naples, and mistress of Horatio Nelson; the knights awarded Lady Nelson, back in England, the title of Dame Petite Croix. Nelson himself was busy blockading the French Channel ports, to counter the threat of Napoleon's invasion of Britain.

Bonaparte's invasion plans. Napoleon, meanwhile, had other ideas. On September 13, 1797, he wrote to Talleyrand, the politically ambitious Bishop of Autun:

"Why don't we take Malta? Admiral Brueys could easily drop anchor there and seize the fortress. The total garrison of Valletta is 400 knights and 500 soldiers. The 100,000 inhabitants are friendly towards us and much estranged from the knights as so many are dying from starvation . . . I have confiscated the Order's possessions in Sicily . . . If we seize Sardinia, Malta and Corfu, we should make ourselves masters of the Mediterranean in its entirety."

And so, early in 1798, the 29-year-old Bonaparte was assembling his fleet in Toulon with the intention of capturing Egypt and then India, and so cripple Britain's growing empire. But now there was an extra task: he'd take Malta in passing.

Nelson's summons. Rear-admiral of the Red, Sir (not yet Lord) Horatio Nelson, aged 40, was at home recovering from the loss of his arm at Tenerife when he received command of the 74- gun *Vanguard* and orders to find out what was happening at Toulon. He sailed from Cádiz on 9 May with a small fleet and on 10 June learned that Bonaparte had left the French port three weeks earlier. Guessing Napoleon's target was Egypt, he sailed at once for Alexandria.

Napoleon arrives. But Bonaparte was in Malta. His fleet of 429 ships from Toulon plus another 70 from Civitavecchia near Rome, had arrived off Valletta on 9 June. Admiral Brueys, true to Bonaparte's suggestion, sent an envoy into Grand Harbour to ask Grand Master von Hompesch for permission to take on water.

Hompesch dithered all that day and into the next, but as night fell the French landed at strategic places around the island: Général Vaubois, already designated Governor of Malta, came ashore at St Julian's and marched on Mdina where he dined with the archbishop; Deslaix landed at Marsaxlokk; Lannes at Marsamxett; and Marmont at Fort Tigné.

Hompesch surrenders. As Nelson was crowding on sail to round Corsica on 11 June, von Hompesch surrendered Malta without a struggle, and saw the French ships of the line enter Grand Harbour and help themselves to the Order's small navy, the *Athénien* and *Dego,* each of 64 guns, the 36-gun frigate *Carthagénaise,* and three galleys, now useless as vessels of war.

It's easy to criticise von Hompesch and call him lacking in courage, but his struggle was far different from Valette's. Valette was fighting for Christianity against Islam, and had the moral support of all Europe, even if reinforcements were lacking. Von Hompesch saw himself as a relic of the old school trying to resist inevitable social change in a Europe that had turned against the nobility. He had already lost the will to resist.

Napoleon lands. The next day Napoleon himself landed at Custom House Steps from the *Orient* and walked up what is now Merchants Street to take the surrender. He gave the Order of St John three days to quit Malta.

The Maltese people welcomed the French as liberators — as they had done the Phoenicians, the Romans, the Arabs, the Normans, and even the Order itself — but once again their hopes were dashed: once again the new masters of Malta were proving no better than the old.

French plunder. The French, if anything, were worse despite their claims to be the saviour of the common man. Napoleon set up home in an auberge he renamed the Palais Parisio — it's now the main post office — and decreed that forthwith French was the official language of Malta. As street names such as *Place de la Liberté* and *Rue des Droits de l'Homme* went up, he imposed extra taxes on a people who were already poor, to pay for the French garrison. He seized the last of the Order's silver plate and melted it down to 3,500lbs (1,600kg) of bullion which he later used to pay his troops in Egypt. He seized the sword Felipe of Spain had given Valette — it's now in a Paris museum — and his troops looted treasure worth 3,000,000 francs, or £240,000 at 1800 values, and loaded it aboard *Orient*.

Then, on 19 June, Bonaparte left Malta in the control of Général Vaubois and 6,000 troops, and sailed for Egypt with the plundered treasure.

Near miss. That night, 180 miles (290km) to the east, Nelson's armada was within hailing distance of Napoleon's fleet without realising it. Bonaparte knew, and ordered total silence until the British sailed on, thus avoiding what would have been the Battle of Malta. Nelson in his ignorance pushed on to Alexandria, back to Sicily and on to the Greek islands before learning that Napoleon's fleet was safe at anchor at Aboukir Bay, Egypt, and his army in control of Cairo.

Battle of the Nile. At dawn on 1 August, Nelson's lookouts sighted a forest of masts at Aboukir on the Nile delta, and that evening Sir

One of the longest balconies in Malta? This is on the Grand Master's Palace fronting on Republic Square.

Horatio fired the opening shots of the Battle of the Nile. The British captured ten of the 13 French ships of the line, including the *Orient*, but she caught fire and was lost with the entire Maltese silver on board. Nelson had 450 casualties to Bonaparte's 4,000 — and the French army was now marooned in Egypt.

Meanwhile, life on Malta was rapidly going from bad to abysmal. Families of men pressed into the French fleet were starving in Valletta while the French troops plundered Malta's splendid churches, then committed the unpardonable sin of introducing civil marriage: divorce is still not allowed in Malta. In late August the French vessels *Guillaume Tell, Diane* and *Justice*, three of the four major ships to survive Aboukir (the other was the *Généraux*), entered Grand Harbour and advertised to the jubilant islanders that Bonaparte had been defeated and that the French garrison in Malta was therefore cut off.

Maltese rebellion. A few days later the French callously tried auctioning the treasures of the Church of Our Lady of Mount Carmel in Mdina and the population rose in revolt, lynched the Mdina garrison and drove the remainder of the French back into Valletta.

Xavier Carnova. Once more the capital was under siege, but this time the Maltese were outside the walls, 4,000 strong and armed with 2,000 muskets. But they knew there were enough provisions in the city to support the 6,000 troops for months: from that point of view von Hompesch needn't have capitulated so quickly. A priest, Xavier Carnova, emerged as the Maltese leader and was later to become Archbishop of the island, but his immediate problem was still how to get rid of the French.

In mid-September Captain Saumarez in *HMS Orion* called into Malta on his way from Aboukir to Gibraltar. He couldn't stay but he gave the islanders 1,200 seized French muskets and summoned help from Gibraltar: the British blockade had begun.

Gozo surrenders. Ten thousand Maltese, swearing allegiance to the King of Sicily, ringed Valletta when Nelson came over on a day trip from Naples and saw Captain Ball, the British unofficial governor, take the surrender of the 217 French troops on Gozo. Back in Naples Nelson said: "Malta is in our thoughts day and night. We shall lose it, I am afraid . . . If we lose this opportunity it will be impossible to recall."

Captain Ball stayed to blockade Valletta for two years and two days while on the broader front England, Austria and Russia went to war against France, and Napoleon marched from Cairo to Damascus and eventually home. Everybody in Malta knew the pangs of hunger; the French, the Maltese, and the British sailors to whom it was no stranger.

Besiegers besieged. In March of 1799 Ball gave the Maltese two of his cannon; in May he had to send his ships to British-held Menorca, and at once the French sailed out of Grand Harbour and besieged the besieging Maltese in Marsaxlokk Bay, until they heard that Ball's ships were coming back.

Nelson returned in November and demanded the French surrender but Général Vaubois said he was "resolved to defend the fortress to the ultimate," so Nelson prepared for a land attack. He called in two British infantry regiments totalling 1,300 men, plus 1,200 Neapolitan troops — but General Thomas Graham who came with them, decided he was still under strength.

Shortly after the siege entered the 19th century a small boat broke the blockade to carry the news to Vaubois that Bonaparte had been appointed Chief Consul of France: in effect, its dictator. A supply ship reached Valletta a few days later and the revitalised French vowed never to surrender.

French resistance. But the siege was to drag on that second year with near-total blockade. Vaubois opened Valletta's gates to kick out the unfortunate Maltese who had been unwillingly sharing the siege, then the French started eating the cats and dogs. Some of the garrison tried escaping at night in their ill-equipped ships; *Diane* was captured but *Justice* made it to Toulon.

But starvation was breaking their resistance and on 4 September, Vaubois surrendered — 235 years all but four days after the Turks had broken off the Great Siege. And 142 years *plus* four days later, Malta's third siege was to end.

The Armoury Corridor in the State Apartments of the Grand Master's Palace has beautiful mosaics.

British rule begins. The French rule was over and the Maltese were angered when they saw French troops carrying away yet more trophies of war, but they had been so impressed with Britain's help over the past two years that they welcomed Captain Sir Alexander Ball as their temporary governor under British rule, while the greater nations decided the island's fate.

The Treaty of Amiens in 1802 brought peace between Britain and France, and restored the Order of St John to Malta with the creation of a Maltese langue. But nobody listened when the Maltese said they didn't want the Order back: they wanted to become part of the growing British Empire.

Malta 'important'. The next year Britain and France forgot the treaty and went to war again. Bonaparte had already told the British Ambassador that he'd rather give up the Faubourg St Antoine in Paris than lose Malta, and the British were now well aware of Valletta's strategic importance. Nelson wrote from Valletta: "I now declare that I consider Malta as a most important outwork to India . . . In this view I hope we shall never give it up."

As the Napoleonic War raged, all merchant ships trading in the Mediterranean had to call in at Valletta for clearance from the Royal Navy, bringing so much business that Maltese warehouses were filled. Grand Harbour became a free port, and the merchants did a million pounds' worth of business in the year 1805.

Treaty of Paris. It was only natural that the Maltese hoped that fortune was here to stay and that, as Nelson said, "they pray never to be separated from England." When Bonaparte went into exile on another little island, the Treaty of Paris of 1814 declared that 'the island of Malta and its dependencies shall belong in full right and sovereignty to His Britannic Majesty.'

British rule had come.

18: BRITISH

The *Greater* Siege

ONCE AGAIN THE MALTESE PEOPLE WERE DISAPPOINTED, although not as much as on other changes of sovereign power. We must remember that Europe's colonial powers put their own interests first, and those of their subject peoples second. The British were interested in Malta almost entirely for its docking potential in Grand Harbour and for its strategic location in the middle of the Mediterranean.

Britain was undoubtedly the best external power to rule the islands, though one can argue whether this was due to policy, to more enlightened times, or to the contrast between the last years of the Order's rule and the disastrous two years under France. At the beginning of the 19th cent no territory as small and as strategically vital as Malta could hope to survive without the protection of an overlord, and the Maltese were grateful their new masters were the best they had ever had.

Those new masters built further gun batteries in St Angelo, Fort Manoel, and in the Cotonera Lines, so that by the mid-19th cent there were 332 guns around Grand and Marsamxett harbours, and in 1882 two enormous 100-ton guns were shipped to Malta and installed at the Cambridge Battery west of Fort Tigné and at the Rinella Battery east of Fort Ricasoli, thus guaranteeing protection for the approaches to Grand Harbour. A third 100-tonner was delivered to Gibraltar where it's still a tourist attraction (see *Discover Gibraltar*), and a fourth was prepared for Dover.

The Rinella gun is still in place, probably to become part of a film studio's tourist attraction; see chapter 20.

Suez Canal. The opening of the Suez Canal in 1869 boosted Grand Harbour's popularity, and as shipping moved from wooden hulls and sail to iron hulls and steam, so the docks of Senglea and Vittoriosa grew. The shipyard built its own iron- hulled sloop between 1883 and 1889 in its spare time between servicing the Navy's vessels, but the Admiralty decided against developing the shipbuilding idea in Grand Harbour.

Malta Railway. In 1883, as work began on the sloop, the British opened Malta's first and only railway. The Malta Railway Company Ltd began its services on 28 February with a 35-minute journey from an underground station in Valletta to Floriana, Ħamrun, Msida, Santa Venera, Birkirkara, Balżan, Attard, and on to Rabat. The line was seven miles (11km) long and the regular services − seven daily in each direction − took 35 minutes, including stopping time. A first-class one-way ticket for the route cost the equivalent of 7p (21pfennig, 14¢ US), giving the company a daily income of around £50 (DM180, US$95). But the stations were badly placed at the bottom of long, steep slopes, and within seven years the company was in financial trouble.

Three 0−6−0 locomotives built by Manning Wardle of Leeds were in use at the start, soon to be joined by one made by Black Hawthorn of Gateshead, and by the end of the century there were six more; the rolling stock came from the Isle of Wight, which is slightly larger than Malta and Gozo together. The island was too small to support a railway at all, and despite government help the trams introduced in 1905 offered too much competition; when motor buses arrived the railway had no option but to close, and the last train ran on 31 March 1931.

The late 19th cent was a time of great progress in heavy engineering massive building, and in 1877 the Inspector General of Forts, General J. Simmons, was called in to report on Malta's defences. "The difficulty of maintaining a fleet in the Mediterranean without the possession of Malta would be insurmountable," he wrote, and urged that "no expense, within reasonable limits," be spared to make the island impregnable.

Victoria Lines. The most obvious result of Simmons's report is the Victoria Lines, straggling across northern Malta along the route of the former Dwejra Lines and protecting most of the island from any army which succeeded in landing on the beaches of Mellieħa or St Paul's Bay.

Breakwater. Victoria's son, Edward VII, came to Malta in 1903, the first reigning monarch to pay a call since Alfonso of Aragon in 1432 − but Queen Adelaide, who had visited Valletta in 1838, had given £10,000 of her own money to build the Anglican Cathedral. Edward VII laid the foundation stone for the Grand Harbour breakwater which was to be an excellent torpedo barrier in two world wars, but he did little for the common man and when the three-year contract was finished, economic depression hit the islands. By now the population had passed the 200,000 mark and could no longer support itself on the sunscorched summer pastures. A sound economy was essential, but lacking.

First World War. Grand Harbour was again the centre of the Mediterranean stage in the First World War, when torpedoes and sea mines came into the battle. The Maltese workforce forgot its

The Great Ditch was dug by Turkish slaves; it now leads to a good car park and the Lascaris War Rooms.

grievances, helped win the war, and in 1921 in return for their effort the people had their first taste of self-government since Roman times.

Self-government. In the 1921 Constitution, Britain controlled defence, foreign relations and immigration, while the 32 members of the Legislative Assembly looked after everything else. It lasted six years, shattered by the fury of the Church ordering its flock not to vote for the Constitutional Party of Lord Strickland, and by arguments over languages.

Every islander spoke Malti, most educated people spoke English, but only 15 percent could speak Italian. Yet knowledge of Italian was essential for anybody hoping for a government job, even if only as a roadsweeper. Most ridiculous was the working of the law courts with people giving evidence in Malti, the judge translating it into Italian for the written record, which might then be translated into English for the defendant or a witness. The lawyers argued in Italian but questioned the witnesses in Malti or English. Finally, the verdict and the sentence were delivered in Italian, and again translated.

Colonial status. By 1936 Malta was again a colony, with a constitution banning Italian as an official language, and with English used in government and Malti in the courts. But thoughts of home rule went into hibernation as Hitler invaded Poland and so started the Second World War.

At once Italy under Mussolini was seen to be a major threat, and as a precaution the leaders of the Nationalist Party were exiled to

Uganda because of their strong Italian links.

Second World War. In the first year of war Malta was undefended. The RAF was fighting the Battle of Britain, the Royal Navy was in Alexandria, and the Army was recovering after the defeat at Dunkirk.

As Italy prepared to enter the conflict the Maltese people made their own preparations. In May 1940, several thousand people quit the towns around Grand Harbour and moved into the country. On Sunday, 9 June, 20,000 people went on pilgrimage to Mdina knowing that war was imminent, but none realised it was to come so soon.

Italy attacks. Mussolini declared war on the Allies the next day, and at 0650 on Tuesday, 11 June, Italian bombers attacked Malta, killing eight people in the first of the day's eight raids.

The War Museum. It was an early taste of what was to come. From that day to the end of September 1943, Malta was at the receiving end of 3,332 air raids. The War Museum by Fort St Elmo tells the story in grim statistics as well as some startling exhibits: in 1940 there were 211 air raids; in 1941, 963; in 1942, 2,031; in 1943, 127; and in 1944 just eight.

The Greater Siege. The Germans called it Blitzkrieg, but the Maltese saw the war as the Greater Siege, beginning in earnest when the aircraft carrier *HMS Illustrious* limped into port early in 1941 and was attacked for seven days by dive bombers before escaping.

Early 1942 was the worst with 282 raids crammed into April; almost 10 a day. In that month alone, 6,728 bombs were dropped, half of them on the dockyard and most of the remainder on the airfields at Luqa, Ta'Qali, and Ħal Far, and the Kalafrana seaplane base. For comparison, the blitz which devastated Coventry took a mere 250 tons of bombs.

Throughout the Greater Siege, 16,000 tons of bombs fell, damaging or destroying 35,000 buildings, killing one person in 200 and injuring one in 70. The RAF destroyed 1,252 enemy aircraft with 383 probables, and ground gunners accounted for 241 with 49 probables, against the RAF's losses of 547 planes in the air and 160 destroyed on the ground.

Within days of the start of the attack, 19,000 of the 31,000 people who'd stayed in Valletta and Floriana, were living underground, either in the old railway tunnel or church crypts. Across the islands, 100,000 people fled the danger areas, and Vittoriosa and Cospicua became ghost towns.

Faith, Hope **and** *Charity.* The Navy sent *HMS Terror* to boost the anti-aircraft gunpower – and somebody realised that a load of packing cases waiting for shipment from Grand Harbour contained four ancient Gloster Gladiator biplanes. Mechanics rebuilt the machines, flying-boat pilots from Kalafrana offered to fly them, and for the first three weeks of the air war the canvas-and-wire stringbags

The Verdala Palace has a commanding view over Malta; here we see the Buskett Gardens and Mdina.

went aloft to fight the Italian air force.

One Gladiator was lost very quickly but the remaining three, dubbed *Faith, Hope* and *Charity*, held out until the RAF managed to send a squadron of Hurricanes to Malta. *Faith* has survived the years since the war and is now on display, minus her wings, in the War Museum.

Conscription. Malta had introduced conscription in March 1941, with all men between 18 and 41 liable to be taken into the army, and by the end of the year 3,872 men were in uniform, their pay as low as 10/− (50p, DM1.50, 90¢ US) a week, a quarter of the average pay for civilians.

Vital base. By early 1942 the strategists in Whitehall realised how vital Malta was to the Allied cause. The island was a midway staging post on the run from Gibraltar to the Suez Canal, and an unsinkable aircraft-carrier just 60 miles south of Italy. Hitler knew he had to capture Malta if he were to win the war in north Africa, and Churchill knew he had to hold the island if he wanted to win the war in the Mediterranean.

The Luftwaffe had more than 500 bombers ready to raid Malta, and frequently sent 200 into action in a day, while U-boats and Stuka dive-bombers attacked the convoys that tried to feed the fortress island. Some convoys were wiped out before they could reach Grand Harbour, but even behind the breakwater there was no escape; the destroyer *Maori* was sunk at anchor, and burning oil from her tanks threatened many other vessels. The Royal Navy lost a further 20 ships in or around Grand Harbour at the peak of the attack; the destroyer *Kingston* was knocked off her stilts in dry dock; and the submarine pens were so battered that during air raids the craft would lie at the bottom of the harbour − but even there, two were hit, never to rise again.

Mosta Church. On 9 April, a 1,000-lb high-explosive bomb crashed through the dome of Mosta Church and rolled past the large congregation, but never blew up. Many islanders saw this as a miracle, redeeming the damage done in Valletta where the Grand Master's Palace, six auberges, the University, the Customs House, St John's Co- Cathedral, six churches, the General Post Office and the Sacred Infirmary had all been damaged or destroyed.

But the worst was yet to come. Convoys were not getting through and people were starving. The basic food ration in Valletta was a third of the allowance in London − and even water was scarce. In June, the Governor and the military heads decided that without more supplies they would have to surrender by September.

Operation Pedestal. Malta's last hope was Operation Pedestal, a convoy due to deliver 35,000 tons of vital stores in August. But the 14 merchantmen would be protected by two battleships, seven cruisers,

30 destroyers, and three aircaft- carriers with 70 planes. In addition, 186 aircraft and several submarines would join the escort for the last part of the journey − and there would be a diversionary convoy from Egypt of 24 ships.

SS Ohio. The Germans sank the first aircaft-carrier near Algiers and damaged another; as the convoy progressed, two cruisers, one destroyer and nine of the 14 cargo vessels were lost. The most important ship of all was the *Ohio*, full of fuel oil and vital for Malta's survival. She was torpedoed and dive-bombed, but she stayed afloat. Her engines were smashed, her steering destroyed, and she was abandoned. But though her decks were awash she was taken in tow for the last 100 miles − then the tow parted within sight of Valletta and the *Ohio* drifted into a minefield. A tug rescued her, and at last she was hauled into Grand Harbour, and the threat of surrender was past.

Italy surrenders. The Allies planned the invasion of Sicily at the Phoenicia Hotel and Fort St Angelo; on 9 July the Allies sailed from Valletta to begin the conquest of Italy and, on 8 September, as the Maltese were celebrating Il-Bambina, the Feast of the Birth of the Virgin Mary, which also marked the end of the Great Siege 378 years earlier, they learned that the Greater Siege was officially over. For on that same date, and only four days after the anniversary of the French surrender in Valletta, the Italians capitulated to the Allies and her navy surrendered, almost within sight of the ramparts of St Elmo; the surrender documents were signed aboard *HMS Nelson* in Grand Harbour.

George Cross. By November 1942 the Allies had landed in north Africa and Malta could return to relative peace: the war had passed by. But the attack on Malta had been so severe that on 15 April, 1942,

Some Maltese buses have travelled more than a million miles, and their drivers are justly proud of them.

King George VI had awarded the George Cross to the island itself in a citation which read:

"The Governor, Malta. To honour her brave people I award the George Cross to the Island Fortress of Malta to bear witness to a heroism and devotion that will long be famous in history."

US President Roosevelt, returning from the Teheran Conference in December 1943, called in at Malta and awarded it his own citation, the texts of both now on plaques on the front wall of the House of Representatives in Valletta.

Prime Minister Mintoff. After the war, when colonialism became a dirty word, Malta was set for its long-promised independence. In 1947 the people tried again with a 40-member Legislative Assembly, though the Governor retained control of defence, currency and immigration. The Malta Labour Party couldn't work with these clauses and split, giving Dom Mintoff his first spell as Prime Minister.

Integration? Mintoff's Labour party went on to press for total integration with Britain, Malta to elect MPs to Westminster, but the Maltese Church was totally opposed to the suggestion, seeing itself swamped by British Protestantism; at one stage priests in the pulpit were condemning a vote for Labour as a mortal sin.

The issue collapsed, and Malta again chose independence, a hazardous road in view of the island's dependence upon the British military presence, the lack of light industry, the over-population, and the terrible war damage to be repaired. Britain gave £30,000,000 in 1947, and £50,000,000 of aid in the 1960s, with £14,000,000 a year in rent from NATO for the bases, and £2,500,000 in aid from Italy.

But an independent Malta had set its aim on the eventual withdrawal of all foreign military, although 12,000 men had worked in the dockyards at peak periods.

Independence. The constitution was revoked in 1959 with the Governor again in control until the next elections in 1962. The Nationalists formed the new government but both parties continued pressing for independence, which came on September 12, 1964, with Queen Elizabeth II becoming Queen of Malta at the islanders' request.

There were numerous minor disagreements between Malta and Britain in the next 10 years, one of the worst being when Britain pulled out all its air traffic controllers at short notice, forcing Prime Minister Dom Mintoff, a friend of Colonel Nasser, to invite controllers over from Egypt. In that instance, the British came back very quickly.

The Republic was formed on December 13, 1974, and British troops were withdrawn on March 31 1979 leaving Malta free of foreign intervention of any kind for the first time since the Phoenicians arrived. It had been a long journey from the Cave of Darkness to the light of the new Republic.

19: RULERS OF MALTA FROM 1530
Grand Masters, Presidents, Prime Ministers

GRAND MASTERS of the Order of St John of Jerusalem:

1530–34: Philippe Villiers de l'Isle Adam (French)

1534–35: Pierino del Ponte (Italian)

1535–36: Didiers de St Jaille (French)

1536–53: Juan de Homedes (Aragonese)

1553–57: Claude de la Sengle (French)

1557–68: Jean de la Valette (French)

1568–72: Pietro del Monte (Italian)

1572–82: Jean de la Cassière (French)

1582–95: Hughes Loubenx de Verdalle (French)

1595–1601: Martino Garzes (Aragonese)

1601–22: Alof de Wignacourt (French)

1622–23: Luis de Vasconcelhos (Portuguese)

1623–36: Antoine de Paule (French)

1636–57: Jean Lascaris Castellar (French)

1657–60: Martin de Redin (Aragonese)

1660: Annet de Clermont Gessan (French)

1660–63: Rafael Cotoner (Aragonese)

1663–80: Nicolas Cotoner (Aragonese)

1680–90: Gregorio Carafa (Italian)

1690–97: Adrien de Wignacourt (French)

1697–1720: Ramón Perellos y Roccaful (Aragonese)

1720–22: Marc Antonio Zondadari (Italian)

1722–36: Manoel de Vilhena (Portuguese)

1736–41: Ramón Despuig (Aragonese)

1741–73: Manuel Pinto de Fonseca (Portuguese)

1773–75: Fransisco Ximenes de Texada (Aragonese)

1775–97: Emmanuel de Rohan de Polduc (French)

1797–98: Ferdinand von Hompesch (German)

French interlude

1798–99: Napoleon Bonaparte

1799: Général Vaubois

British rule

Civil commissioners:

1799–1801: Captain Alexander Ball, RN

1801: Maj-General Henry Pigot

1801–02: Sir Charles Cameron

1802: The Order of St John of Jerusalem (nominally only)

1802–10:

1810–13: Lt-General Sir Hildebrand Oakes

Governors:

1813—24: Lt-General The Hon Sir Thomas Maitland

1824—26: General the Marquess of Hastings

1826—36: Maj-General The Hon Sir Frederic Ponsonby

1836—43: Lt-General Sir Henry Bouverie

1843—47: Lt-General Sir Patrick Stuart

1847—51: The Rt Hon Richard More O'Farrell

1851 58: Maj-General Sir William Reid

1858—64: Lt-General Sir John Gaspard le Marchant

1864—67: Lt-General Sir Henry Storks

1867—72: General Sir Patrick Grant

1872—78: General Sir Charles van Straubenzee

1878—84: General Sir Arthur Borton

1884—88: General Sir Linton Simmonds

1888—90: Lt-General Sir Henry Torrens

1890—93: Lt-General Sir Henry Smyth

1893—99: General Sir Arthur Freemantle

1899—1903: Lt-General Lord Grenfell

1903—07: General Sir Mansfield Clarke

1907—09: Lt-General Sir Henry Grant

1909—15: General Sir Leslie Rundle

1915—19: Field-Marshal Lord Methuen

1919—24: Field-Marshal Viscount Plumer

1924—27: General Sir Walter Congreve

Two citations that praise Malta for its stand during the Greater Siege.

1927−31: General Sir John du Cane
1931−36: General Sir David Campbell
1936−40: General Sir Charles Bonham-Carter
1940−42: Lt-General Sir William Dobbie
1942−44: Field-Marshal Viscount Gort

Independence, September 12, 1964
Governors-General:
1964−71: Sir Maurice Dorman
1971−74: Sir Anthony Mamo

Republic, December 13, 1974
Presidents:
1974−76: Sir Anthony Mamo
1976−81: Dr Anthony Buttiġieġ
1981−82: Dr Albert Hyzler
1982−87: Miss Agatha Barbara
1987−89: Mr Paul Xuereb
1989−   : Dr Vincent Tabone

1944−46: Lt-General Sir Edmond Schrieber
1946−49: Sir Francis Douglas, *later* Lord Douglas
1949−54: Sir Gerald Creasey
1954−59: Maj-General Sir Robert Laycock
1959−62: Admiral Sir Guy Grantham
1962−64: Sir Maurice Dorman

PRIME MINISTERS from 1921
1921−23: Joseph Howard
1923−24: Fransesco Buhagiar
1924−27: Sir Ugo Mifsud
1927−32: Sir Gerald Strickland, *later* Lord Strickland
1932−33: Sir Ugo Mifsud
1933−47: colonial status
1947−50: Dr Paul Boffa
1950: Dr Enrico Mizzi
1950−55: Dr Giorgio Borġ Olivier
1955−58: Dominic Mintoff
1958−62: constitution revoked
1962−71: Dr Giorgio Borġ Olivier
1971−84: Dominic Mintoff
1984−87: Dr Carmelo Mifsud Bonniċi
1987−   : Dr Eddie Fenech Adami

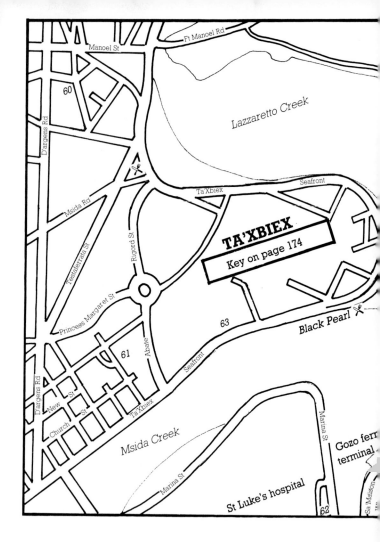

DISCOVER MALTA

20: THE VALLETTA AREA

Around Grand and Marsamxett harbours

THE PENINSULA OF SCIBERRAS, dividing Grand Harbour from Marsamxett Harbour, was an obvious choice for a capital city from the moment mankind knew how to smooth the headland's rugged surface. The first practical suggestion came in 1551, just 21 years after the Order of St John arrived on the island. There was already a small watch-tower and a simple beacon at the promontory, the 'light at the tip' which gives Sciberras its name. Other plans were made in 1559 and 1562, but nothing had been started when the Turks made their attack in 1565.

A year later, with the Great Siege behind them, the knights revived the plans and laid the foundation stone of their new capital city on 28 March, 1566. The problem was that they had not allowed enough time to flatten the headland, so Valletta is now endowed with some of the world's steepest streets, several of them a series of steps.

The twin harbours had been the focal point of Malta's commerce and economy since Phoenician times, so when the Order of St John began the massive fortifications of Fort Tigné, Fort St Elmo and Fort Ricasoli, it was obvious that the merchants, the artisans, the shipwrights and the diplomats — everybody except the peasantry — would gravitate to the area. Birgù and L'Isla, now renamed Vittoriosa and Senglea, were already there on Grand Harbour, soon to be joined by Sliema, Ġżira, Msida and the other villages lining the inlets of Marsamxett Harbour.

Today, the area within a radius of 1.5 miles (2.5km) from Valletta city gates is Malta in miniature, holding everything of commercial and economic significance except Freeport and Luqa Airport.

VALLETTA

Valletta is one of the most architecturally interesting capitals of the world, with the advantage of being convenience-packed into a mere 900m by 500m; you can drive around it in half an hour by *karrozzin* or in minutes by bus, then you can go out on foot and explore the city centre.

Republic Street. The main thoroughfare was the Strada San Giorgio of the Order of St John, becoming Rue de la République under the French, then changing to Strada Reale under the later Italian influence. The British translated this almost literally to Kingsway, and the independent Maltese have opted for Republic Street. It runs straight as an arrow's flight from City Gate to Fort St Elmo and at a little more than 900 metres is Valletta's longest street and the focal point of the country.

At its beginning it crosses the **Great Ditch,** a cleft averageing 55ft deep by 30ft wide (17m by 9m), hacked from the solid rock by Turkish slaves. The ditch runs for 2,660ft (875m) across the peninsula, making a formidable obstacle to any land-based invader, but today it is an ideal car park, with 56 steps leading up to emerge on Freedom Square beside the **tourist office.** (To park there, drive north along Great Siege Rd, Floriana, and turn right by a sign to the Lascaris War Rooms.)

Cross Ordnance St, named from the knights' gun foundry which stood on the left corner, and on the right you see the gaunt remains of the Royal Opera House, destroyed in 1942 and now used as a car park.

On the right is **St Barbara's Church,** built by the Langue de Provence and now used by non-Maltese Catholics. Diagonally opposite, beyond Melita St (formerly Britannia St), is the **Auberge de Provence,** designed by Girolamo Cassar, the man who completed the street plan of Valletta and saw the city rise. Finished in 1575, the building is now home to the National Museum of Archaeology.

NATIONAL MUSEUM OF ARCHAEOLOGY.

The museum holds the great majority of Malta's archaeological treasures that were not taken away by earlier enthusiasts; entry is 15c for adults, but ♿ visitors have several steps to overcome. The Prehistoric Gallery holds relics from Għar Dalam and the Neolithic temples, with a massive bowl, carved from limestone around 4,500 years ago, as the centrepiece; this is similar to a giant stone bowl of the same age found in Amathus, Cyprus.

The Tarxien Room holds stone tools and copies of sculpture, and leads to the Bronze Age Room with exhibits from Borġ In-Nadur. At the other end of the museum and up a short flight of stairs are two small rooms devoted to Roman and Punic times, including the only artefact yet found with Punic and Greek script, which provided the clue to understanding the Phoenician language.

A quarter the way along Republic St, St John's Street leads right into the charming and tree-shaded St John's Square with steps leading up to the main entrance of St John's Co-Cathedral; in 1816 Pope Pius VIII elevated it to share the honour of being the state cathedral with St Paul's in Mdina.

St. JOHN'S CO-CATHEDRAL

The cathedral's exterior is impressive, with a clockface and a calendar face marking time, day and date, as in many Maltese churches. At ground level two small cannon symbolically guard the doors, as you also find at the other co-cathedral.

But the interior of the cathedral is amazingly detailed and ornate, even considering the high quality of interior decoration of the island republic's lesser churches. St John's, however, excels — as it should. Built between 1573 and 1577 to Girolamo Cassar's design, and financed by Grand Master Jean de la Cassière, it is a museum to the splendour and opulence of the Order of St John in their years of glory, although it later lost many of its treasures to Napoleon's troops, and the silver altar rails of the East Chapel of the Blessed Sacraments (the last chapel on the south side) might have been stolen as well if they hadn't been painted black to disguise their true worth — or so legend claims.

Tombs of grand masters. Built as a simple basilica, St John's has 12 side chapels, seven of which were devoted to the langues of the Order of St John; reading anticlockwise from the entrance they are Castille, Léon and Portugal (2nd chapel on the south side) who share the patronage of St James, San Jaime; Aragon, Catalonia and Navarra (4th) sharing St George, San Jorge; Auvergne (5th) with San Sebastian; Provence (7th, on the north side), patron St Michel; France (8th), St Paul; Italy (9th), and St Catherine who was crucified on a wheel; and Germany (11th) under the patronage of the Magi. The German langue's chapel was the English langue's until 1631, and ironically it was only one damaged by German bombing.

Many contain lavish sculptures commemorating the grand masters of their langue who died after the creation of Valletta, while the tombs of 11 of the first 12 grand masters are in the **crypt,** accessible from the Chapel of Provence. Only Didiers de St Jaille (1535-36) is missing, but in his place is Sir Oliver Starkey, not a grand master but the only Englishman buried in the cathedral; he was Valette's secretary. The last grand master, Ferdinand von Hompesch, died penniless in Montpellier, France, in 1805, and was buried in a softwood coffin.

The **Chapel of the Holy Relics** of the Anglo-Bavarian langue is in an alcove off the Provence Chapel, near the stairs down to the crypt, its prize possession being a wooden carving of St John the Baptist, the cathedral's patron saint, rescued from the *Great Carrack,* the ship in which the Order left Rhodes in 1522.

Art lovers may appreciate the *Beheading of St John,* painted by Caravaggio and claimed to be Malta's most important work of art. The artist was created a knight in 1608, but expelled from the Order after

KEY TO VALLETTA MAP

1 Archbishop's Palace
2 Auberge d'Aragon
3 Auberge de Bavarie
4 Auberge de Castille
5 Auberge d'Italie
6 Auberge de Provence
7 Embassy of the Order of St John
8 Government Craft Centre
9 Grand Master's Palace & Armoury
10 House of Representatives
11 Department of Information
12 Malta Library
13 Manoel Theatre
14 Mediterranean Conference Centre
   and Malta Experience
15 Ministry of Foreign Affairs
16 National Museum of Archaeology
17 National Museum of Fine Arts
☎ Telemalta

18 War Museum
Church, Cathedral:
19 St Andrew's Ch
20 St Barbara's Ch
21 St Catherine's Ch
22 St John's Co-Cathedral
23 St Paul's Anglican Cathedral
24 St Paul's Shipwreck
**Embassy, Consulate,
   High Commission:**
25 Austria
26 Belgium
27 Canada
28 Denmark
29 Finland
30 Netherlands
31 Sweden
32 Switzerland

Key to map on pages 164-5

he attacked another knight.

The **floor** is no less ornate, holding more than 400 memorial slabs to the dead knights who lay beneath them. But these are no ordinary slabs; each is a mosaic of marbles of many colours, reproducing the heraldic arms of their owners.

In the **museum,** open Mon-Sat 0930-1300, 1500-1730, are the ceremonial robes of many of the grand masters, some of the lavish gifts made the knights made on their admission to the Order, and the Belgian-woven tapestries, based on paintings by Poussin and Rubens, which are hung in the main cathedral for the feast of St John on 24 June. Grand Master Ramón Perellos paid for them, and as a small token is depicted on one.

Returning to Republic Street we soon enter **Great Siege Square,** where the Law Courts stand on the site of the **Auberge d'Auvergne,** destroyed during the Greater Siege this century. Beyond lies **Republic Square,** known as Queen's Square in colonial days, and where Queen Victoria still sits in stone effigy. Behind her, in the **Malta Library** (usually open Mon-Sat 0830-1300), are most of the archives of the Università and the Order of St John; Napoleon ordered them to be burned but, as with Hitler and Paris, somebody with a sense of history disobeyed the command.

Republic Street leads into **Palace Square** – St George's Square under the British – where 33 dissident Maltese were executed on Napoleon's orders in 1798. On the north were the barracks of the

Grand Master's Guard, recently used as offices of the Libyan People's Institute and Cultural Centre. After the US air attack on Tripoli, Libya fired a missile at the US navigation beacon on the Italian island of Lampedusa. It missed, but it reminded the Maltese that the beacon had earlier been on their islands and they could have been dragged into somebody else's war. Relations with Libya worsened after a Maltese oil rig drilled in waters that Libya claimed, so Libya protested by banning Maltese exports, Malta's retaliation to which included the closing of Libya's offices on Palace Square.

On the south side of the square is the Grand Master's Palace, now the House of Representatives and the seat of the Maltese Government.

GRAND MASTER'S PALACE

The palace stands on a site given to the Order by the Inguanez family, which is today the oldest surviving of Maltese aristocratic families; the Inguanezes asked a price of five grains of wheat and a glass of water to be offered in person by the first inhabitant, Grand Master Pietro del Monte (1568-72). Every successive grand master lived here, until von Hompesch surrendered the islands to Napoleon.

The building is of a rather gaunt design, another example of the work of Girolamo Cassar, and today its 292ft (89m) frontage carries three small pieces of history; the two **citations** to Malta during World War Two, one from King George VI awarding the George Cross, and the other from President Roosevelt praising Malta for its stand against Hitler and Mussolini. The third plaque is in Malti and commemorates independence on *21 ta'Settembru 1964.* And the south-western wall, facing Republic Square, has one of the largest continuous first-floor (2nd floor US) wooden balconies in the islands.

The main entrance leads into the **Neptune Courtyard,** which in turn leads to the **Armoury,** one of the most spectacular museums of ancient weaponry in the world. Among the 6,000 items on display that remain from the original 25,000 pieces stored here during the Order's sovereignty (from 1551 all armour was kept in one spot and maintained at common expense) are Valette's half-armour and the sword of the corsair Dragut. In modern times the Armoury has become home to an excellent collection of toy soldiers fighting a selection from famous battles in world history.

Tickets. Entry, Mon-Sat 1 Oct-15 Jun, 0830-1300, 1400-1630; no afternoon opening Jun-Oct; closed Sun, &; fee 15c adults. The Armoury ticket office also issues tickets for the first-floor **State Rooms.** Here, amid the opulence of the elected monarchy, you can see lifesize portraits of several grand masters hanging on the walls, flanked by suits of their armour. The **Throne Room,** known as the Hall of St Michael and St George in colonial times, was the Order's

Marsamxett Harbour

St MICHAEL'S COUNTERGUARD

St MICHAEL'S BASTION

St ANDREW'S BASTION

SPENCER'S BASTION

SALVATORE BASTION

St Andrew's St

Sappers St

74

M.A.Vassalli St

Matija Preti Sq

Marsamxett St

Carmelite St

St Mark's St

St Patrick's St

Windmill St

17

Old Mint St

St JOHN COUNTERGUARD

29

Medina St

St JOHN'S CAVALIER

Old Bakery St

Orchard St

19

Strait St

South St

Pope Pius V St

16   6

Carts St

St John's St

St Lucia St

City Gate

Republic St

Gt Siege Sq

Republic Square

20

Zachary St

St JAMES'S CAVALIER

Victory St

32

31 28
      30

St John Sq

22

12

21   5

Merchants St

8

Medina St

4

11   St Paul's St

72

24

St JAMES'S COUNTERGUARD

71

St Ursula St

Girolamo Cassar St

70   73

Battery St

St Anthony St

East St

St BARBARA'S BASTION

Lascaris Hill

SCALE

| 0 | 100 | 200 | 300 | 400 metres |

| 0 | 100 | 200 | 300 | 400 | 500 | 600 | 700 | 800 | 900 feet |

KEY TO HOTELS

70 British
71 Castille
72 Cumberland
73 Grand Harbour
74 Osborne

Key on page 162

St SEBASTIAN BASTION

ENGLISH CURTAIN

St Michael's St

West St

Bounty St

Old Mint St

3

St Charles St

Bull St

Bakery St

St Christopher's St

FRENCH CURTAIN

Strait St

Fountain St

St Joseph's St

St George St

Republic St

St Elmo Pl

18

St GREGORY CURTAIN

St GREGORY BASTION

BALL'S BASTION

FORT St ELMO

ABERCROMBIE'S BASTION

Republic St

Frederick St

85

St Dominic's St

St Nicholas's St

Old Hospital St

North St

ABERCROMBIE'S CURTAIN

Merchants St

St Christopher's St

St Paul's St

14

St LAZARUS'S BASTION

St Ursula's St

26

Mediterranean St

St LAZARUS'S CURTAIN

Old Wells St

N

Grand Harbour

VALLETTA

supreme court; as its name implies it now holds the presidential throne. Nearby, the **Gallery** still has seven vast paintings of British royalty hanging on the walls.

Manoel Theatre. A little way north along Old Theatre Street stands the Manoel Theatre, started and finished in 1731 by the Portuguese Grand Master Antonio Manoel de Vilhena, whose statue graces the foyer. It was out of use and favour for 96 years from 1866, at one stage serving as a beggars' home, but now in restoration it is claimed to be the oldest theatre in the Commonwealth. The home of the National Theatre of Malta, it is worth a visit either to see the building itself — there are guided tours Mon-Fri at 1045, 1130 and 1630 — or to see live theatre or opera. The booking office is open Mon-Fri 1000-1200, 1600-1900, and tickets are much cheaper than for similar theatres in continental Europe.

Carmelite Church. Turn into Old Mint Street and you see the dome of the Carmelite Church, which dominates the Valletta skyline from Sliema. This dome is unusual in that it is not circular; its north-west to south-east diameter is less than its north-east to south-west.

And north-west of it, on West St, **St Paul's Anglican Cathedral** stands on the site of the Auberge d'Allemagne, the German Auberge, demolished in 1838. Queen Adelaide, the widow of William IV of England, gave from her own pocket the £10,000 needed for the building, which was completed in 1841. The organ? It came from Chester Cathedral.

Auberges. When the Order of St John moved into the newly-built Valletta it had seven auberges or hostelries for its langues, for by then Henry VIII of England had abolished the eighth langue, that of England. Only four of the auberges remain and of them only that of Provence, on the corner of Republic and Cart streets, is open to the public, in its role as the National Museum of Archaeology, mentioned above.

The oldest survivor is the **Auberge d'Aragon** in Independence Square, now serving as government offices; the grandest is the **Auberge de Castille y León** on Castille Place, formerly British Army HQ and now the Prime Minister's office. It was built for Grand Master Emmanuel Pinto de Fonseca (1741-'73), who was Portuguese, not Castillian. The **Auberge d'Italie** is today's General Post Office on Merchants Street and is undoubtedly the least spectacular from the outside — yet that's the one Napoleon chose for his palace.

Old Theatre Street's extension on the other side of Republic St is known as Old Treasury St, the setting every weekday morning for a **street market** which overflows into Merchants Street. The next parallel road on the southern side is St Paul's St where you find the church of **St Paul Shipwrecked,** whose right front door has a motif recalling the legend of the snake emerging from the fire (see chapter

13). The church is closed 1300-1600 Mon-Sat, but at any other time you can see the gilded wooden statue of the saint which is carried in procession through the streets on 10 February, the Feast of St Paul Shipwrecked, which the Maltese believe to be the anniversary of the event.

St Paul's St ends in Old Hospital St, an unglamorous name for what was one of the greatest achievements of the Hospitaller Knights.

SACRED INFIRMARY

The Sacred Infirmary was the inspired work of the brothers Cotoner, Rafael being Grand Master from 1660 to 1663, and his successor Nícolas from 1663 to 1680.

The Great Ward is the infirmary's principal feature, for not only did it have the two longest rooms in 17th-cent Europe — one above the other, 502ft long by 36ft wide (152.6m by 11m) — but it was renowned as the best hospital in the world, drawing its patients from the aristocracy of Europe.

Three centuries ago, the patients ate their meals off silver plate in the manner to which the knights themselves had become accustomed for decades, while the surgeons boiled their instruments before use, believing it made operations less painful but not realising they were probably the first doctors in the world to practise sterilization. Yet there were other lessons in hygiene that the surgeons had not learned, for Black Death struck the islands in 1675, 11 years after ravaging London, and killed 11,000 people including several patients in the Sacred Infirmary.

French theft. Napoleon's generals stole the silver plate from here as well as from the cathedral, melting it down and using the raw metal to pay the troops during the dictator's ill-fated campaign into Egypt.

British stables. During the British rule, the infirmary became a military hospital, with the lower part of the great ward later seeing use as a stable for horses. In 1919 the building became the headquarters of the Malta Constabulary — a police training college is still across the road outside — to be abandoned in 1940 at the start of the Greater Siege. The place was derelict until restoration in the 1970s when most of it became the Mediterranean Conference Centre.

Mediterranean Conference Centre. A major fire severely damaged the centre's Republic Hall in 1987 but it reopened in 1989 incorporating several improvements, such as a large stage which backs onto Old Hospital St and therefore allows access for major exhibits in commercial promotions. The new hall is a splendid modern theatre with seating for 654, built to a design that has character in keeping with its setting in the historic hospital: one of the first events staged after the refit was a meeting of the Order of the Knights of St John.

Beneath the theatre is a new auditorium used for performances and presentations to smaller audiences, and the smart **Valletta Restaurant** is open Mon-Fri 1130-1600.

Exhibition hall. The centre's exhibition hall, **Dar-il-Wiri,** (&), was the upper of those two identical rooms forming the Great Ward in the original hospital. Today it's used as an occasional exhibition gallery, its high and flat ceiling giving plenty of space, while the lower room, now about 20ft shorter and much lower under its barrel-vaulted stone ceiling, serves as a banqueting hall of immense proportions for charity events, commercial functions, or government promotions. It's used about once a month with up to 250 guests paying up to Lm25 for a ticket, which may include a brass band, waiters in period costume, and a fireworks display from Fort St Elmo.

The lower room still retains traces of coats of arms painted on the walls, each with the number of the appropriate bed, from the days of the Sacred Infirmary's era of grandeur.

Entry. When not in use, both halls are open to the public, free, by asking a security guard in the entrance to the building.

The Malta Experience. Upstairs, an excellent audio-visual show brings to life Malta's history from prehistoric times to the present. Shows start on the hour from 1100 to 1500, Mon-Fri, and at 1100 and 1200 on Sat, with headphones for the commentary of your choice in English, Italian, German, French, Norwegian or Dutch. Shows last 50 minutes, and the Malta Experience costs Lm1.

The **Fort St Elmo** you see today was rebuilt after the Great Siege, with further work in 1687, 1790 and 1871-'75, and is not open to the public, which means you cannot see the tomb of Captain Ball, the first British administrator. But an annexe, holding the **War Museum,** is open. This is an unusual attraction, its exhibits collected and displayed by the National Museum Association which is independent of the government; entry is by purchase of the 50c handbook, which tells the story of the Greater Siege in words and pictures; &. The main exhibit is undoubtedly *Faith,* one of the three Gloster Gladiator biplanes of the RAF which fought off the Italian air force during the opening raids of World War Two. Wingless she may be, but she shows how ill-prepared Britain was in 1939 and into 1940.

Other exhibits include parts of allied and axis war planes, such as the engine of a Spitfire which was lost over Gozo in 1942 because one oil pipe was ruptured. There is *Husky,* the Jeep that General Eisenhower used before his invasion of Sicily in July 1943 — and you may even see the George Cross that George VI gave to the island.

OTHER SIGHTS OF VALLETTA

The **Museum of Fine Arts,** on the corner of South and Old Mint streets, was originally a private house in early Valletta, but the Order took it over to accommodate some of its knights, remodelling it in

The Inland Sea is really an oversized paddling-pool; through the tunnel is the other sea.

1761-'63. The building was the official home to both French and British admirals on the Malta station during Malta's colonial times.

As a museum its main exhibit is a collection of religious paintings, with Room 8 holding some of the largest canvases in the art world. Entry, summer, daily, 0830-1330, 1400-1700; winter, 0830-1300, 1400-1630.

The **Church of Our Lady of Victory** commemorates the end of the Great Siege and stands on Victory Square near the Auberge de Castille; this is where Valette's body lay until the co-cathedral was finished.

The **Lascaris War Rooms** in the Great Ditch, with access from Great Siege Rd, have been prepared as a museum to show the command bunker used during the Greater Siege, and where the attack on Sicily was planned, marking the Allied forces' first foothold in continental Europe after Hitler's conquest.

Here in Valletta you are in one of the most strongly fortified cities in the world, excluding the concrete monstrosities of the 20th cent. You can comfortably walk around the **fortifications** in half a day, allowing time to look out across Marsamxett and Grand harbours, to study the cannons used as bollards along Barreira Wharf where the fish market has replaced the quarantine area, and to begin to appreciate something of the history of this remarkable city. Finally, why not relax in the Upper or Lower **Barraca Gardens** and look at those other fortresses across the water, St Angelo and Ricasoli?

FLORIANA

Grand Master Antoine de Paule saw the threat of another Turkish attack in 1634, and welcomed the architect Paolo Floriani whom Pope Urban VIII sent over. Floriani's defensive lines protecting Valletta's landward approach were begun in de Paule's last year, 1636, but halted to allow for work on the Margherita Lines behind the Three Cities. Almost a century passed before Floriani's lines were completed, leaving a large open area beyond the defences, a 'killing ground' which an enemy army invaded at its peril. With the defences and the killing ground in place, Grand Master Antonio Manoel de Vilhena laid out the town of Floriana, his Portuguese ancestry explaining the architecture which wouldn't be out of place on a main avenue in Lisbon.

Pall Mall. Vilhena kept the special recreation area that Jean Lascaris Castellar, de Paule's successor, had created: an alley where the over-energetic knights could play the ball game of *pallamaglio*, 'ball-mallet,' later known in English as pall mall. Floriana's main street is still known as The Mall, and nearby are the **Maglio Gardens,** with Vilhena's statue presiding over them — though they were the work of Castellar.

The large open area in front of **St Publius's Church,** named from the Roman governor who became Malta's first bishop, was the underground granary of the Order of St John, with each bottle-shaped silo capped by a large coin-shaped stone.

Floriana's other attractions are the **Argotti Botanic Gardens,** noted for their cacti, and the RAF memorial just off The Mall.

THE THREE CITIES

The three cities south of Grand Harbour have seven names. Before the Order of St John arrived the cities were L'Isla (or L'Isola) on the promontory between today's French and Dockyard creeks, Birgù at the base of the narrow point ending in Fort St Angelo, and Bormla at the head of Dockyard Creek and virtually joining the other two cities.

After the Great Siege the Order renamed them respectively **Invitta,** the Unconquered; **Vittoriosa,** in honour of the victory; and **Cospicua,** for the conspicuous role the town played in the defence. To complicate matters, L'Isla (Invitta) was later renamed Senglea from Grand Master Claude de la Sèngle, and that's the name that has stuck.

The Maltese today use all seven names, but Invitta is rare, and they're not keen on the 'Three Cities' title which Napoleon invented.

War damage. The British developed the old Gallery Creek of the knights' era into the biggest dockyard in the Mediterranean and so made the Three Cities a prime target for the Luftwaffe; most of the houses had been destroyed in the Great Siege and most of their successors were flattened in the Greater Siege, but the area has been rebuilt so tastefully you'd not guess it. Remarkably, many of the major buildings escaped the Axis bombs.

L'Isla, Invitta, Senglea. The Church of Maria Bambina, the 'Nativity of Our Lady,' in the Parish Square, was a victim of World War Two but has been rebuilt, its impressive square façade carrying reproductions of the scrolls of honour of the knights who were killed in 1565 defending **Fort St Michael** at the tip of the peninsula. The fort was demolished in 1922 and has given way to the Safe Haven Garden, but one single watchtower survives, with the eye and ear of Osiris keeping guard over Grand Harbour. Beneath this little belvedere you may just see the remains of the anchoring point of Valette's great harbour chain of 1565.

Birgù, Vittoriosa. The name of the 'Town of the Castle,' *Il Borgo del Castello,* had been corrupted to the Malti **Birgù** by the time the knights of St John arrived and made it their capital city.

They built their first seven modest auberges here, but only four survive: those of France, Auvergne and Provence; Castile; Portugal; and England, all to the east and south-east of Victory Square. The three city gates are still intact with their carvings restored; the Advanced Gate of 1722, the Covered Gate (Couvre Porte) built a year later, and the Vittoriosa Gate of 1727, leading into Triq Il-Boffa where stands the notorious Palazzo del Sant'Uffizio, the **Inquisitor's Palace,** open summer daily 0830-1330, 1400-1700 (closed Tues, Thur, Sat, Sun afternoons); winter, 0830-1300, 1400-1630, for 15c. To avoid confusion, remember that the building over by the Dingli cliffs is the Inquisitor's *Summer* Palace.

Museum of the macabre. The palace was enlarged in the 16th and 17th cents from a much older building, but retains the **Bir tas-Skieken,** the horrible knife pit where many victims ended their days. Farewell messages still adorn the walls in death row, and elsewhere there are coats of arms and dates of office of all the inquisitors, save the date of departure of the last, Julius Carpineo, who left in too much of a hurry when Napoleon arrived. The Inquisition was one of those gruesome inventions of the Catholic Church for suppressing heresy, and was responsible for the slaughter of uncounted thousands of American Indians as well as large numbers of Europeans.

Death by fire. Vittoriosa's parish church of St Lawrence contains a large tableau of the saint preparing for his martyrdom by fire; the townspeople carry this figure through the streets on the Sunday nearest 10 August. Roger the Norman, who snatched the islands from Islam, founded the original church on this site, and the present building, dating from the 16th cent, served the Order until St John's conventual church (later the Co-Cathedral) in Valletta, was finished. A small oratory across the square holds the hat and sword that Valette wore for the 1565 victory parade.

Fort St Angelo. At the tip of the peninsula stands the mighty Fort St Angelo, officially with no public access following the closure of the hotel on the site.

Roger the Norman built a chapel here in 1090, and the church of Sant'Angelo was completed in 1274. A small palace was on the headland when the Order of St John arrived, and the grand masters used it as their residence until after the Great Siege; four of the earlier masters were buried here but were moved to St John's Co-cathedral with the building of Valletta.

The present structure is late 17th cent and includes the dungeons where the knights imprisoned their galley slaves; some of the slaves mutinied here in 1530. The Spanish builder Carlos Grunenberg incorporated much of the Chapel of St Anne where the first Grand Master prayed, and the British added an enormous Maltese Cross to the outside of the bastion when it served as the 'stone frigate' *HMS St Angelo*, a fully-commissioned 'ship' of the Royal Navy. The cross, like the Navy, has gone.

Bormla, Cospicua. The Church of the Immaculate Conception was the only part of residential Cospicua (pronounced kos-*pik*-wa) left standing after the Second World War, but the historic Margherita and Cotonera lines survived. Grand Master Lascaris Castellar started the **Margherita Lines** in 1639 when the architect working on the Floriana defences realised that an enemy who managed to seize Santa Margherita hill, south-east of Vittoriosa, could fire on the Three Cities and dominate Grand Harbour. The work began straight away, and three of the bastions were finished by 1641 when the Turks plundered Gozo and briefly landed on Malta itself. The Turks threatened attack again in 1645 and in 1669.

After this last scare, the grand master decided that the Margherita Lines were not adequate, and he financed the start of the **Cotonera Lines** beyond the first defences. These massive bulwarks with eight bastions were to stretch in a semicircle for three miles (5km) and enclose sufficient land to hold the entire civilian population of 40,000 and their livestock. Nicolas Cotoner died before the project was completed, and the funds died with him, which meant that the ravelins — V-shaped outworks — were never built although the remainder of the plan was completed, including the **Żabbar Gate,** which now stands isolated on a traffic island.

AROUND RICASOLI

Kalkara. Kalkara is not part of the Three Cities but is an overgrown fishing village that's become fashionable. Beside it is **Fort Ricasoli** (pronounced ri-*cah*-s'li) which Giovanni Ricasoli gave to the Order of St John in return for his admission as a knight. Building began in 1670 and with its compound, stretching back 500m from Gallows Point,

Ricasoli was at one time the largest fort in the British Commonwealth. Mutineers blew up the magazine in 1807, a storm did more damage in 1821, and today the vast fortress is near-derelict, its only point of interest being the large carved columns which flank the locked main gate.

The Hundred-Ton Gun. From the end of the Great Siege until the development of missiles, the problem with making guns has always been to have one which would outrange and outshoot your enemy's. By the time your planned 10-ton gun is ready, your enemy has a 12-tonner, so you start a 15-tonner which again comes too late. Between 1865 and 1877 gun calibre (the diameter of the barrel) rose from 7 inches to 17.75in; and the weight of the barrel went from 6.5 tons to 102.25, with a massive leap from 38 to 81 tons.

The British firm of W.G. Armstrong of Newcastle-upon-Tyne built the monster 102-ton — commonly called the Hundred-Ton gun — in 1877 but the Admiralty was working on its 81-tonner, and refused the larger weapon. So Armsrtong sold two to the Italian Navy. As soon as Their Lordships realised their mistake they decided that Britain must have the Hundred-Tonner as well, two of them to be sited on Malta to deter the Italian Navy, another on the Rock of Gibraltar, and the fourth at Dover. Another gun foundry offered plans for a 160-tonner and a 220-tonner, but soon found that technology had reached its limits with the Hundred-Tonner.

Specification. Armstrong's monster had a barrel 32ft 7in long (9.96m) capable of firing a 1,995lb (904.7kg) shell a maximum range of 14,000yds (13.78km) with a muzzle speed of 1,548ft-sec (472m-sec). The shell could go through 26in (67cm) of solid wrought iron at a range of 1,000m.

By 1881 the Malta Garrison had decided the guns should command the approaches to Valletta, one on the Rinella Battery near Ricasoli, and the other at the Cambridge Battery near Fort Tigné. The first gun arrived in Malta on 10 September 1882 (the second came the following August), was offloaded in Valletta onto a sled and dragged to its site at Rinella, getting there on 4 December.

The guns were fired only in practise, and in 1904 the Cambridge Battery was abandoned; today neither the gun nor the battery remains. The Hundred-Ton gun at Rinella Battery was fired for the last time on 5 May 1905, then left to nature. As I write, the underground magazine rooms are derelict and the gun itself is rusting, with little of its black paint left.

The future. But there are plans for the monster gun. The conservation group *Din Liart Helwa*, has done some work, and the Mediterranean Film Studios wants to restore it as a tourist attraction and put a living museum and video show in the magazine. Until this is done, **access** to the gun is on foot (&), through a crude metal-faced door at the west end of a long stone wall fronting the road between Ricasoli and Fort St Rocco.

Mediterranean Film Studios. The Rank Organisation came to Malta in 1951 to film *The Malta Story*, and realised the island's photographic potential. In 1964 a British special-effects man, Jim Hole, started Malta Film Facilities with a surface shooting tank as his main attraction. This particular tank is 400ft (122m) by 302ft (92m) max, on which film producers can float their ships, be they full-scale or models, and simulate any kind of weather. But *this* tank is the only one in the world that doesn't need articifial backdrops: it has the Mediterranean Sea and, from certain camera angles, the ships in the tank can appear to be in mid-ocean, and have a natural horizon.

You must have seen the tank. It was used in *Christopher Columbus, Orca The Killer Whale, Shout At The Devil, Raise The Titanic*, and many other films, plus television commercials and the BBC television series *Howards' Way*.

Jim Hole's company, now the Mediterranean Film Studios, has another tank, 351ft (107m) in diameter, for underwater shots; it was built specially for *Raise The Titanic* and holds 9,500,000 gallons (36,000 cu m) of sea water. And you can see both tanks from the Hundred-Ton gun.

Special effects. You want to explode a speeding car? The studio's special effects and locations have appeared in around 100 productions, including *Casino Royale, Murphy's War, Sea Wolf, Warlords of*

KEY TO HOTELS

Key to maps on pages 158, 175, 17●

Atlantis, Force Ten From Navarone, Airline, and many commercials shown around the world. It also built the US$1,200,000 **Popeye Village** in Anchor Bay in six weeks for the 1979 film *Popeye.* You can go and see Popeye Village but the studio is **not open** to the public.

AROUND MARSAMXETT HARBOUR

Ħamrun. Ħamrun's main interest to the visitor is its shops, which are almost as good as those in Sliema and Valletta but with far less visitors. There is a thriving cut bloom nursery at the Żammit Gardens, and towards Santa Venera a craft centre where blind people produce

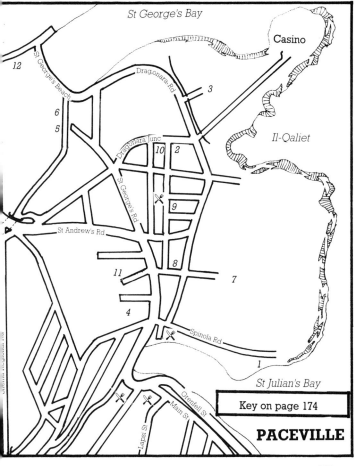

SLIEMA

Key on page 174

baskets.

Qormi. The large village of Qormi (pronounced ¦or-mi) on the fringe of Valletta was earlier known as Casal Fornaro, the Baker's Village, and the name still has roots in the Italian for 'oven' — forno. Among the interesting old-town architecture amid the narrow streets is the Palazzo Stagno of 1589.

Sliema. Sliema is the dominant town on the north shore of Marsamxett Harbour and holds some of the most popular holiday attractions in the islands. The town takes its name from the greeting *Sliem!* which sailors called to the Church of Our Lady at Tigné Point; the word comes from the Arabic greeting *Salaam*. The Order of St John built Fort Tigné in 1793 as its last major work, but it wrapped the defences around the church so that just five years later the Maltese had to destroy Our Lady's church in order to train the fort's guns on the French troops occupying Valletta. The fort is now derelict, but a small circular tower, It-Torri, built by Emmanuel de Rohan (1775-'97), survives. Nearby is a reverse osmosis desalination plant for the Water Works Board.

Sliema today, with its suburbs of **St Julian's, Ġzira** (jiz-*ear*-uh) and **Paceville** (*patchy*-vil) is the heart of tourist Malta with many of the self-catering flats, the pick of the restaurants, the prime of the nightlife, and many of the best hotels, including the Malta Hilton and the Dragonara Palace, the latter noted for its casino and enormous pool.

Although Sliema's promenade is called The Strand, there is no 'strand' here at all. The beaches front onto the open sea on the other side of Sliema protected by a fence, a locked gate, and a sign declaring *Tigné Beach; for members of Union Club and Marsa Sports Club.* Season tickets are available at the gate, which is open 0930-1830 in summer. If you want **water sports,** try St George's Bay where you can rent a canoe for 25c, a paddle boat for 50c, or go windsurfing for 75c, all per hour. St George's and St Andrew's barracks, formerly home for British troops, are now flats for Maltese families.

Or you can go boat-gazing. From The Strand to Manoel Island, and on around Ta'Xbiex (tash-beesh), luxury yachts and motor cruisers are at their moorings, with the impressive skyline of Valletta forming a picturesque background.

Manoel Island. A short causeway joins Manoel Island to the mainland, but you can also reach it by ferry from The Strand. The main attraction is a factory making glass souvenirs, but there is also the crumbling stonework of Fort Manqel, built in 1726 by the Portuguese Grand Master Manoel de Vilhena and designed by Réné Tigné, the Knight Grand Cross who also designed Fort Tigné. Manoel Island has a quarantine station dating from 1613, and the headquarters of the Yacht Club, which claims to have the finest moorings in the Mediterranean.

21: SOUTH MALTA

Żabbar to Żurrieq

THE SOUTHERN TIP OF MALTA is dominated by the urban overflow from Valletta into Paola and Tarxien; by the island republic's two airfields, whose runways are only a mile (1.6km) apart; and by the activities of the freeport of Kalafrana.

Żabbar. Żabbar's twin attractions are the Hompesch Arch built in 1798 on the road to Fgura and Paola, and the Żabbar Gate in the Cotonera Lines on the Cospicua road. The village grew in the 17th cent as the threat of pirate raids diminished, and a new village meant scope for a new church. Our Lady of Grace is another on the massive scale, dominating the centre of the village; work began in 1641 and lasted for 40 years. Beside it is a small museum of religious art, in fact a collection of paintings giving thanks to the Virgin of Graces for delivery from storm or piracy. Ask the parish priest if you want to see the paintings.

Marsaskala. A good road runs from Żabbar east to the small village of Marsaskala which fills the available flat land around Marsaskala Bay. It's a colourful place but the beach is tiny.

St Thomas's Tower, a legacy of the Order of St John and now converted into the It-Torri restaurant, looks down on Marsaskala and on **St Thomas's Bay**, a resort and a beach in the making. A narrow road leads on south to the 100-ft chalk cliffs of Il-Munxar.

North of Marsaskala the knights' **Fort Leonardo**, much strengthened during the Second World War, is derelict.

Żejtun. South of Żabbar lies the older village of Żejtun, the only community to resist the demands of the inquisitors, and it was the first village that the invading Turks occupied in 1565. It has an impressive parish church dating from 1692 as well as the original St Gregory's Church of 1463, which has several additions in differing styles. Neighbouring Għaxaq (*ash*-ak) has a church dating from 1655.

Għaxaq lies on the main road from Paola in the north to Birżebbuġa in the south. **Paola,** sometimes spelled 'Pawla,' is a newish dormitory suburb of Valletta built on a similar grid-plan. The town of more than 12,000 inhabitants has some light industry, but for the tourist the main attraction is the **Hypogeum,** described in chapter 11. Paola merges with **Tarxien,** noted for its Tarxien Temples, also described in chapter 11.

Birżebbuġa. South, then, to Birżebbuġa (bear-zee-*boo*-zha) on Marsaxlokk Bay, a summer resort popular with foreigners and those Maltese who have a second home, this being a favourite place for it. It's colourful, with a pleasant but small beach at St George's Bay to the north, and a better beach at Pretty Bay to the south. Sadly, the sight of Kalafrana's giant dock equipment and large container ships means Pretty Bay isn't pretty.

Birżebbuġa's name means 'Well of Olives,' the Malti *bir* being identical to the Arabic for 'well.' There are few olives today, but you can see some of the island's history in the Pinto Battery on the promenade, St Julian's Tower on the headland opposite, and at Fort Benghisa (ben-*ee*-sa) on the southern cliffs, all relics of the Order of St John.

The area also has some of Malta's more intriguing relics: **Għar Dalam,** the 'Cave of Darkness,' and the inaccessible Bronze Age village of **Borġ In-Nadur** with its megalithic wall and cart ruts, both detailed in chapter 11.

Marsaxlokk. East lies the pretty village of Marsaxlokk (*mar*-sash-lok), where the Turks landed at the start of the Great Siege in 1565. After defeating the invaders the knights of St John strengthened the area around the bay with Fort St Lucien and Fort Delimara, the latter also known as Zondadari Tower from its builder, Grand Master

Wingless she may be, but 'Faith' of the faithful three lives on in the War Museum in Fort St Elmo.

Zondadari (1720-'22). But the defences were useless when the will to resist had gone, so Napoleon calmly brought his fleet into the bay in 1789 and put his troops ashore.

The village's name is a corruption of *marsascirocco,* the south wind, the only one which could enter the near-landlocked Marsaxlokk Bay. The new breakwater has tamed the scirocco, but the wind can still throw an occasional surprise.

This is the best place to see large numbers of the Maltese fishing boat known as the *luzzu,* and there's usually a small market on the waterfront.

The Delimara Peninsula. You'll probably need to ask for the road to Delimara; I have been directed to drive the wrong way along a one-way street, with no other option apparent. Don't try looking for the **Tas Silġ** hilltop site unless you're a committed archeologist, but if you head south along the tarmac road you should find on your left, opposite the new power station, a narrow lane leading to **Peter's Pool,** a pleasant bathing-spot in a secluded bay facing east.

Kalafrana. South of Pretty Bay, Kalafrana was the site of the seaplane base in World War Two and is now Malta's second port, built with help from China and handling tankers and container ships. The large new breakwater keeps the Scirocco wind out of the bay.

Għar Hassan. Beyond Kalafrana on Malta's southernmost point is Hassan's Cave, where you can let your imagination run loose. The cave is well signed, right to the pathway leading down over the cliff edge. Access is unrestricted in the absence of any person to operate the government franchise, and ♿ visitors can negotiate the path, but a torch would be useful in the cave.

Hassan was an Arab who lived in this cavern long after Roger the Norman had reclaimed the islands for Christianity. He clambered to the surface by night to abduct the local beauties one by one, and kept them imprisoned deep in the grotto before lowering them by rope to a waiting boat to begin their long voyage into slavery. Hassan's enterprise failed, says local legend, when one brave girl urged him to make love to her so she could seize his dagger and kill him.

On the plateau above stands **Ħal Far** airfield, Malta's only military base and one of the three aerodromes used in World War Two; the others were Luqa and Ta'Qali.

I find the road from Ħal Far to Żurrieq the least interesting in the islands, but Żurrieq makes up for it.

Żurrieq. Most villages whose names begin with Ż display their ancient origins − Żabbar is the exception − and Żurrieq can trace its beginnings back to the Roman era though the only relic remaining is part of a Punic temple incorporated into the wall of a house beside the parish church.

The early 14th-cent **Ħal Millieri Chapel** at the north of the village is an example of what a builder does when he's not sure of the strength of his materials. In this case the builder didn't know the loadbearing limits of the globigerina limestone so the arches are no more than an arm's span wide.

Much of the honey-coloured limestone used in modern architecture is quarried at **Mqabba** (im-ḷabba); you may catch a glimpse of it from the air, but a closer approach at ground level shows exactly how the building blocks are cut from the solid rock with giant circular saws.

North-east of Żurrieq is Kirkop, standing beside the main runway of Luqa Airport; near the south end of the tunnel under the runway is the former gun-running Constellation aircraft that is now an unusual restaurant.

West of Żurrieq is **Qrendi,** (ḷrendi) a picturesque village with rambling streets that defy your sense of direction. In Tower St is the Cavalier Tower, the only eight-sided fortress in Malta. South of the village is Il-Maqluba (ilma-ḷlooba), a large hole around 150ft (50m) deep, created when the roof of a cave collapsed.

The **Blue Grotto** is one of the main attractions of rural Malta, reached by boat from Wied Iż−Żurrieq at the end of the steep road from Żurrieq itself. Cruises around the grotto take the visitor first into Zazu's Cave, then under The Leg, an intriguing natural arch rather like the flying buttress of a cathedral, and finally into the Blue Grotto itself.

The name isn't just a good publicity hype. As you cruise slowly towards the grotto and dip your hand into the water, you notice it appears pale blue due to the diffusion of light. Blood−red anemones clinging to the rocks just below the waterline also have a faint blueish tinge. A green chain-link fence on the road up from Wied Iż-Żurrieq marks a parking area from where you have a splendid clifftop view of The Leg, but not of the grotto.

The boat fare is Lm1.75 per person, but boats don't go to the cave when there's an onshore wind; if in doubt, ☎826947 to check.

And west of Qrendi along a mixture of roads, are the two most impressive ancient temples on the island of Malta: **Ħaġar Qim** and **Mnajdra,** detailed in chapter 11.

22: CENTRAL MALTA

Behind the Victoria Lines

MALTA'S GEOLOGY SHOWS A LARGE RIFT FAULT across the island from the headland of Rass Ir-Raħab on the west coast to just south of the Splash Park on the east. This diagonal split in the earth's crust has the high plateau to the south-east, including Malta's highest point at 826ft (252m) on the Dingli cliffs, and the lower and more fertile land to the north-west, crossed by a series of parallel hills known as the Wardija Ridge, the Bajda Ridge, the Mellieħa Ridge and the Marfa Ridge. Between the hills, deep bays indent the coast, giving ideal landing beaches for invaders.

During the Victorian era, the British reinforced the line of the rift by building forts at Binġemma, Nadur, Targa, Mosta, Għargħur, and Fort Madliena, and adding large defensive stone bastions between them, creating the formidable **Victoria Lines,** which are still visible in several places, notably between Mġarr and Rabat.

Għargħur. The most northerly village to nestle behind the protection of the Victoria Lines is Għargħur (ʹar-ʹur), where human bones are visible in a plaster moulding beneath the church altar. The moulding shows a saint, but he is not Bartholomew, the village's patron. The church has another unusual appendage outside – a sundial. Despite the endless blue skies of summer, sundials are rare in Malta; time isn't that important.

Naxxar. The road from Għargħur leads to Naxxar, which boasts a church with two dials, but these are both clock faces. One is (or was) in working order; the other is fixed, to confuse the Devil. The village's name means 'to dry,' and it is here, according to legend, that the Apostle Paul dried his clothes after his shipwreck. Better not question the accuracy too much and merely accept that every village wants to get in on the act somewhere. However, Naxxar may have a claim to be the first village in Malta to accept Christianity and could therefore be the seat of Christendom in Europe.

The Maltese **International Trade Fair** is held in Naxxar in July, and at **San Pawl Tat Targa** 800m north and near the Victoria Lines, is the Torre Tal-Kaptan, the 'Captain's Tower,' a watchtower built by the Order of St John. St Paul preached in the little village, hence its name.

Mosta. In 1833 the people of Mosta began building St Mary's Church on a prime site in the centre of the village. When they finished it in 1860 they had created the third largest dome in the world, beaten only by St Peter's in Rome and Santa Sophia in Istanbul, but in 1971 the people of Xewkija on Gozo completed an even larger dome and thrust Mosta into fourth place. Now, of course, domes are much easier to build, the world's largest as I write being the Louisiana Superdome in New Orleans, with a diameter of 680ft (207m). Britain's largest is in Perth, Scotland, at 222ft (67m) — but these are not built in self-supporting hemispheres of stone as Malta's church domes are. For a truer comparison, consider the Pantheon in Rome, in AD112, with a dome 142ft (43m) across.

It's not really true to say the church *has* a dome: St Mary's *is* a dome, topping the neo-classic circular walls, the only other feature being the façade with its six tall Ionic columns and a belfry at each side, the left belfry carrying a calendar-clock and the right a clock that marks the hours and minutes.

The Maltese people love their churches, and lavish great wealth on them. Most were built, like Mosta's, with unpaid labour and financed by the parishioners at considerable personal sacrifice. The ornamental bas-relief sculpting on Mosta church's exterior hints at a lavish interior, but the reality exceeds expectation. The dome, built without any scaffolding, carries a vast painting worthy of the greatest cities of the world, and the sculpting and decor of the walls is only a little less proud. Commanding one of the six chapels is a larger-than-life tableau of the Virgin Mary which is the centrepiece at the Feast of the Assumption.

The 1,000-lb bomb which fell through the roof on 9 April 1942, and rolled across the floor without exploding or injuring any of the 300 congregation, is now on display in the vestry. The dome and floor have been repaired so well there's no trace of the damage.

Three Villages. East of Mosta are Lija, Balzan, and their sister community Attard, collectively known as the Three Villages. The trio originally lived by farming and horticulture but are now dormitory villages as they are on the western edge of the conurbation that spreads from Valletta, yet they still retain something of their earlier tranquility.

The first of the Three Villages is **Lija** whose main attraction is its splendid firework display marking the Feast of the Saviour on the Sunday after 6 August. Some people claim the Tal-Mirakli Church (Our Lady of Miracles) west of the village is the furthest you can get from the sea in Malta, but that's not so; the centre of the island is 800m south-west.

Balzan's Church of the Annunciation, built between 1669 and 1695, is particularly worth a visit when decorated for the Feast of the

Popeye Village cost US$1,200,000 to build in 1979 — plus the cost of the spinach.

Annunciation in early June. The small Church of St Roque, built during the plague, is a century older and plain in contrast. Nearby, in Three Churches St, is the private Ermina House, formerly a church.

Attard, which takes its name from the rose — you've heard of attar of roses? — has the the bougainvillea-draped **San Anton Palace,** built in lavish style by Grand Master Antoine de Paule (1623—36) and used as the seat of revolutionary government while Napoleon's troops were besieged in Valletta. It is now the official home of the President of Malta and is closed to the public, but the **San Anton Gardens** are open free every day until 1800hrs, ⅄. Walk through the gateway, built in 1882, and you enter a large garden containing many species of plants unusual to Malta, including the *phoenix canariensis,* the Canary date, and the *washingtonia robusta* from California. These, and many other specimens, are named.

Local people leave unwanted cats and kittens in the gardens, other people looking for a pet come here to choose, and many visitors bring food for the resident felines.

Birkirkara. Birkirkara, often shown on maps and road signs as B'kara, is a modern industrial town and dormitory suburb for Valletta. Its parish church of St Helena has some elegant carvings that make it the most important church in Malta in its class. The road into Santa Venera seems to hold many of Malta's motor dealers, several of whom sell cars that, in Britain, would be classics and prized by collectors.

When Valletta and its neighbour villages began to grow, the supply of fresh water became so serious a problem that Alof de Wignacourt

185

ordered the building of an aqueduct from Rabat to Valletta. The 9-mile (15km) **Wignacourt Aqueduct** was built between 1610 and 1614 and served the capital until modern methods of water supply took over. A large section of the aqueduct survives, alongside the road between Attard and Santa Venera.

Ta'Qali. The RAF fighter base at Ta'Qali (ta-¦ahli) was almost in the centre of Malta, which makes the old airfield a suitable place for the **Ta'Qali Craft Centre.** Sadly, the service buses stop on the main Attard−Rabat road, leaving the visitor a 600m walk each way. Tourist coaches drive into the centre where there is a good car park (give a tip).

The craft centre is aimed at the tourist market, producing and selling a wide range of souvenirs from delicate filigree silverwork to a full-size suit of medieval armour − to be looked at rather than worn. Here you can see pots being thrown (turned) on the wheel, glass being blown, lace being woven, iron being wrought (forged), and wood being carved.

There's no entry fee to the centre, which is housed in the original RAF nissen huts, and ♿ visitors can get around with reasonable comfort although many shops have steps. There's an on-site lavatory.

Mdina. The horizon to the west of Ta'Qali is dominated by the impressive fortress-city of Mdina, one of the smallest cities in the world and with a population fewer than 500. The residents, by the way, are the only people allowed to take cars into the city as its streets are not only short − Mdina is 400m on its longest axis − but also narrow and crooked, so archers couldn't shoot down them. In truth, Mdina is a miniature capsule of all that's good in Maltese architecture, containing five so-called palaces, some of which are now private houses; three museums; three churches; plus a chapel, a convent, and the Rennaissance Co-Cathedral of St Peter and St Paul.

The Romans saw the strategic importance of this rocky crag, and built their capital city on it, where Rabat stands today; they called it *Melita,* which was also their name for the island. The Arabs reduced Melita to the size of the present Mdina and are responsible for its present name; *medina* is Arabic for 'town,' although this town is called 'Im-deena.'

This was where Roger the Norman was acclaimed as the island's liberator in 1090; this was where Alfonso the Magnanimous of Aragon thanked the Maltese in 1428 when they gave him the 30,000 florins he needed to redeem the islands; this was where Don Mesquita lined the women and children on the city walls and persuaded Mustapha Paşa to abandon the Great Siege; and this was where the ordinary citizens rose in revolt against their French overlords in 1798. Mdina's role is important in Malta's history.

The city almost certainly took its other name, **Città Notabile,** the

N

Bastion Sq

Co-cathedral   MDINA

Magazines St

Villegaignon St

Mesquita St

Casa
Inguanez

Greeks Gate
Sq

Inguanez St

museum

rail tunnel

Roman Villa Mus

Museum Rd

Point
de Vue

Saqqajja

Racecourse St

St Augustine's St

Judge's Box

St Paul's St

Hospital St

Victory St

Main St   RABAT

Parish Sq

St Paul's Ch
grotto

St Paul's
catacombs

College St

Busket Rd

**RABAT
&
MDINA**

↓
St Agatha's catacombs

187

noteworthy city, as a reward for its stand against the Turks in the Great Siege, but some authorities claim this name was a gift from Alfonso of Aragon, while others say the name honours Carlos V of Spain who was also the Holy Roman Emperor. There is no doubt that when Valletta became the capital, Mdina took on yet another name, **Città Vecchia,** the old city, and in its quieter role it has also come to be known as the silent city, perhaps its most charming name.

Access to the old, silent, noteworthy city, on foot or in a *karrozin*, is through **Mdina Gate,** an essay in stone just begging to be photographed, which dates from 1724 in the grand mastership of Manoel de Vilhena. Above the carriageway on the inside you can see the coat of arms of Antonio de Inguanez, put here in 1886 to replace the arms the French destroyed in 1798. And the dry moat you have just crossed is not as solid as it looks, as a tunnel for the defunct railway runs beneath it.

Inside the gate lies St Publius's Square, surrounded by tall, almost windowless walls, which emphasise the silence − unless a *karrozzin* goes by, with bell tinkling and horse's hoofs clattering. On the right the former Magisterial Palace, used as a hospital for much of the British era, is now the **National Museum of Natural History,** open summer 0800-1330, winter 0830-1630 for 15c; ♿ (but steps at the door), photography forbidden.

The Benedictine Convent stands on the corner in an early-15th-cent building, then **Villegaignon St,** Mdina's main road, opens in front of you. Nicolas Durand de Villegaignon, born around 1510 in France, founded the city of Nouvelle-Genève in Brazil (when the Portuguese captured the territory they renamed the city Rio de Janeiro), before joining the Order of St John and defending Mdina against a Turkish raid 14 years before the Great Siege.

On the left is the private **Casa Inguanez,** home of the most aristocratic family in Malta and hereditary governors of Mdina before the Order of St John came. The present owner of the house has self-catering flats for rent, which may give you an excuse to see inside the house. You'll be in good company, for Alfonso the Magnanimous stayed here in 1432, and Alfonso XIII was here in 1927.

Again on the left, beyond Mesquita St, is the 17th-cent **Casa Viani,** from whose balcony the Mdina citizens threw the commander of the French garrison on 2 September 1798 for the crime of auctioning treasure looted from the Carmelite Convent, further down on the left.

And then comes **St Paul's Co-Cathedral** (♿, but steps at the door), sharing the honour of being Malta's state cathedral with St John's Co-Cathedral in Valletta. Built of warm-coloured globigerina, the cathedral dominates St Paul's Square in the centre of the tiny city, but this is a relatively new building, completed in 1702 and replacing the cathedral destroyed in the 1693 earthquake. It has preserved the Maltese tradition of having a clock on one belfry and a calendar on

This is the upper part of the Great Ward of the Sacred Infirmary.
Compare it with the lower part on page 192.

the other.

On this site, according to long-standing belief, stood the house of Publius, the Roman chief of the islands, to be replaced in the 4th century by a church which Roger the Norman restored in the 11th century – and ancient belief also claims that the Norman doors, carved from Irish bog-oak, survive in the present sacristy.

The cathedral is impressive inside, lacking the majesty of St John's in Valletta and indeed of many parish churches, but it has the royal arms of Spain, put here in 1530 when Carlos V gave Malta to the Order of St John, and under the south aisle lies the body of Lord Strickland, prime minister from 1927 to '32.

Outside, the two cannon were a gift from the British Army's Artillery Museum in Woolwich.

The **Cathedral Museum** (& after the steps) across Archbishop Square is the treasure-house for the relics we would normally expect to find in the cathedral itself; there are engravings by Dürer and Goya, and a set of silver statuettes stolen by Napoleon but redeemed. An unexpected exhibit is the cross that Godfrey de Bouillon carried on pilgrimage to Jerusalem in 1099, but the museum is an exhibit in its own right, as a former Maltese mansion of architectural merit. Entry summer 0930-1300, 1400-1730, in winter closes half hour earlier; 15c ticket also covers St John's Co-Cathedral Museum, Valletta.

Further along Villegaignon Street is the **Carmelite Convent** which earned a place in history when its bells gave the signal for the

Maltese uprising in 1789 against Napoleon's troops who had just plundered the convent's church.

The palazzos (palaces) include **Santa Sophia,** on the opposite side of St Paul's Square from the cathedral and dating from 1233 and, at the north of Villegaignon Street, the **Palazzo Falzon** or Norman House, whose ground floor rooms were built around 1495. For safety, these rooms have no windows looking onto the road, drawing light and air from the central courtyard or from the more recent first floor. The Falzon Palace is believed to be the first home of Grand Master de l'Isle Adam on his arrival in Malta in 1530, but it is now a privately-run museum of medieval life, open Mon-Fri 0900-1300, 1400-1630.

You are now almost at **Bastion Square,** Pjazza Tas-Sur, the northernmost tip of Mdina, from where you have a splendid view from Valletta in the east to Gozo in the north-west, and on a really clear day you might see the snows of Mt Etna in Sicily. No wonder the early conquerors of Malta chose this spot for their capital.

If you walk back along Magazines St you will notice Roman numerals on the houses, relics from the time when these were indeed magazines for gunpowder and shot. And at Greeks Gate Sq you'll find Greeks Gate, which takes you down into the moat and so into Rabat.

Rabat. The path from Greeks Gate leads through the Howard Gardens to the wide Museum Road, almost outside the **Roman Villa Museum,** open summer 0800-1330, winter 0830-1630 for 15c, ♿ after the steps. The Roman town house — it's not a 'villa' in the strict sense — which was excavated in 1881, revealed a wealth of mosaics and statuary, including a marble bust of the Emperor Tiberius, all on display here.

If you continue south down St Paul's St you reach **St Paul's Church** on Parish Sq. This late-17th-cent church is on the site of the Chapel of St Publius, built at the beginning of that century, but its main interest lies in the **Grotto of St Paul,** under the church; go through the doorway on the right of the church's front wall. It's nominally open 1430-1630 daily for a donation, but I recommend leaving your companion outside, as I got locked in. The grotto is legendarily the place where St Paul stayed while in Rabat, which explains the saint's large alabaster statue in the centre of the cave. Chambers have been cut into the rear wall, and another legend claims that the mineral can cure certain ills. Yet another legend states that the grotto stays the same size no matter how much stone is cut away. There's much more truth in the story about Giovanni Beneguas who came to Malta to join the Order, built the Chapel of St Publius, then decided to spend his life as a hermit in St Paul's grotto.

A street on the west side of Parish Sq leads to St Cataldus's Church and on to the signposted **St Paul's Catacombs,** not to be confused with the saint's grotto. The catacombs are 4th-cent burial chambers, open daily in summer 0830-1330, plus 1400-1700 Tues, Thur, Sat, Sun; in winter 0830-1330, 1400-1630 daily, for 15c. A little further on are **St Agatha's Catacombs,** open daily 0900-1200, 1400-1545, named from a young woman who fled from the attentions of a Roman emperor.

Two other features of interest in Rabat are the heavily-gilded barrel-vaulted ceiling of St Augustine's Church in the street of that name, and the **Judge's Grandstand,** built in 1696 for the grand masters of the day to watch the finish of the horse and donkey races of Mnarja on 29 June. The box is now incorporated in the wall of the main Mosta–Dingli road, between the main turn-off to Mdina, and the very steep and narrow alley which makes a short-cut to the silent city. Both streets meet on the tree-lined square above the Judge's Box, an area known as the **Saqqajja,** the car park for Mdina, the bus terminal for Rabat, the base for *karrozzini,* and a good spot for buying petrol.

The road from Rabat to Attard is called Racecourse Street because of its links with the Mnarja donkey races, but our road leads south, to Dingli.

Dingli. Sir Thomas Dingli, an English knight in the Order of St John, was granted permission to build a hunting lodge near the cliffs on Malta's west coast. A few Maltese people built their homes nearby, and Dingli village was founded. It now has around 2,500 people and is Malta's highest village, convenient for the splendid **Dingli Cliffs,** dominated here by the former RAF radar station.

A strip of cultivated land used as small allotment gardens lies near the bottom of the precipice but the best access to the sea is where Roger the Norman presumably landed, at Baħrija to the north-west.

There are several churches along this coast; the windswept Annunciation Chapel at Ġebel Ċiantar is now derelict, and the **Maddalena Chapel,** on the island's highest point, is used only once a year, on 22 July, the feast of St Magdalene. Legend claims that the chapel was built by a noble in 1546 as thanksgiving for his daughter's recovery from a fatal illness, and it is one of many small churches to carry an inscription warning would-be fugitives that they could not find sanctuary from the law here, as they could in larger churches.

Verdala Palace. East of Dingli, and on a separate road from Rabat, the Verdala Palace is a brilliant example of architecture from the Order of St John, with many surprises.

The palace is the president's summer residence, but is open the year round Tues and Fri, 0900-1200, 1400-1700. There's no fee, but you're expected to leave a donation for your guide; from observation 25c to 50c appears to be the rate.

Built in 1586 for Grand Master Hugues Loubenx de Verdalle, probably the most ostentatious of the elected monarchs and the only one to become a cardinal (Valette was offered the title, but refused), this is an elegant fortified medieval mansion, surrounded by a dry moat. The large front door is the first unusual feature: it has no hinges, instead swinging easily on a pivot. The main spiral staircase is another oddity: it's oval, not circular. Note the way the steps are fashioned, with each one different. Look at the steps themselves, shallow enough to allow a man to climb them in full armour, then study the ceiling over the stairs, a complex barrel-shaped ovoid with each piece of masonry specially shaped.

The ground floor (1st floor, USA) has an elegant hall leading to a superb dining room with murals showing Verdalle's rise from artillery officer to grand master and on to cardinal. The painting on the vaulted ceiling showed scenes from Greek mythology, which Lady Bonham-Carter, wife of the governor, decided did not match those on the walls. So in 1938 she had them painted over. They are now being restored with great difficulty. The room has two built-in corner cupboards made from translucent marble from a quarry in Gozo.

Marshal Tito stayed in the palace in 1979, one of many important people who slept here in the decade when the palace was a guest house for visiting dignitaries. But the short-legged Tito had a special low lavatory pan installed in his bathroom, set in a turret at one corner of the palace.

The first floor has another dining room with a ceiling 25ft (7.5m) high. This was the presidential suite, but three stone slabs in its floor, with chess and solitaire game boards carved into them, recall that French officers were once imprisoned in this room.

The brilliantly-lit lower section of the Great Ward still has bed-numbers on its walls.

A secret staircase built into the wall of one bedroom leads down to the moat, a convenient escape route. Another secret stair leads to the torture chamber where prisoners were tied to the walls and poisoned by sulphur fumes.

A third stair leads to the roof, from where there is an impressive view across the island to Valletta, down into the grounds and the Chapel of St Anthony the Abbot — he's the San Antonio Abad after whom so many Spanish villages are named — and across to the **Buskett Gardens** 100m away.

The gardens, always open and with no entry fee, are the most densely wooded part of Malta, the name originating in the Italian *boschétto*, a 'small wood.' Here are Aleppo pines, cypresses, oak, ash, and dozens of orange trees — and on 29 June you'll also find large crowds celebrating Imnarja.

As you leave the Buskett Gardens, turn left and left again, and soon you see signs pointing to **Clapham Junction,** the name that Dr David Trump, a Malta University lecturer, gave to the intricate series of cart ruts covering several acres of rugged limestone country.

Nobody knows who carved these parallel slits in the rock, nor why. Were they for the runners of Bronze Age sleds? For Copper Age carts using wheels carved from volcanic lava? Your guess may be as good as any the experts have made.

A mile (1.5km) south-east is the **Inquisitor's Summer Palace,** built in 1625 by Honoratus Visconti, one of the early inquisitors. Once an elegant mansion, it fell into disrepair but has been restored less tastefully than the place deserves. Visitors are not allowed.

This summer palace never saw the grimmer side of life which is so starkly in evidence in the main palace in Vittoriosa, but legend claims that the domestic staff had to sleep in ancient cave dwellings in the village of Għar Il-Kbir, 'Great Cave,' to prevent them learning too much. The British rehoused the dwellers in 1835, claiming that the caverns were unfit for human habitation. Shortly after the evacuation the roof of the main cave collapsed.

A lonely lane runs east from the summer palace, meets a main road, and so gives the choice of destinations: Żebbuġ or Siġġiewi. We'll take the northern route.

Żebbuġ. The ancient village of Żebbuġ takes its name from the olive groves that were here in byegone centuries — the Arabic for 'olive' is *zitoun* — and if you venture into the maze of narrow streets in the village centre you're bound to lose your way.

The Church of St Philip, completed in 1599, is attributed to Vittorio Cassar who, like his father Gerolamo, designed many of Malta's churches in the period after the Great Siege. The lesser chapels, St Roque's (1593) and Ta'l Abbandunata (1758) would interest students of church history, but the **de Rohan Arch** at the eastern entrance to

The old windmill lends a touch of history to Xagħra, Gozo.

Żebbuġ catches everybody's eye. It commemorates the last grand master but one.

The village is the birthplace of Bishop Caruana, prominent in the revolt against the French, and of Dun Karm, the composer of the Maltese national anthem.

Siġġiewi. And then there is Siġġiewi, a pleasant farming village with a modern bypass. The Secretary to the Inquisitor lived here in the Villa Sant'Cassia in St Margaret's Street, the house today identifiable by its distinctive porch. The parish church of St Nicholas has probably the best baroqe architecture in the islands.

South of the village, at Tal Providenza, the road forks left to the Blue Grotto and Ħaġar Qim, and right to the rocky bay of **Għar Lapsi**, 'Ascension Cave,' a popular bathing spot with a tiny beach, a small restaurant, and views out to the craggy rock of Filfla.

194

23: NORTH MALTA

Mellieħa and Buġibba

THE NORTHERN PART OF MALTA was almost uninhabited until British times. Mellieħa was created a separate parish in 1436 but soon abandoned in the face of pirate raids; the village of St Paul's Bay had only a few fishermen's huts, and Buġibba was non-existent.

Although the threat of invasion dominated Maltese thinking until the surrender of the Italian Navy in World War Two, the risk was much smaller after the French pulled out in the early 19th cent.

The Order of St John had built watch towers in the north of the island, notably the **Red Tower,** Torri L-Aħmar, and the **White Tower,** Torri L-Aħrax, both on Marfa Ridge; the Red Tower was recently used by the Armed Forces of Malta. These lookouts were in visual contact with the **Comino Tower** and similar defences on Gozo, as well as with 'A' Tower near Gillieru's Restaurant in St Paul's Bay, Għallis Tower, the tower at Għajn Tuffieħa, and others around the coast and along the crest where the British were to build their Victoria Lines.

The **Selmun Palace** and the **Zammitello Palace** were the only major buildings to go up in north Malta during the supremacy of the Order of St John, the Selmun, on Mellieħa Ridge, having a commanding view out to sea and over much of the countryside. Built in the design of the Verdala Palace, it was the property of the *Monte di Redenzione,* a charity established in 1607 to buy Christians from slavery on the Barbary Coast (see *Discover Morocco* in this series for white slavery). In the late 1980s the large Selmun Palace Hotel was built nearby, enjoying those same views; the original palace and its chapel are still accessible.

The Zammitello Palace near Mġarr was in the hands of the family who owned St Paul's Islands, but it has been near-derelict for several years and is now just a shell.

Splash Park. Coming along the coast road from Valletta you are not aware of crossing the ridge dividing high from low land, but you're in north Malta when you see the Splash Park. Billed as Malta's only leisure park, the Splash Park opened in summer 1987 at Baħar Iċ-Ċagħaq (☎342724; open daily 0900-2200, but in midwinter opening only when there's demand; adults Lm3, children Lm2, ♿ spectators) with what is claimed to be the largest water chute in the Mediterranean, a children's park, lagoon pool, bumper-boat pool, and restaurant. It also has *El Paso*, the only passenger-carrying train in the islands.

The road continues around **Salina Bay,** where salt has been dried from seawater since the 16th cent; it was formerly a monopoly of the grand masters of the Order of St John. The faint smell comes from rotting seaweed, not from the salt pans. The road passes the shady **John F. Kennedy Memorial Grove,** built in 1966 in tribute to the late US president, before reaching the entry to Buġibba, one of the main tourist villages of the Maltese islands.

Buġibba. Buġibba and Qawra (ḷaw-ra) have merged to become one community, occupying the entire peninsula; and a ribbon of houses stretches west along St Paul's Bay to take in the village of the same name, known in Malti as San Pawl Il-Baħar. Bugibba is the modern tourist resort, perhaps more resembling Spain's Torremolinos than anywhere else in Malta, though still with a long way to go, while St Paul's Bay is the old village, lining the waterfront with picturesque old houses along a crooked street, now bypassed. Buġibba's northern suburb of Qawra has among its many hotels the Dolmen, with prehistoric standing stones as the main display in the gardens and an exhibit of Maltese palaeontology in the foyer.

It's arguable whether the 16th-cent Church of St Paul is in St Paul's Bay or Buġibba, but San Pawl's *parish* church of Our Lady of Sorrows is supposedly on the spot where Paul landed after his shipwreck and performed the miracle detoxification of the snake venom, and it's near **Għain Rasul**(ḷain rasul), the Apostle's Fountain, where he struck a rock and conveniently produced flowing water.

At the head of St Paul's Bay you have a choice of roads: west, across the fertile Pwales Valley, or north to Mellieħa.

The Pwales Valley is Malta's most fertile land, cropped the year round with the help of water drawn from boreholes. Its western end holds the tiny resort of **Għajn Tuffieħa,** 'Apple Valley,' with, in my opinion, the most impressive coastal scenery on the island of Malta. **Golden Bay** has an excellent beach for sunbathing, castle building, swimming and windsurfing – but beware the warning flag when the wind is in the wrong quarter, as this creates dangerous undercurrents. A path gives access to Għajn Tuffieħa Bay, and another path, with steps, takes you with some difficulty to the secluded sands at the north of **Gnejna Bay.**

The main road winds back inland, passing the **Roman baths** (open daily 1030-1700, but ☎476127 before 0800 to advise that you are coming). You needn't go into the site to see the open-air Roman lavatories as these are visible from the road which looks down on the ruins. And the road continues south-east to Żebbieħ, for the Skorba Temples, Mġarr and the Ta' Ħaġat Temples (both described in

ST PAUL'S BAY

BUGIBBA

Tower

Gillieru's

Parades St

Islet Prom

Bugibba Rd

Bay Sq

Qawra St

Pioneers Rd

Mosta Rd

Bypass

Dolmen

KEY TO HOTELS
1 Bugibba
2 Charella
3 Chez Francis
4 Concorde
5 Crystal
6 Dolmen
7 Flora
8 Hyperion
9 International
10 Liliana
11 Mediterranea
12 St Paul's Court
13 San Pawl
14 Seaview
15 Topaz
16 Villa Mare

197

chapter 11), and finally down an extremely steep hill to the southern sands of **Ġnejna Bay.**

But there was that other road from St Paul's Bay, leading north to Mellieħa, via Xemxija, where the large Church of St Joseph the Worker has been demolished because of structural problems in the dome.

Mellieħa. Mellieħa has now been bypassed, but the village is well worth a visit. Its large church of the Nativity of Our Lady, built of warm pink stone and occupying a dominant position on the top of the ridge, is on three levels. Beneath the church, and accessible from the main car park, is the crypt, its walls carrying scores of thank-you paintings done by ordinary people who have received spiritual help. The art is sometimes poor, but the message is plain.

Go down more steps to the main road, cross over, and open a blue-painted door in the wall opposite. A further 77 steps lead down to the **Grotto of the Madonna,** where children's clothes, dolls, toys, and simple letters give thanks for young people who have recovered from serious illness or accident.

There are rumours that the nymph Calypso stayed in a cave in this immediate area; if there is any truth in the legend, then this was presumably her hideout. If, of course, she existed outside mythology.

The main roundabout at the south of the village, leads east to the Selmun Palace and on, via narrow lanes, to another headland called Blat I-Bajda — or you can get here by driving to Mistra Bay and then walking over the headland.

Either way, in front of you lie **St Pauls's Islands,** home to thousands of rabbits and the giant statue of the saint, built in 1845. Access on normal occasions is by chartering a boat in St Paul's Bay, or by swimming across the narrow channel, but once a year pilgrims sail over in a fleet of fishing boats to pray at the base of the statue. If you come under the right weather conditions it's possible to stand at the base of the cliffs on St Paul's main island, Selmunett, talk quietly to someone on the mainland salt pans 200m away, and hear that person relay your message to another person 200m along the shore. How do I know? I've done it.

Go west from that main roundabout and the Mellieħa bypass takes you downhill to a narrow lane leading to **Anchor Bay** and **Popeye Village,** a film set built by the Mediterranean Film Studios in 1979. Popeye Village desperately needs a good coat of paint, but its rickety houses are still a considerable tourist attraction, open daily 0900-1800 for 50c adult, 25c child; ⑤ in part. Anchor Bay has a tiny beach, within the confines of Popeye's village, and there is a riding stable nearby.

North, **Mellieħa Bay** has a splendid beach at Għadira, particularly popular with windsurfers. The road climbs past the Mellieħa Holiday Village and ends at the Ċirkewwa ferry terminal for access to Gozo.

24: GOZO and COMINO

Calypso's isle

THE BEAUTIFUL ISLAND OF GOZO, known in Malti as Għawdex (ļow-desh), is not just a continuation of Malta across the azure Gozo Channel. The island has a different character, is greener, hillier, and the pace of life is decidedly slower. Agriculture is still the main industry, with a tankerload of milk going on the morning ferry to Malta and early vegetables sometimes hitting the British market. Honey and cheese come from the smaller holdings, delicious Gozitan bread is still baked in brick ovens over a faggot fire — although it's becoming difficult to find — and lacemaking thrives as a cottage industry with most of its products selling to the tourist industry.

Victoria. The only town is Victoria, officially known as Rabat until 1879 and still known as that to most Gotizans who would never confuse it with that *other* Rabat in Malta. Victoria is roughly in the middle of the island where, in byegone centuries, it was relatively safe from attack by passing pirates; the islanders had warning of any approaching enemy and could evacuate themselves to Victoria's near-impregnable Citadel if the threat appeared great. The Citadel stands on a peak more than 500ft (150m) high, beaten for the Gozitan altitude record only by a hill reaching 600ft exact (183m) near Għasri. The view is impressive, taking in most of the 11 villages and some of the steep-sided valleys which separate them, but never giving a glimpse of vulnerable landing places on the island's coast.

The **Citadel,** begun in Roman times, developed into an impregnable fortress similar to Mdina in Malta, but fell to the corsair Dragut in 1551, 14 years before he joined the Great Siege. Six thousand Gozitans, almost the entire population, were carried away to slavery, a mere 300 escaping down ropes the night before the capitulation. A plaque in Latin and Italian in the Archaeological Museum on Gozo remembers Bernard Deopuò who killed his wife and two daughters rather than lose them into slavery, then died as Dragut's men stormed the defences. No wonder that for the next 86 years the islanders went into the Citadel each evening, hauled up the drawbridge, and slept peacefully. Despite this nocturnal inconvenience the Gozitans managed to repopulate their island.

The **Archaeological Museum,** in the former Palazzo Bondì, beside the cathedral but at the foot of its steps, traces the island's history from the earliest times to the rule of the Order of St John; open summer daily 0830-1300, plus 1400-1700 Tues, Thur, Sat and Sun; winter, daily 0830-1300, 1400-1630, for 15c.

Gozo citadel's **cathedral,** rebuilt between 1697 and 1711 as the Church of the Assumption from the ruins of the 1693 earthquake, became head of the diocese in 1866. Externally it is much plainer than Malta's two co-cathedrals, the Spanish hint in its architecture coming

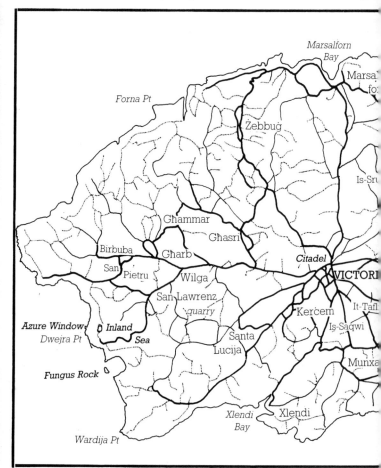

from the grand master of the time, Perellos y Roccaful, whose coat of arms is over the main door. Shortage of money compelled it to be built without a dome, but the artist who painted the ceiling has created the illusion of one; and among its chapels is one dedicated to the island's patron saint, Ursula, a Briton martyred by the Romans. It's also a small cathedral, mainly because of the absence of space to expand, but it looks majestic when you first see it through the modern arch in the citadel's walls. The 31 steps make ♿ access near impossible.

To the right of the cathedral is the **Natural Science Museum,**

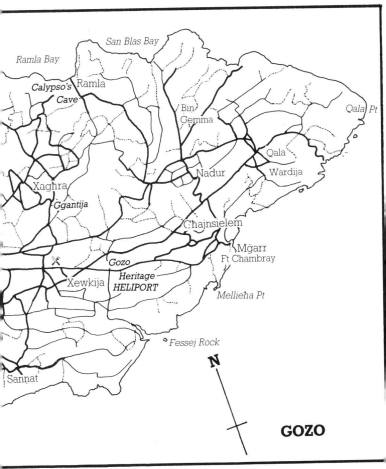

covering the geology and biology of Gozo; further down the narrow street to the left of the cathedral, but on the right side, the **Cathedral Museum** holds the treasures used during special services; while in a side-alley on the left is the **Folklore Museum,** showing how the average Gozitan peasant lived until the age of mass travel. All the museums have thresholds making ♿ difficult; their hours vary around the core of Mon-Sat 0830-1630, Sun 0830-1500, with entry costing 15c.

Other buildings in the Citadel are in poor repair, including the ramparts, in many places so eroded that the globigerina limestone

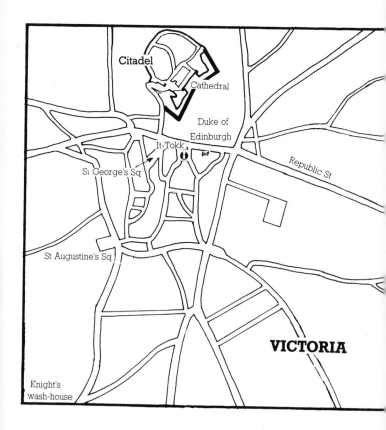

looks like the straw reinforcing of mud bricks after the soil has been washed away. The ruins have for several years provided the setting for two firework displays held each summer.

Castle Hill leads steeply down to It-Tokk, the 'meeting place' or main square, as quiet as Republic Square in Valletta and a convenient place for buying knitwear – at a price. Until recently there was a roadsign here giving distances in leagues to most of the island's villages, an indication of the Gozitan timelessness.

The **tourist office** is to the east, downhill, in a backstreet on the shady side of the road, open Mon-Sat 0715-1900, Sun 0800-1300, and beyond it is the Duke of Edinburgh Hotel, which hasn't found the need to change its Victorian façade. The appointment of a Minister for Gozo since the last election has resulted in a better tourist office and, as you will see, improved road signs throughout the island, but the walking-pace tempo survives for this is what makes Gozo so special.

RURAL GOZO

Gozo's most spectacular coastline – it's probably the most spectacular in the Maltese islands – lies at the end of the road west out of Victoria. Half a mile (1km) along the road, the new *Auberge Chez Armand* and Wilderness Piano Bar night club strike a slight discord in the rural tranquility, but they're popular. Opposite, across the fields, are the remains of Gozo's aqueduct, and ahead is another of those towers built in the latter years of the Order of St John. **Wilga** and **Gharb** – the name means 'west' – are just off the road, which goes through tiny **San Lawrenz,** retirement home of Nicholas Monsarrat, author of *The Cruel Sea* and *The Kappilan of Malta,* to end at Dwejra Point.

Inland Sea and Azure Window. And here are several beauty spots, as if nature forgot how to stop. The Inland Sea, *Il-Qawra*, &, is a beautiful freak, a tiny bay with its own shingly beach, cut off from the open sea by a 60ft (20m) wall of solid rock. A tunnel, conveniently at sea level, allows fishing and tourist boats to come in and shelter on the beach – but in May 1986 the roof gave way and blocked the tunnel for much of that season. The lagoon is shallow and always calm, making this an ideal place for children and for people learning to swim. If the sea outside is equally calm you can hire a boat here and sail through the tunnel to explore the Azure Window.

On the other side of that wall of rock the headland of Dwejra Point ends in the spectacular and cathedral-like natural arch known as the Azure Window, *Tieqa Zerqa* (tee-ay¦ah tser-¦ah); & travellers can get close enough to see it. Its opening is 100ft (30m) wide by 100ft high, and people with a sense of adventure can walk out over the span. But the arch is getting thinner as its underside slowly crumbles, much like the collapse of the Inland Sea's tunnel, a reminder that this phenomenon is only a fleeting feature in geological time.

Fungus Rock. To the south, Fungus Rock stands proudly in the middle of its own little bay, giving a greenish appearance. This is the fungus which since the Roman era is believed to be able to staunch bleeding, and the Knights of St John sensibly stocked up with it before the Turks began their siege in 1565.

If you study the coastline around here you'll soon see plenty of evidence that not so many millennia ago the shore was around 150ft (50m) higher than at present. Part of the top of Fungus Rock is seaworn, there are several small wave-cut cliffs at the higher level, and beneath them fossils up to 4in (10cm) across have been exposed by water erosion of the limestone. Now look back at the Azure Window and imagine the sea once again at that higher level; it's obvious how the natural arch was formed.

Back now to Wilga, noting the tiny craft village of **Ta'Dbieġi** on the right, and turn left towards Għammar and **Ta'Pinu** church, &, a landmark for miles around. Ta Pinu, standing alone in the open countryside, marks the spot to which Carmela Grima and Francesco Portelli were summoned in 1883 by the voice of God. The original 16th-cent chapel is incorporated in the present building which went up between 1920 and 1936. And the name recalls the first chapel's custodian, the Filippino named Gauci — Pinu for short. Opposite the church a footpath leads to a series of statues marking the Stations of the Cross.

A good road leads through Għasri to **Żebbuġ,** which has the reputation of being the home of the island's blanket weavers, but they also knit some of the thick sweaters sold in It-Tokk. The question is: where are the sheep that produce the wool? You will occasionally see small flocks of sheep or goats on Gozo but most livestock throughout the islands is penned up in summer and let out to graze in winter.

North from Żebbuġ the road plunges steeply down into tiny Xwieni Bay and the salt pans before swinging into **Marsalforn,** the 'baker's harbour' that is now the most popular coastal resort on Gozo. The beach is shingly but the bathing is good.

Don't be confused by the Hotel Calypso in Marsalforn, for Calypso's Cave is on the headland overlooking Ir-Ramla Bay, signposted from Xagħra. The cave is really a cleft in the clifftop, with carved steps giving access to a jagged hole that scarcely provides shelter from northerly storms. Why should the nymph choose such a spot to serenade Ulysses and charm him for seven years — unless they spent their time on the beach? There's no fence, so no entry fee — and there's no road down to the beach.

Back in Xagħra you have the unusual marvels of **Ninu's Cave** and Xerri's Grotto, both on private property. Ninu's Cave, in January Street near the village centre, was discovered when the present owner's

This was Calypso's view of Ramla Bay, northern Gozo.

grandfather began digging a well in 1888. Instead of water he came into a cave of alabaster festooned with stalactites and in despair he moved 20ft (6m) away, dug again, and struck what he wanted 70ft (20m) down. His descendants now profit by showing visitors around his useless find: open 0700-1900 daily for 15c. **Xerri's Grotto,** discovered in near-identical circumstances in 1923, is open 0700-1115, 1430-1900 (closed Sunday afternoon) for 15c.

Leaving Xaghra on the road south you find an unexpected windmill at the end of Triq Il-Bambina on the way to the Ggantija Temples overlooking the Ramla Valley — they're described in chapter 11 — then there's an interesting road going round the back of the village and down the valley to **Ramla Bay** and its beach of red sand, a pleasant spot that sees fewer visitors than it deserves.

A good road takes you back inland to **Nadur,** a village over-shadowed by its impressive 18th-cent Baroque church. By the way, the village quarry yielded stone for the Catholic Cathedral in Liverpool.

A narrow lane goes north-east to the tiny fishing hamlet of **Dahlet Qorrot,** but a better road runs east to **Qala,** which had one of the last working windmills in the Maltese islands. It still stands sentinel over the village, but its sails, like those of the Xaghra mill, no longer turn.

South of Nadur down a steep hill, lies **Mgarr,** the ferry terminal where a stone breakwater protects Gozo's only harbour. Overlooking the port is the massive Fort Chambray, the gift in 1749-'60 of the knight Jacques François de Chambray, Governor of Gozo. Built as a miniature town in the style of Victoria's Citadel, it failed to attract inhabitants. The fort resisted the French in 1798 and saw brief duty under the British, but it's now a hospital.

Gozo Heritage. Mġarr merges with **Għajnsielem** (ain-*see*-elem), on whose western edge stands the Gozo Heritage, formerly a large farmhouse but since October 1988 the home of an impressive computerised light-and-sound museum tracing Gozo's story from Punic times to Independence. The waxworks are lifesize, either made here or bought from Madame Toussaud's in London, but other exhibits, such as a fertility goddess from Tarxien in Malta, and the face of the Turkish pirate Dragut, are dramatically much larger than life. The heritage is well designed, and open daily 1000-1700 for Lm1.50, &; but you can come into the bar and boutique without paying the admission fee.

The Gozo Heritage is close to the knights' Santa Cilja Tower, beside which a lane leads to the **Gozo heliport.**

Inland, to the south of the road to Victoria, lies **Xewkija,** Gozo's oldest village and the setting for the third largest dome in Europe. The present church was begun in November 1951 and finished in June 1971, built by local voluntary labour around the earlier structure which served as scaffolding. With the new church completed, its dome 82ft (25m) in internal diameter, rising to 245ft (74.5m) with its cupola, and with an internal headroom of 225ft (68.5m), the old church was demolished. So why replace a perfectly good 17th-cent building that was already big enough to hold the parishioners three times over? Because Xewkija can now claim to have the largest dome in the islands. And to understand *that* is to understand the Maltese and the Gozitan way of life.

South-west lies **Sannat,** the lace-making village on the road to Ta'Ċenċ where, surprisingly, a luxury hotel stands at the end of the tarmac road. But there's a grand walk down rough tracks to Mġarr Ix-Xini, a fjordlike inlet offering secluded swimming.

Sannat leads west to **Munxar** and west again to **Xlendi,** a tiny fishing village on another deep inlet, with a sheltered beach. A watchtower built by the Order of St John stands on the headland guarding Xlendi Bay.

From here there's a long but scenically-rewarding walk to Wardija Point, Gozo's south-western headland with its Roman sanctuary and carving of the goddess Tanit, or by road back to Victoria, passing the public **wash-house** attributed to the Order of St John and still in daily use by the local women. Finally, there's a loop road to **Kerċem** and **Santa Lucija,** and some impressive quarries where potatoes grow on the reclaimed stone floor.

COMINO

Comino takes its name from cumin, a herb similar to fennel, anise and caraway, which the Romans found growing here; the seed is used for flavouring. The summer-parched land of Comino produces nothing of commercial value today though the derelict farm near the island's centre shows that somebody tried and failed.

Quiet dereliction is probably the theme on Comino; the cemetery, standing on the highest point, thankfully lacks custom, and the three or four houses in Congreave Street, the island thoroughfare, look as if history has passed them by. The isolation hospital at the end of the street stands empty, like a ghost from a previous century, and the Comino Tower, also known as St Mary's Tower, built in 1618, has an air of neglect; you can climb to the parapets if the guardian is around.

Yet there is life and industry. The Comino Hotel flourishes, the self-catering chalets of Santa Marija, the only real village, attract lovers of solitude, and on the eastern tip of the island there's a pig farm. Downwind evidence indicates this is also a thriving business. And if you look carefully around the south landing you'll see where the electricity, telephone and water essential for these industries are piped ashore from Malta.

For many people the charm of Comino is its isolation. Rough tracks lead across the island, past terraces that nature has recolonised and where swallowtail butterfiles and even the occasional snake bask in the sun. Other visitors come on the cruisers from Sliema and spend their afternoons swimming in the Blue Lagoon or basking on the rocks.

The **Blue Lagoon** is between waist and shoulder deep with a bed of fine white sand which reflects the sunlight and gives the water the illusion of being palest pastel blue, a sharp contrast to the deep ultramarine of the surrounding sea. It's justly listed as one of Malta's beauty spots, and is a fitting place to end our tour of the islands.

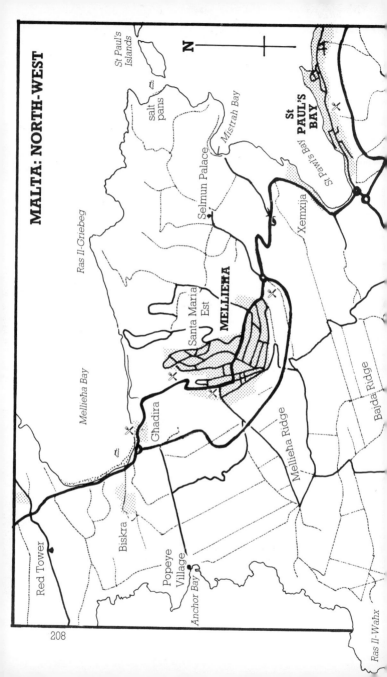

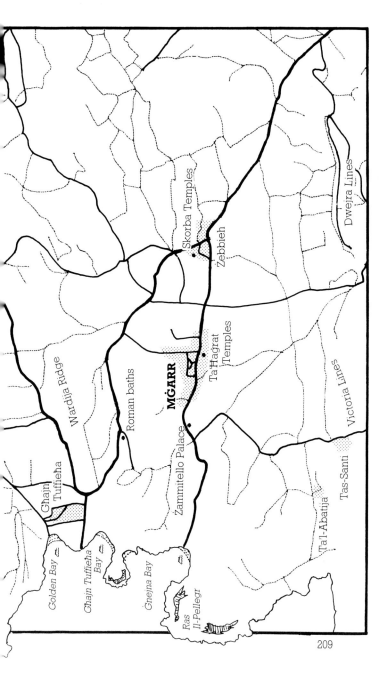

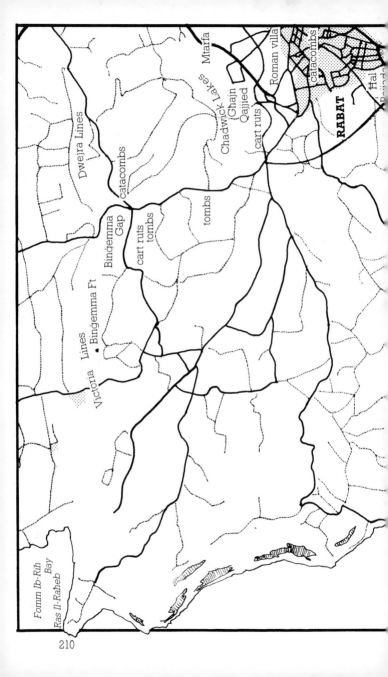

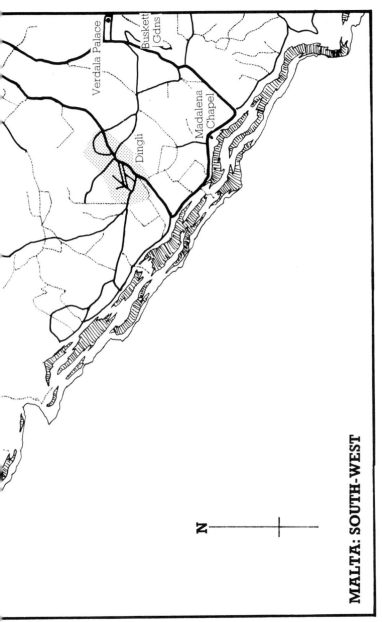

MALTA: SOUTH-WEST

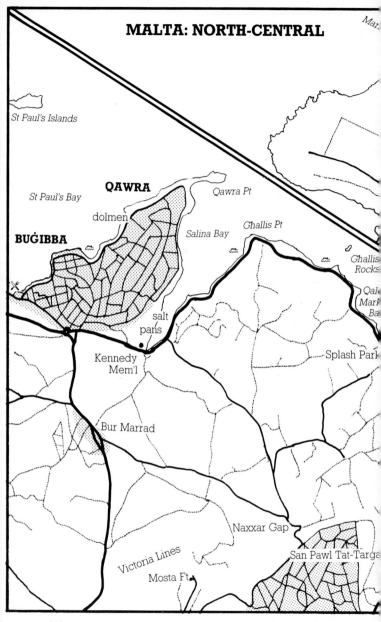

MALTA: NORTH-CENTRAL

St Paul's Islands

QAWRA

St Paul's Bay *Qawra Pt*

dolmen

BUĠIBBA *Salina Bay* *Ghallis Pt*

Ghallis Rocks

Qal... Mar... Ba...

salt pans

Kennedy Mem'l Splash Park

Bur Marrad

Naxxar Gap

San Pawl Tat-Targa

Victoria Lines

Mosta Ft

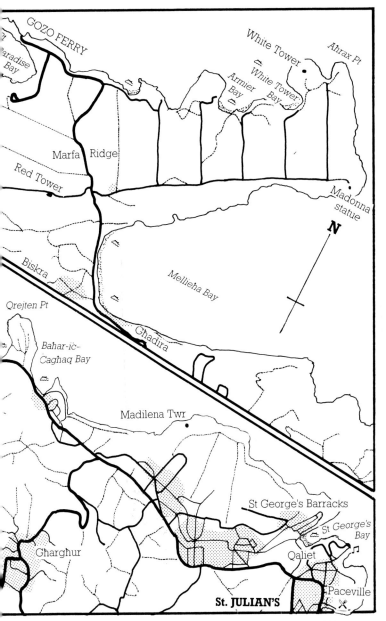

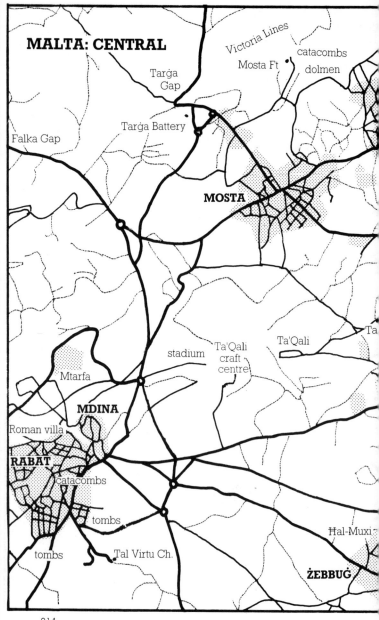

MALTA: CENTRAL

Victoria Lines
catacombs
Mosta Ft
dolmen
Targa Gap
Targa Battery
Falka Gap
MOSTA
Ta
Ta'Qali
stadium
Ta'Qali craft centre
Mtarfa
MDINA
Roman villa
RABAT
catacombs
tombs
Hal-Muxi
tombs
Tal Virtu Ch.
ŻEBBUĠ

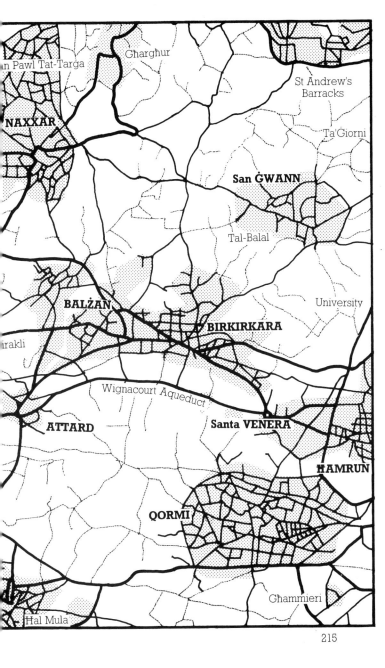

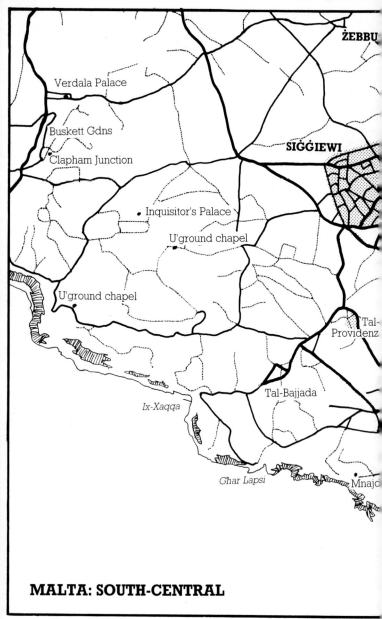

MALTA: SOUTH-CENTRAL

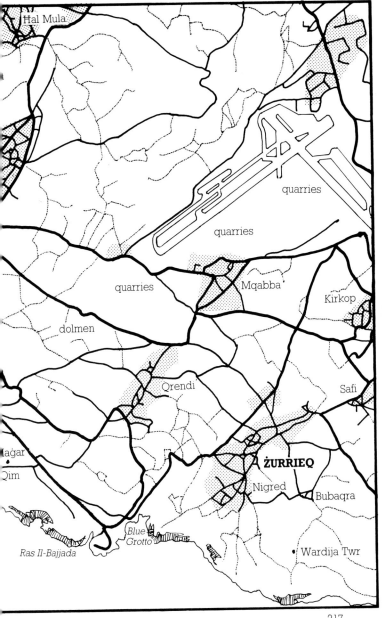

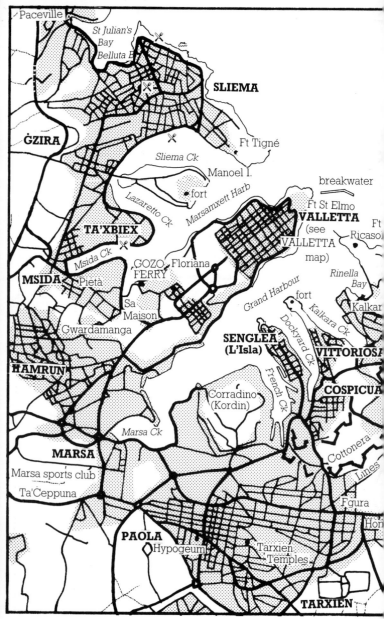

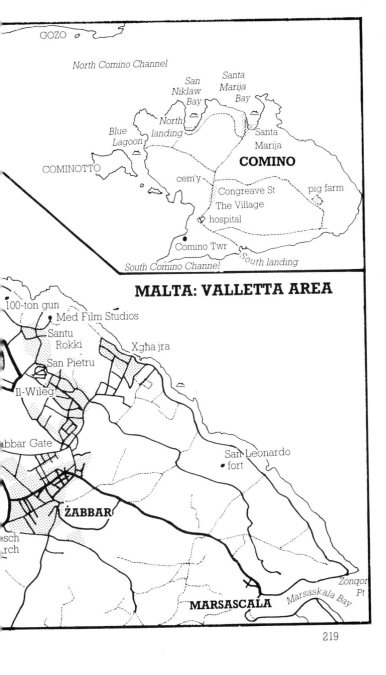

GOZO

North Comino Channel

San Niklaw Bay

Santa Marija Bay

North landing

Blue Lagoon

Santa Marija

COMINOTTO

COMINO

cem'y

Congreave St

The Village

pig farm

hospital

Comino Twr

South Comino Channel

South landing

MALTA: VALLETTA AREA

100-ton gun

Med Film Studios

Santu Rokki

Xgħajra

San Pietru

Il-Wileg

San Leonardo fort

bbar Gate

ŻABBAR

sch rch

Zonqor Pt

MARSASCALA

Marsaskala Bay

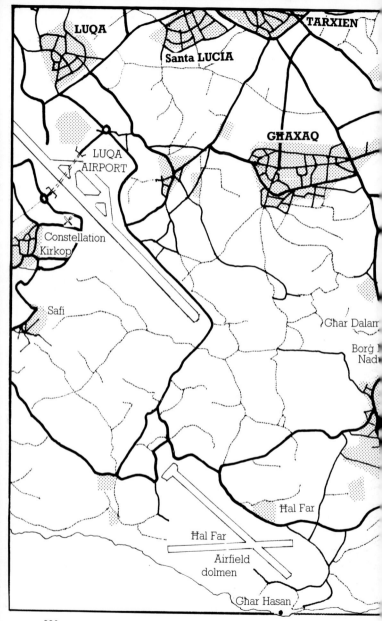

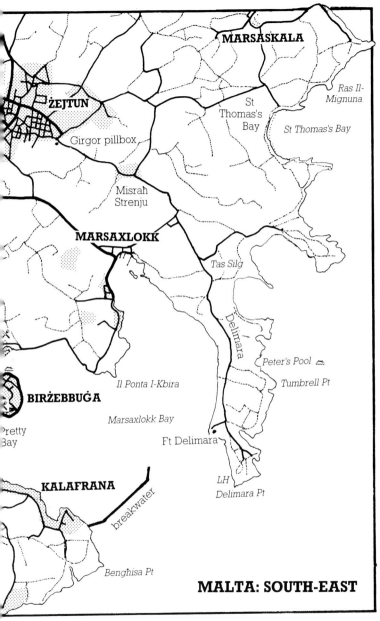

MALTA: SOUTH-EAST

INDEX